Looking at Latin

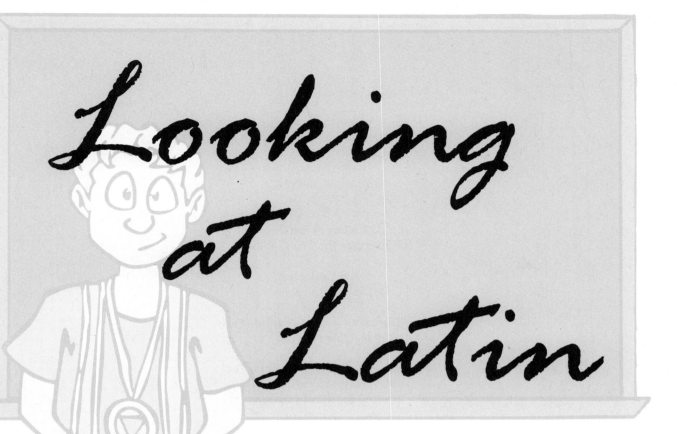

Looking at Latin

A GRAMMAR FOR PRE-COLLEGE

by

Anna Andresian

Bolchazy-Carducci Publishers, Inc.
Wauconda, Illinois USA

General Editor:
LeaAnn A. Osburn

Cover Design:
Adam Phillip Velez

Looking at Latin
A Grammar for Pre-College

Anna Andresian

© 2006 Bolchazy-Carducci Publishers, Inc.

Bolchazy-Carducci Publishers, Inc.
1000 Brown Street, Unit 101
Wauconda, Illinois 60084
www.bolchazy.com

Printed in Canada
2006
by Friesens

ISBN-13: 978-0-86516-615-8
ISBN-10: 0-86516-615-3

Library of Congress Cataloging-in-Publication Data

Andresian, Anna.
  Looking at Latin : a grammar for precollege / Anna Andresian.
      p. cm.
  ISBN-13: 978-0-86516-615-8 (pbk. : alk. paper)
  ISBN-10: 0-86516-615-3 (pbk. : alk. paper)
  1. Latin language--Grammar. I. Title.

PA2080
478.2'421--dc22

                                                              2006004113

TABLE OF CONTENTS

VERBS

INTRODUCTION TO VERBS
Verb Terminology

INTRODUCTION TO VERB FORMS
Personal Endings

Connector Vowels 158

Voice

INDICATIVE VERB FORMS AND MEANINGS
Systems of Tenses: Meanings

Present Tense

Imperfect Tense

Future Tense

Perfect Tense

Pluperfect Tense

Future Perfect Tense

Systems of Tenses: Forms

REGULAR VERB CONJUGATIONS

IRREGULAR VERBS

OTHER VERB FORMS

VERB MOODS

INDICATIVE MOOD

IMPERATIVE MOOD
Imperative Forms

INFINITIVE MOOD
Infinitive Forms

Infinitive Constructions

Infinitive in an Indirect Statement

PARTICIPIAL MOOD
Participles

PREFACE

Looking at Latin is an illustrated grammar aid intended for young classicists studying at the middle and upper school levels. This project evolved over the course of my teaching career at the Rocky Hill School in East Greenwich, Rhode Island, as I prepared each week to conduct my classes. The goal of these pages is to provide students with essential form paradigms and grammatical explanations, comprehensive example sentences, and useful hints, all arranged in a visually appealing and unintimidating layout whose primary objective is clarity. It is my hope that this book will help students both learn and review Latin grammar and that it will enhance their ability to find answers and clarify confusion independently.

Since *Looking at Latin* is intended for middle and upper school students, I have omitted some details on the grounds that they fall outside the scope of what is fundamental to a pre-college curriculum. For example, there is no discussion of conditions in indirect statement or of the conative force of the imperfect. Students are encouraged to consult a larger reference grammar when they come upon scenarios not covered here. Another important resource that students should own is a Latin dictionary, as practical constraints have not allowed me to treat individual vocabulary words of particular interest in depth (such as *ut, quam,* and correlative adjectives and adverbs).

The topics in this book are arranged by category. Since *Looking at Latin* does not impose any particular order, it can be used as a companion to any other textbook. On the other hand, teachers who have developed their own set of practice exercises and who do not use a traditional textbook may find *Looking at Latin* an appropriate resource for presenting grammar to their students. This book is suitable for those who are just beginning their study of Latin and for those who have moved on to literature, as upper level students may find it a useful reference tool in which information is conveniently arranged and consolidated.

Looking at Latin was designed with particular attention to visual cues, as I believe that their mnemonic power will facilitate students' acquisition of Latin grammar. I have included abundant illustrations, multicolored text, and arrows pointing the way in an attempt to make the contents of this book less intimidating, more memorable, and more clear.

The study of Roman antiquity is well worth the time and effort it requires, as it enhances students' language and logic skills, sets the scene for an examination of more recent developments in human affairs, and both challenges and delights the curious mind.

GUIDELINES FOR USING THIS BOOK

1. **Locating a Topic:** Turn to the table of contents, find the relevant section (nouns, adjectives, verbs, etc.) and browse for the desired item.

2. **Page Layout—Where to Begin:** Start in the large text box at the top of the page and work your way down.

3. **Page Layout—Arrows:** Pay close attention to the arrows that link one piece of information with another or with example sentences.

4. **Page Layout—Color:** Particularly important information is highlighted in red, purple, or blue.

THIRD DECLENSION

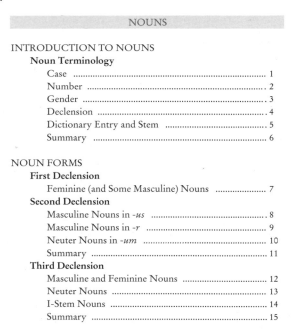

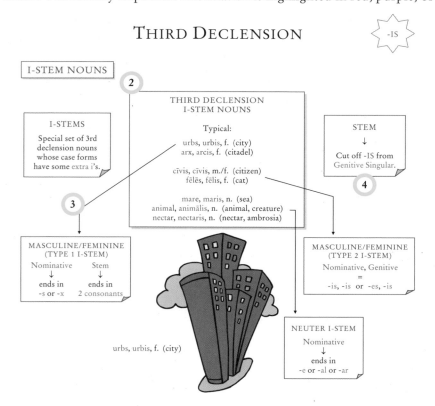

NOTATIONAL REMARKS

ALPHABET: (See p. xiv)

In this book, both consonantal *i* (pronounced as in "yellow") and vocalic *i* (pronounced as in "green" and "in") are represented by the letter *i*. Consonantal *v* (pronounced as in "water") is represented by *v* whereas vocalic *v* (pronounced as "pool" and "foot") is represented by *u*.

GENITIVE SINGULAR OF -IUS/-IUM NOUNS:

In all vocabulary lists, this book gives -iī as the genitive singular ending rather than -ī (see p. 11).

PRINCIPAL PARTS OF INTRANSITIVE VERBS:

Intransitive verbs such as currō (to run) are generally listed in dictionaries in one of the following ways:
- currō, currere, cucurrī, cursum (fourth principal part = supine)
- currō, currere, cucurrī, cursūrus (fourth principal part = future active participle)

This book gives all fourth principal parts in -us:
- currō, currere, cucurrī, cursus (fourth principal part = perfect passive participle)
- Although some verbs never actually appear in perfect passive participle form, the form is given as the fourth principal part for the sake of uniformity and simplicity.

MARKERS & SYMBOLS:

Recurring notational features are described on p. xiii.

THE TABLE OF CONTENTS:

- The words in black all caps indicate general categories of topics.
- The words in boldface correspond to the titles at the top of each page.
- The sub-headings under the boldface words correspond to the sub-titles that appear below on some pages.
- Each page has a footer with its general category, title, and subtitle.
  - For example, the footer of p. 20 is: Noun Forms – Irregular Nouns – *Domus*.

PEDAGOGICAL REMARKS

NOUN CASE INTRODUCTIONS:

For each noun case, this book presents an introductory overview of forms and usage (see pp. 25, 29, 44, 57, 65). First declension, second declension (masculine), and third declension (masculine/feminine) forms are provided. These lists are not meant to be comprehensive and aim simply at supplying quick reference to help students practice declining the most common nouns. A comprehensive list of all noun endings can be found on p. 22.

PRESENT STEM:

The present stem is traditionally defined in the following manner:
- First Conjugation: remove -re from second principal part (amāre → amā-).
- Second Conjugation: remove -re from second principal part (tenēre → tenē-).
- Third Conjugation: remove -ere from second principal part (mittere → mitt-).
- Fourth Conjugation: remove -re from second principal part (audīre → audī-).

This book attempts to simplify the treatment of the present stem as follows:
- All Conjugations: remove last three letters (-xRE) from second principal part.
- Stem vowels (called "connector vowels" in this book) are then added as a second step (see p. 158).

A NOTE ON THE ILLUSTRATIONS

While the result is by no means perfect, every effort has been made to select illustrations that reflect the diversity of our society. To that end, this book depicts people of a variety of ages and ethnic backgrounds engaged in a wide range of activities. This is not a perfunctory show of political-correctness but rather a sincere attempt (motivated by convictions that spring from my own experience) to bring it about that diverse users of this book may in some form see themselves and their realities in it.

ACKNOWLEDGMENTS

I am grateful to my students for their humor, enthusiasm, and fellowship. I very much appreciate Kathy Todd's technical advice and the assistance rendered by Joe Pucci and John Penney in later stages of revision (any errors remaining in this book are entirely my own). Indeed, I am indebted to Joe for many years of support and guidance. Finally, I thank my parents for encouraging me in the study of Classics from high school through college and beyond.

Anna Andresian
Worcester College, Oxford
anna.andresian@worcester.oxon.org

NOTATION

PREPOSITION MARKERS	For uses of the Ablative and some uses of other cases, a star appears in the upper right corner indicating what preposition is used.	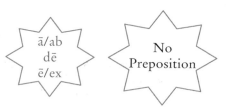

NOUN DECLENSION MARKERS — For each noun declension, a star appears in the upper right corner indicating the declension's genitive singular ending.

ADJECTIVE DECLENSION MARKERS — For adjectives, a star appears in the upper right hand corner indicating the standard nominative singular endings.

VERB CONJUGATION MARKERS — For each verb conjugation, a star appears in the upper right corner indicating the conjugation's present active infinitive ending.

PRINCIPAL PART MARKERS — For each verb tense, a star appears in the upper right corner indicating what principal part of the verb is used for the active or passive voice.

SUBJUNCTIVE MARKERS — For uses of the subjunctive, a star in the upper right corner lists the subjunctive tenses that are used and indicates whether the construction is an independent or a dependent clause.

CONNECTOR VOWEL CHARTS — The vowels used to connect verb endings to verb stems are presented by charts described in greater detail on p. 158.

IMPERFECT
CONNECTOR
VOWELS

a		e
1		2
	3	4
(i)e		ie

SYMBOLS

-◇RE → Refers to the last three letters of the present infinitive, which may be -āre, -ēre, -ere, or -īre (see pp. 153, 162-167).

1° → Primary Sequence ⎤
2° → Secondary Sequence ⎦ (See p. 231)

ALPHABET AND PRONUNCIATION

THE LATIN ALPHABET
The alphabet used by the ancient Romans includes almost all of the letters in the modern English alphabet.
Note that j and w are missing and that v is pronounced quite differently in Latin than it is in English.

LONG MARKS
A mark (called a "long mark" or a "macron") may appear over a vowel to indicate that it is long (ā) rather than short (a).
The sound produced by a long vowel is slightly different from that of a short vowel and is held for a longer duration.

	Consonants	Vowels		Diphthongs
A		(ā) father	(a) Similar to long ā, but of shorter duration.	(ae) eyebrow
B	bridge			(au) plow
C	score (not as in "cellar")			
D	drama			
E		(ē) fiancé	(e) egg	(ei) they
F	father			(eu) eh-oo – pronounced as one syllable.
G	game (not as in "age")			
H	home			
I	yellow	(ī) green	(i) in	
K	key			
L	laugh			
M	mother			
N	name			
O		(ō) open	(o) on	(oe) boy
P	spine			
Q(u)	quiet			
R	river			
S	stable			
T	enter			
V	water	(ū) pool	(u) foot	(ui) oo-ee – pronounced as one syllable.
X	index			
Y		(y/ȳ) Originally pronounced as French *u*, later as Latin *i/ī*.		
Z	zoom			

I and V
Regularly serve as consonants between vowels (Āiāx, avis) and at the beginning of a word if followed by a vowel (iam, vīta).

Ch	core
Ph	pine
Th	table

These three sounds are known as "aspirates," which means that the c/p/t sound is accompanied by a breathy release of air. The difference between c and ch, for example, can be heard in the English words "score" (similar to Latin c) and core (similar to Latin ch, though Latin aspiration is even more forceful).

NOUN TERMINOLOGY

CASE

ENGLISH	LATIN
Word order **tells you** what is going on in a sentence.	Word endings **tell you** what is going on in a sentence.
↓	↓
Flavia eats a bean.	Flāvia fabam devōrat.
A bean eats Flavia.	Flāviam faba devōrat.
Subject: comes before verb Direct Object: comes after verb	Subject: ends in -a Direct Object: ends in -am
(Subject → Verb → Direct Object)	(Flexible word order)

CASES

CASE
Different word forms
(Flāvia vs. Flāviam)
are called "cases."
The case of a word
reveals its grammatical
role in the sentence.

NOMINATIVE: SUBJECT
⬧Andrew⬧ likes ketchup.

GENITIVE: POSSESSION
⬧Courtney's⬧ hair is brown.

DATIVE: INDIRECT OBJECT
You gave a CD ⬧to Ashley⬧.

ACCUSATIVE: DIRECT OBJECT
You saw ⬧Matthew⬧ in the halls.

ABLATIVE: ---[Many different uses]---
André surprises Sue ⬧with flowers⬧.
Barney and Anne live ⬧in New York⬧.
Julian walks back ⬧from the bus stop⬧.

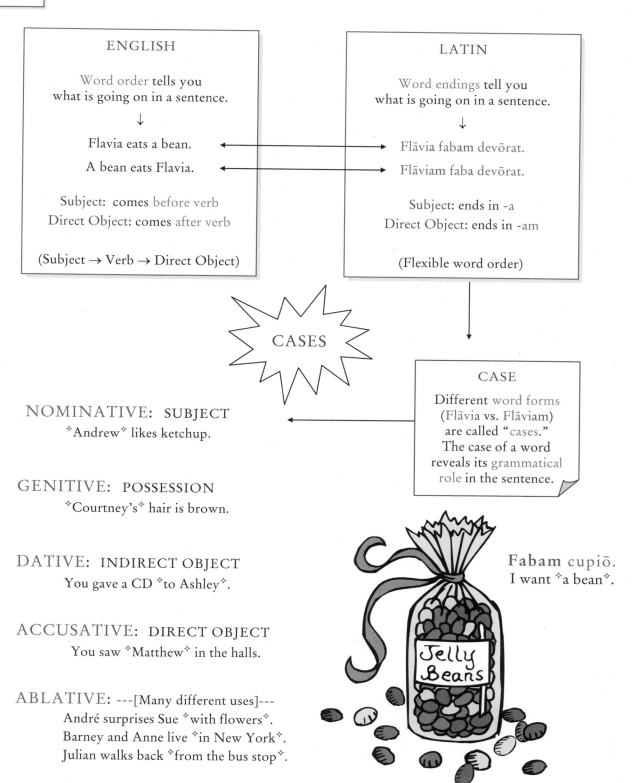

Fabam cupiō.
I want ⬧a bean⬧.

Noun Terminology

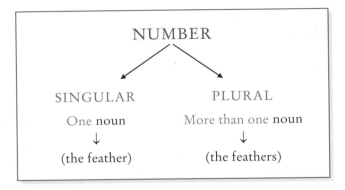

NUMBER

SINGULAR   PLURAL

One noun   More than one noun

↓   ↓

(the feather)   (the feathers)

plūma
nominative singular

plūmae
nominative plural

The ending of a noun
reveals its case and number.

Every noun has a set of
singular case forms and a set
of plural case forms.

NOUN TERMINOLOGY

GENDER

GENDER

↙ ↓ ↘

Masculine   Feminine   Neuter

The gender of a noun is sometimes but not always related to the meaning of the noun.

RELATED MEANING & GENDER

puella - girl → feminine
puer - boy → masculine

UNRELATED MEANING & GENDER

vīcus - village → masculine
urbs - city → feminine
oppidum - town → neuter

IDENTIFYING A NOUN'S GENDER

Some genders are obvious (*puer* - boy → masculine), but in many cases, you must look in the dictionary to find the gender of a noun.

Typical noun dictionary entries

stella, stellae, **f.** (star)

astrum, astrī, **n.** (star)

GENDER MATTERS!

Different genders use slightly different endings, so you may misunderstand a noun's form if you do not know its gender.

puer**um** (boy)
↓
masculine
↓
accusative singular

verb**um** (word)
↓
neuter
↓
nominative or accusative singular

NOUN TERMINOLOGY

DECLENSION

DECLENSION

"Declension" is simply a word that means
"Noun Type."

There are 5 different types of nouns in the Latin language,
each of which has its own set of case endings.

IDENTIFYING A NOUN'S DECLENSION

Every declension has a genitive singular form that is different from the genitive singular forms of other declensions.

Look at a noun's dictionary entry to find its genitive singular form.

stella, stellae, f. (star)

astrum, astrī, n. (star)

GENITIVE SINGULAR ENDINGS

-ae → 1st Declension

-ī   → 2nd Declension

-is → 3rd Declension

-ūs → 4th Declension

-eī → 5th Declension

DECLENSION MATTERS!

It will be difficult to interpret noun endings correctly if you do not know the noun's declension.

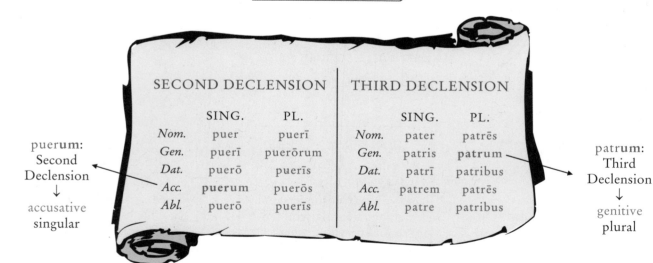

	SECOND DECLENSION		**THIRD DECLENSION**	
	SING.	PL.	SING.	PL.
Nom.	puer	puerī	pater	patrēs
Gen.	puerī	puerōrum	patris	**patrum**
Dat.	puerō	puerīs	patrī	patribus
Acc.	**puerum**	puerōs	patrem	patrēs
Abl.	puerō	puerīs	patre	patribus

puerum:
Second
Declension
↓
accusative
singular

patrum:
Third
Declension
↓
genitive
plural

Noun Terminology

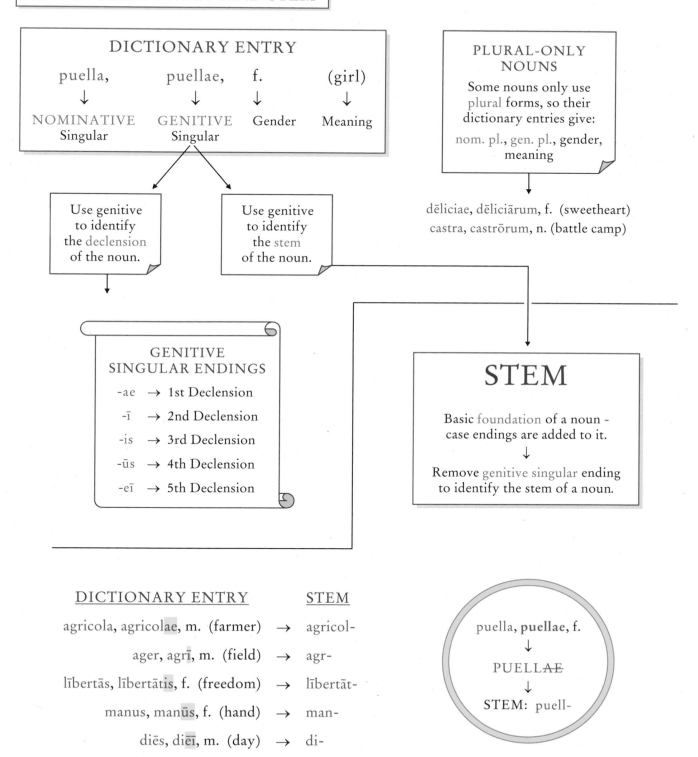

DICTIONARY ENTRY AND STEM

DICTIONARY ENTRY

puella,   puellae,   f.   (girl)
↓   ↓   ↓   ↓
NOMINATIVE   GENITIVE   Gender   Meaning
Singular   Singular

PLURAL-ONLY NOUNS

Some nouns only use plural forms, so their dictionary entries give:

nom. pl., gen. pl., gender, meaning

dēliciae, dēliciārum, f. (sweetheart)

castra, castrōrum, n. (battle camp)

Use genitive to identify the declension of the noun.

Use genitive to identify the stem of the noun.

GENITIVE SINGULAR ENDINGS

-ae → 1st Declension

-ī → 2nd Declension

-is → 3rd Declension

-ūs → 4th Declension

-eī → 5th Declension

STEM

Basic foundation of a noun - case endings are added to it.
↓
Remove genitive singular ending to identify the stem of a noun.

DICTIONARY ENTRY   **STEM**

agricola, agricolae, m. (farmer) → agricol-

ager, agrī, m. (field) → agr-

lībertās, lībertātis, f. (freedom) → lībertāt-

manus, manūs, f. (hand) → man-

diēs, diēī, m. (day) → di-

puella, **puellae**, f.
↓
PUELLAE
↓
STEM: puell-

NOUN TERMINOLOGY

CASE	Reveals grammatical function of noun.	Nominative, Genitive, Dative, Accusative, Ablative
NUMBER	Indicates whether there is one or more than one.	Singular, Plural
GENDER	Plays a role in determining what case endings are used.	Masculine Feminine Neuter
DECLENSION	Type of noun: different declensions use different case endings.	1st, 2nd, 3rd, 4th, 5th
STEM	Basic foundation of noun: case endings are added to it.	Cut off ending of genitive singular form
DICTIONARY ENTRY	Reveals declension, stem, gender, and meaning of noun.	Nominative, Genitive, Gender, Meaning

FIRST DECLENSION

-AE

FEMININE (AND SOME MASCULINE) NOUNS

FIRST DECLENSION

Typical:
aqua, aquae, f. (water)

Genitive Singular: -AE

*LONG MARK

↓

Nominative Sing.: -A
Ablative Sing.: -Ā

STEM

↓

Cut off -AE from
Genitive Singular.

1ST DECLENSION ENDINGS		
	Singular	Plural
Nominative	-a	-ae
Genitive	-ae	-ārum
Dative	-ae	-īs
Accusative	-am	-ās
Ablative	-ā*	-īs

aqua, aquae, f. (water)

1ST DECLENSION aqua, aquae, f. (water)		
	Singular	Plural
Nominative	aqua	aquae
Genitive	aquae	aquārum
Dative	aquae	aquīs
Accusative	aquam	aquās
Ablative	aquā	aquīs

Most first declension nouns are feminine, but several are masculine:

agricola → farmer
nauta → sailor
poēta → poet

SECOND DECLENSION

-Ī

MASCULINE NOUNS IN -*US*

Nouns in -US
↓
Masculine
(Plants, trees, cities
are feminine.)

SECOND DECLENSION
MASCULINE (-US)

Typical:
animus, animī, m. (mind, heart, soul)
nūntius, nūntiī, m. (messenger)

Genitive Singular: -ī

STEM
↓
Cut off -Ī from
Genitive Singular.

nūntius, nūntiī, m.
(messenger)

2ND DECLENSION MASCULINE ENDINGS (-US)

	Singular	Plural
Nominative	-us	-ī
Genitive	-ī	-ōrum
Dative	-ō	-īs
Accusative	-um	-ōs
Ablative	-ō	-īs

Nouns in -IUS
have an "i" at
the end of their
stems. Do not
cut this off.

2ND DECLENSION MASCULINE (-US)
animus, animī, m. (mind, heart, soul)

	Singular	Plural
Nominative	anim**us**	anim**ī**
Genitive	anim**ī**	anim**ōrum**
Dative	anim**ō**	anim**īs**
Accusative	anim**um**	anim**ōs**
Ablative	anim**ō**	anim**īs**

2ND DECLENSION MASCULINE (-IUS)
nūntius, nūntiī, m. (messenger)[†]

	Singular	Plural
Nominative	nūnti**us**	nūnti**ī**
Genitive	nūnti**ī**	nūnti**ōrum**
Dative	nūnti**ō**	nūnti**īs**
Accusative	nūnti**um**	nūnti**ōs**
Ablative	nūnti**ō**	nūnti**īs**

[†]See p. 11 for important information about an alternative genitive singular form for -ius nouns.

SECOND DECLENSION

-Ī

MASCULINE NOUNS IN -R

> **SECOND DECLENSION**
> **MASCULINE (-R)**
>
> Typical:
> puer, puerī, m. (boy)
> ager, agrī, m. (field)
> vir, virī, m. (man)
>
> Genitive Singular: -ī

> Nouns in -R
> ↓
> Masculine

> **STEM**
> ↓
> Cut off -Ī from
> Genitive Singular.

puer, puerī, m. (boy)

2ND DECLENSION MASCULINE ENDINGS (-R)

	Singular	Plural
Nominative	-r	-ī
Genitive	-ī	-ōrum
Dative	-ō	-īs
Accusative	-um	-ōs
Ablative	-ō	-īs

> **NOTE:**
> Some nouns drop an "e" from their stems.
>
> The dictionary entries below indicate that puer keeps the "e" in its stem but that ager drops it.

2ND DECLENSION MASCULINE
puer, puerī, m. (boy)

	Singular	Plural
Nominative	puer	puerī
Genitive	puerī	puerōrum
Dative	puerō	puerīs
Accusative	puerum	puerōs
Ablative	puerō	puerīs

2ND DECLENSION MASCULINE
ager, agrī, m. (field)

	Singular	Plural
Nominative	ager	agrī
Genitive	agrī	agrōrum
Dative	agrō	agrīs
Accusative	agrum	agrōs
Ablative	agrō	agrīs

SECOND DECLENSION

-ī

NEUTER NOUNS IN -*UM*

Nouns in -UM
↓
Neuter

SECOND DECLENSION
NEUTER (-UM)

Typical:
signum, signī, n. (sign)
auxilium, auxiliī, n. (help)

Genitive Singular: -ī

STEM
↓
Cut off -ī from
Genitive Singular.

gaudium, gaudiī, n.
(joy)

2ND DECLENSION NEUTER ENDINGS (-UM)		
	Singular	Plural
Nominative	-um	-a
Genitive	-ī	-ōrum
Dative	-ō	-īs
Accusative	-um	-a
Ablative	-ō	-īs

★
NOMINUSATIVE
★

"Nominusative" is a made-up word to help you remember that neuter nominative and accusastive look the same. (It is *not* a separate case.)

For all neuter nouns, the "nominusative" plural is -A.

2ND DECLENSION NEUTER signum, signī, n. (sign)		
	Singular	Plural
Nominative	signum	signa
Genitive	signī	signōrum
Dative	signō	signīs
Accusative	signum	signa
Ablative	signō	signīs

2ND DECLENSION NEUTER gaudium, gaudiī, n. (joy)†		
	Singular	Plural
Nominative	gaudium	gaudia
Genitive	gaudiī	gaudiōrum
Dative	gaudiō	gaudiīs
Accusative	gaudium	gaudia
Ablative	gaudiō	gaudiīs

†See p. 11 for important information about an alternative genitive singular form for -ius nouns.

SECOND DECLENSION

-ī

SUMMARY

2ND DECLENSION MASCULINE

	Singular	Plural
Nominative	-us, -r	-ī
Genitive	-ī	-ōrum
Dative	-ō	-īs
Accusative	-um	-ōs
Ablative	-ō	-īs

MASCULINE
VS.
NEUTER

Differences appear
in the nominative and
the accusative.

2ND DECLENSION NEUTER

	Singular	Plural
Nominative	-um	-a
Genitive	-ī	-ōrum
Dative	-ō	-īs
Accusative	-um	-a
Ablative	-ō	-īs

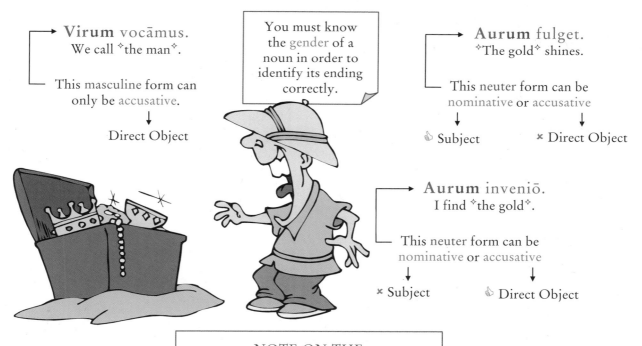

Virum vocāmus.
We call ⋄the man⋄.

This masculine form can
only be accusative.
↓
Direct Object

You must know
the gender of a
noun in order to
identify its ending
correctly.

Aurum fulget.
⋄The gold⋄ shines.

This neuter form can be
nominative or accusative
↓   ↓
👍 Subject   ✗ Direct Object

Aurum inveniō.
I find ⋄the gold⋄.

This neuter form can be
nominative or accusative
↓   ↓
✗ Subject   👍 Direct Object

NOTE ON THE
GENITIVE SINGULAR

For nouns with -ius and -ium in the
nominative singular, there are two
possible forms for the genitive singular:

nūntius, nūntī, m. - early form
nūntius, nūntiī, m. - Augustan form

This book will use the Augustan -iī.

THIRD DECLENSION

MASCULINE AND FEMININE NOUNS

> Masculine and feminine nouns use the same case endings.

> ### THIRD DECLENSION MASCULINE/FEMININE
>
> There is no "typical" noun.
> The nominative singular varies.
>
> soror, sorōris, f. (sister)
> flōs, flōris, m. (flower)
> māter, mātris, f. (mother)
>
> Genitive Singular: -IS

> ### STEM
>
> ↓
>
> Cut off -IS from Genitive Singular.

3ᴿᴰ DECLENSION MASCULINE/FEMININE ENDINGS

	Singular	Plural
Nominative	-varies-	-ēs
Genitive	-is	-um
Dative	-ī	-ibus
Accusative	-em	-ēs
Ablative	-e	-ibus

> ### 3ᴿᴰ DECLENSION STEMS
>
> Some stems keep the entire nominative:
> soror → sorōr-
>
> Some stems change letters in the nominative:
> flōs → flōr-
>
> Some stems drop letters from the nominative:
> māter → mātr-

3ᴿᴰ DECLENSION MASCULINE/FEMININE
flōs, flōris, m. (flower)

	Singular	Plural
Nominative	flōs	flōrēs
Genitive	flōris	flōrum
Dative	flōrī	flōribus
Accusative	flōrem	flōrēs
Ablative	flōre	flōribus

flōs, flōris, m. (flower)

THIRD DECLENSION

-IS

NEUTER NOUNS

THIRD DECLENSION NEUTER

There is no "typical" noun.
The nominative singular varies.

lūmen, lūminis, n. (light)
caput, capitis, n. (head)
onus, oneris, n. (burden)

Genitive Singular: -IS

All nouns
with nominatives
ending in -men
are neuter.

STEM
↓
Cut off -IS from
Genitive Singular.

3ᴿᴰ DECLENSION NEUTER ENDINGS

	Singular	Plural
Nominative	-varies-	-a
Genitive	-is	-um
Dative	-ī	-ibus
Accusative	-varies-	-a
Ablative	-e	-ibus

★
NOMINUSATIVE
(See p. 10)

3ᴿᴰ DECLENSION NEUTER
onus, oneris, n. (burden)

	Singular	Plural
Nominative	onus	onera
Genitive	oneris	onerum
Dative	onerī	oneribus
Accusative	onus	onera
Ablative	onere	oneribus

onus, oneris, n. (burden)

THIRD DECLENSION

I-STEM NOUNS

**THIRD DECLENSION
I-STEM NOUNS**

Typical:

urbs, urbis, f. (city)
arx, arcis, f. (citadel)

cīvis, cīvis, m./f. (citizen)
fēlēs, fēlis, f. (cat)

mare, maris, n. (sea)
animal, animālis, n. (animal, creature)
nectar, nectaris, n. (nectar, ambrosia)

I-STEMS

Special set of 3rd declension nouns whose case forms have some extra i's.

STEM
↓
Cut off -IS from Genitive Singular.

**MASCULINE/FEMININE
(TYPE 1 I-STEM)**

Nominative
↓
ends in
-s or -x

Stem
↓
ends in
2 consonants

**MASCULINE/FEMININE
(TYPE 2 I-STEM)**

Nominative, Genitive
=
-is, -is or -es, -is

NEUTER I-STEM

Nominative
↓
ends in
-e or -al or -ar

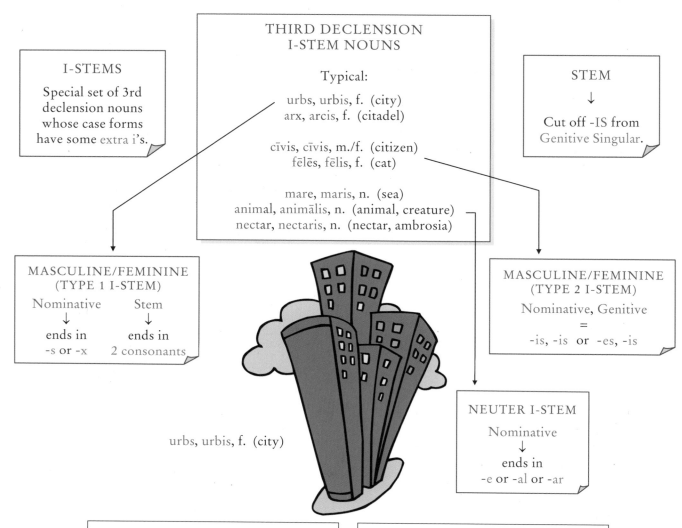

urbs, urbis, f. (city)

MASCULINE/FEMININE I-STEM ENDINGS	Singular	Plural
Nominative	-varies-	-ēs
Genitive	-is	-ium
Dative	-ī	-ibus
Accusative	-em	-ēs / -īs
Ablative	-e	-ibus

NEUTER I-STEM ENDINGS	Singular	Plural
Nominative	-varies-	-ia
Genitive	-is	-ium
Dative	-ī	-ibus
Accusative	-varies-	-ia
Ablative	-ī	-ibus

THIRD DECLENSION

-IS

3RD DECLENSION MASCULINE/FEMININE

	Singular	Plural
Nominative	-varies-	-ēs
Genitive	-is	-um
Dative	-ī	-ibus
Accusative	-em	-ēs
Ablative	-e	-ibus

3RD DECLENSION NEUTER

	Singular	Plural
Nominative	-varies-	-a
Genitive	-is	-um
Dative	-ī	-ibus
Accusative	-varies-	-a
Ablative	-e	-ibus

3RD DECLENSION MASCULINE/FEMININE I-STEM

	Singular	Plural
Nominative	-varies-	-ēs
Genitive	-is	-ium
Dative	-ī	-ibus
Accusative	-em	-ēs / -īs
Ablative	-e	-ibus

3RD DECLENSION NEUTER I-STEM

	Singular	Plural
Nominative	-varies-	-ia
Genitive	-is	-ium
Dative	-ī	-ibus
Accusative	-varies	-ia
Ablative	-ī	-ibus

BEWARE OF NEUTER NOUNS!!

The unusual-looking nominatives of the 3rd declension might actually be accusative if the noun is neuter!

Animal tē terret.
⬩The animal⬩ scares you.
(Neuter Nominative)

Animal vidēs.
You see ⬩the animal⬩.
(Neuter Accusative)

FOURTH DECLENSION

-ŪS

MASCULINE NOUNS

> Nouns in -US
> ↓
> Masculine
> except for:
> manus, f. (hand)
> domus, f. (house)
> +
> a few other
> feminine nouns.

> FOURTH DECLENSION
> MASCULINE
>
> Typical:
> fluctus, fluctūs, m. (wave)
>
> Genitive Singular: -ŪS

> STEM
> ↓
> Cut off -ŪS from
> Genitive Singular.

4ᵀᴴ DECLENSION MASCULINE ENDINGS

	Singular	Plural
Nominative	-us	-ūs
Genitive	-ūs*	-uum
Dative	-uī	-ibus
Accusative	-um	-ūs
Ablative	-ū	-ibus

> NOTE:
> Accusative
> Singular → -UM
> Genitive
> Plural → -UUM

> *LONG MARK
> Nominative
> Singular → -US
> Genitive
> Singular → -ŪS

4ᵀᴴ DECLENSION MASCULINE
fluctus, fluctūs, m. (wave)

	Singular	Plural
Nominative	fluctus	fluctūs
Genitive	fluctūs	fluctuum
Dative	fluctuī	fluctibus
Accusative	fluctum	fluctūs
Ablative	fluctū	fluctibus

fluctus, fluctūs, m. (wave)

FOURTH DECLENSION

-ŪS

NEUTER NOUNS

Nouns in -Ū
↓
Neuter

FOURTH DECLENSION NEUTER

Typical:
cornū, cornūs, n. (horn, wing of an army)

Genitive Singular: -ŪS

STEM
↓
Cut off -ŪS from Genitive Singular.

4TH DECLENSION NEUTER ENDINGS		
	Singular	Plural
Nominative	-ū	-ua
Genitive	-ūs	-uum
Dative	-ū	-ibus
Accusative	-ū	-ua
Ablative	-ū	-ibus

★
NOMINUSATIVE
(See p. 10)

4TH DECLENSION NEUTER cornū, cornūs, n. (horn, wing of an army)		
	Singular	Plural
Nominative	cornū	cornua
Genitive	cornūs	cornuum
Dative	cornū	cornibus
Accusative	cornū	cornua
Ablative	cornū	cornibus

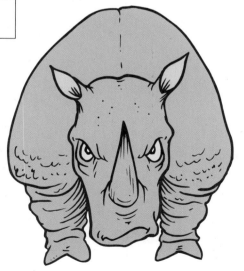

cornū, cornūs, n. (horn)

FOURTH DECLENSION

-ŪS

4ᵀᴴ DECLENSION MASCULINE

	Singular	Plural
Nominative	-us	-ūs
Genitive	-ūs	-uum
Dative	-uī	-ibus
Accusative	-um	-ūs
Ablative	-ū	-ibus

MASCULINE VS. NEUTER

Major differences in the singular, "nominusative" differences in the plural.

4ᵀᴴ DECLENSION NEUTER

	Singular	Plural
Nominative	-ū	-ūa
Genitive	-ūs	-uum
Dative	-ū	-ibus
Accusative	-ū	-ūa
Ablative	-ū	-ibus

MASCULINE NOUNS: -US vs. -ŪS

-US
↓
Nominative Singular

-ŪS
↓
Genitive Singular
Nominative Plural
Accusative Plural

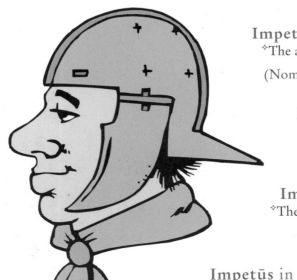

Impetus nōs terruit.
◇The attack◇ scared us.

(Nominative Singular)

Ēventum **impetūs** exspectāmus.
We await the outcome ◇of the attack◇.

(Genitive Singular)

Impetūs hostium ācerrimī erant.
◇The attacks◇ of the enemies were very fierce.

(Nominative Plural)

Impetūs in patriam nostram faciētis.
You (pl.) will make ◇attacks◇ against our fatherland.

(Accusative Plural)

FIFTH DECLENSION

-EĪ

FEMININE (AND SOME MASCULINE) NOUNS

Most fifth declension nouns are feminine, but a few are masculine:

diēs → day
merīdiēs → midday

FIFTH DECLENSION

Typical:
rēs, reī, f. (thing, matter, situation)
diēs, diēī, f. (day)

Genitive Singular: -EĪ

STEM
↓
Cut off -EĪ from Genitive Singular.

diēs, diēī, m. (day)

5TH DECLENSION ENDINGS		
	Singular	Plural
Nominative	-ēs	-ēs
Genitive	-eī	-ērum
Dative	-eī	-ēbus
Accusative	-em	-ēs
Ablative	-ē	-ēbus

Some nouns have an "i" at the end of their stems. Do not cut this off!

(Notice also that these nouns have ēī with a long ē in the genitive and dative singular.)

5TH DECLENSION rēs, reī, f. (thing, matter, situation)		
	Singular	Plural
Nominative	rēs	rēs
Genitive	reī	rērum
Dative	reī	rēbus
Accusative	rem	rēs
Ablative	rē	rēbus

5TH DECLENSION diēs, diēī, m. (day)		
	Singular	Plural
Nominative	diēs	diēs
Genitive	diēī	diērum
Dative	diēī	diēbus
Accusative	diem	diēs
Ablative	diē	diēbus

IRREGULAR NOUNS

DOMUS

DOMUS, DOMŪS, F.
(house, home)

This noun belongs
to the 4th declension,
but it often uses some
2nd declension endings.

STANDARD ENDINGS:
4ᵀᴴ DECLENSION

	Singular	Plural
Nom.	dom**us**	dom**ūs**
Gen.	dom**ūs**	dom**uum**
Dat.	dom**uī**	dom**ibus**
Acc.	dom**um**	dom**ūs**
Abl.	dom**ū**	dom**ibus**

COMMON SUBSTITUTIONS:
2ᴺᴰ DECLENSION

	Singular	Plural
Nom.	dom**us**	dom**ūs**
Gen.	dom**ī**	dom**ōrum**
Dat.	dom**ō**	dom**ibus**
Acc.	dom**um**	dom**ōs**
Abl.	dom**ō**	dom**ibus**

Domūs aedificābimus.
We will build our ⬦homes⬦.

Domōs aedificābimus.
We will build our ⬦homes⬦.

IRREGULAR NOUNS

VĪS
↓
force,
violence

VĪS, VĪS, F.
(force, violence)

This noun is a 3rd declension I-Stem
with some unusual singular forms
and very unusual plural forms.

In fact, vīs looks completely different
in the plural and has a different
meaning as well.
↓
VĪRĒS, VĪRIUM, F.
(strength) - plural of vīs

VĪRĒS
↓
strength

VĪS, VĪS, F.
(force, violence; strength [pl.])

	Singular	Plural
Nom.	vīs	vīrēs
Gen.	vīs	vīrium
Dat.	vī	vīribus
Acc.	vim	vīrēs
Abl.	vī	vīribus

Vīrēs ursī timēmus.
We fear ✧the strength✧ of the bear.

NOUN CASE OVERVIEW

1ST DECLENSION

	Singular	Plural
Nom.	-a	-ae
Gen.	-ae	-ārum
Dat.	-ae	-īs
Acc.	-am	-ās
Abl.	-ā	-īs
Voc.	-a	-ae

2ND MASCULINE

	Singular	Plural
Nom.	-us/-ius, -r	-ī
Gen.	-ī	-ōrum
Dat.	-ō	-īs
Acc.	-um	-ōs
Abl.	-ō	-īs
Voc.	-e/-ī, -r	-ī

2ND NEUTER

	Singular	Plural
Nom.	-um	-a
Gen.	-ī	-ōrum
Dat.	-ō	-īs
Acc.	-um	-a
Abl.	-ō	-īs
Voc.	-um	-a

3RD MASC./FEM.

	Singular	Plural
Nom.	---	-ēs
Gen.	-is	-um
Dat.	-ī	-ibus
Acc.	-em	-ēs
Abl.	-e	-ibus
Voc.	---	-ēs

3RD NEUTER

	Singular	Plural
Nom.	---	-a
Gen.	-is	-um
Dat.	-ī	-ibus
Acc.	---	-a
Abl.	-e	-ibus
Voc.	---	-a

See p. 88 for more information on the vocative case.

3RD I-STEM MASC./FEM.

	Singular	Plural
Nom.	---	-ēs
Gen.	-is	-ium
Dat.	-ī	-ibus
Acc.	-em	-ēs / -īs
Abl.	-e	-ibus
Voc.	---	-ēs

3RD I-STEM NEUT.

	Singular	Plural
Nom.	---	-ia
Gen.	-is	-ium
Dat.	-ī	-ibus
Acc.	---	-ia
Abl.	-ī	-ibus
Voc.	---	-ia

4TH MASCULINE

	Singular	Plural
Nom.	-us	-ūs
Gen.	-ūs	-uum
Dat.	-uī	-ibus
Acc.	-um	-ūs
Abl.	-ū	-ibus
Voc.	-us	-ūs

4TH NEUTER

	Singular	Plural
Nom.	-ū	-ua
Gen.	-ūs	-uum
Dat.	-ū	-ibus
Acc.	-ū	-ua
Abl.	-ū	-ibus
Voc.	-ū	-ua

5TH DECLENSION

	Singular	Plural
Nom.	-ēs	-ēs
Gen.	-eī	-ērum
Dat.	-eī	-ēbus
Acc.	-em	-ēs
Abl.	-ē	-ēbus
Voc.	-ēs	-ēs

NOUN CASE OVERVIEW

The chart below presents
the basic translation
of each noun case.

	SINGULAR	PLURAL
Nominative	the noun (subject)	the nouns (subject)
Genitive	OF the noun	OF the nouns
Dative	TO/FOR the noun	TO/FOR the nouns
Accusative	the noun (direct object)	the nouns (direct object)
Ablative	*_____* the noun	*_____* the nouns

There are many words that
may be used when translating
ablatives into English.

Some examples are:
by, with, from, in, within,
because of, and than.

Often, one form may
represent several
different cases.

In a sentence, context
clues will help you
determine the correct
interpretation.

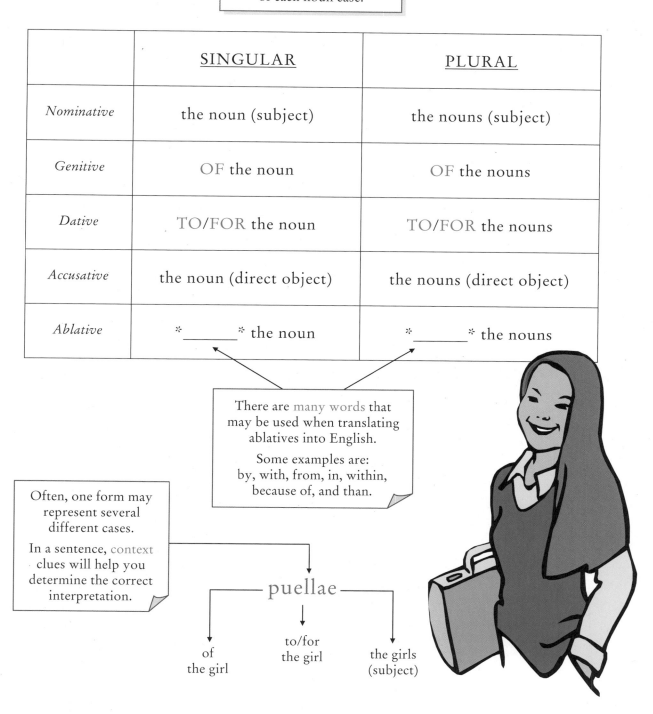

puellae

of
the girl

to/for
the girl

the girls
(subject)

ARTICLES

ARTICLES

"The" is referred to as the
definite article.

"A/An" is referred to as the
indefinite article.
↓
Latin does not have words
for "the" or "a/an,"
so you must add them
into your English translation
whenever it seems appropriate.

Puer dormit.
⬦The boy⬦ sleeps.

Your instincts and context
clues will help you decide
whether to add "the" or
"a/an" to a noun.

Often, "the" will sound best
if the noun has already
been mentioned.

Puer nōn in **lectō** dormit.
⬦The boy⬦ does not sleep on ⬦a bed⬦.

INTRODUCTION TO THE NOMINATIVE CASE

NOMINATIVE CASE

Acts as the subject of the verb.

OR

Is linked to the subject by "is."

Subject
Nominative

Antōnia currit.
⋄Antonia⋄ runs.

Predicate
Nominative

Antōnia **dēfessa** est.
Antonia is ⋄tired⋄.

1ST DECLENSION NOMINATIVES		
	M./F.	
Sing.	-a	
Pl.	-ae	

2ND DECLENSION NOMINATIVES		
	M.	*N.*
Sing.	-us	-um
Pl.	-ī	-a

3RD DECLENSION NOMINATIVES		
	M./F.	*N.*
Sing.	-varies-	-varies-
Pl.	-ēs	-a

SUBJECT NOMINATIVE

> **SUBJECT NOMINATIVE**
>
> SUBJECT:
> Noun that performs the verb - appears in the nominative case.

Puella lūdit.
⬦The girl⬦ plays.

Puellae lūdunt.
⬦The girls⬦ play.

> **SINGULAR**
>
> "The girl" = "She" –
> 3rd person singular
> ↓
> Verb ends in: -T

> **PLURAL**
>
> "The girls" = "They" –
> 3rd person plural
> ↓
> Verb ends in: -NT

> **1ST & 2ND PERSON VERBS**
>
> When the subject of a verb is
> I, you, we, or you (pl.),
> you will usually not find a
> subject nominative.

> **3RD PERSON VERBS**
>
> If the subject of the verb is
> he/she/it and there is no
> nominative, use context to
> figure out whether to say
> "he", "she", or "it."

Dormīre parāmus.
⬦We⬦ prepare to sleep.
↓
No nominative is required
because the verb ending indicates
that "we" is the subject.

Titus dormīre parat.
⬦Titus⬦ prepares to sleep.

In lectō iacet.
⬦He⬦ lies down on the bed.

PREDICATE NOMINATIVE

LINKING
VERB:
am, is, are
was, were
will be

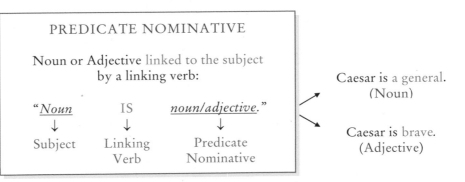

PREDICATE NOMINATIVE

Noun or Adjective linked to the subject
by a linking verb:

"*Noun*	IS	*noun/adjective*."
↓	↓	↓
Subject	Linking Verb	Predicate Nominative

Caesar is a general.
(Noun)

Caesar is brave.
(Adjective)

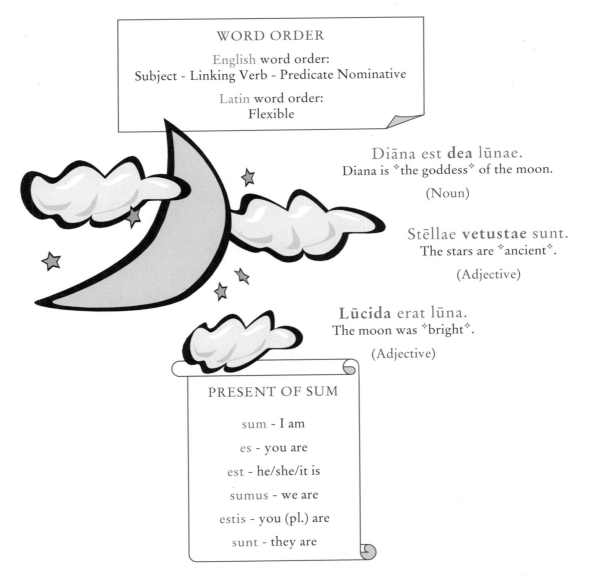

WORD ORDER

English word order:
Subject - Linking Verb - Predicate Nominative

Latin word order:
Flexible

Diāna est **dea** lūnae.
Diana is ⋄the goddess⋄ of the moon.

(Noun)

Stēllae **vetustae** sunt.
The stars are ⋄ancient⋄.

(Adjective)

Lūcida erat lūna.
The moon was ⋄bright⋄.

(Adjective)

PRESENT OF SUM

sum - I am

es - you are

est - he/she/it is

sumus - we are

estis - you (pl.) are

sunt - they are

PREDICATE NOMINATIVE

WITH PASSIVE OF "CALL," "NAME," "MAKE"

LINKING
VERB:
Passive of
call, name,
make

PREDICATE NOMINATIVE

"Noun	IS CALLED IS NAMED IS MADE	*noun/adjective."*
↓	↓	↓
Subject	Linking Verb	Predicate Nominative

You were named king.
(Noun)

You were called the best
of all students.
(Adjective)

PREDICATE NOMINATIVE TRIGGERS

vocō, vocāre, vocāvī, vocātus (to call)
appellō, appellāre, appellāvī, appellātus (to name)
fīō, fierī, factus sum (to be made, become)

Equus **Pēgasus** appellātur.
The horse is named ✧Pegasus✧.

(Noun)

Pēgasus ab omnibus **optimus equus** vocātur.
Pegasus is called ✧the best horse✧ by everyone.

(Adjective + Noun)

INTRODUCTION TO THE GENITIVE CASE

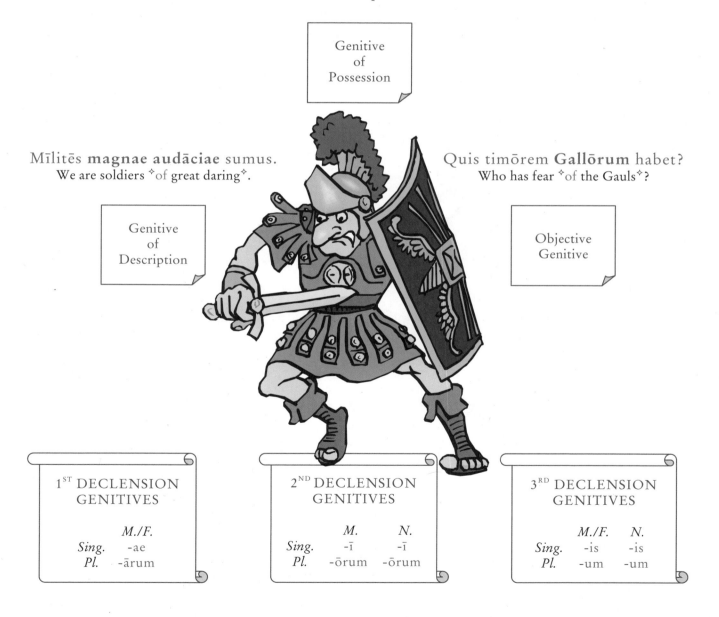

GENITIVE CASE

Often translated
into English
by adding
"OF."

Castra **Rōmānōrum** dēfendēmus.
We will defend the camp ⬦of the Romans⬦.

Genitive
of
Possession

Mīlitēs **magnae audāciae** sumus.
We are soldiers ⬦of great daring⬦.

Quis timōrem **Gallōrum** habet?
Who has fear ⬦of the Gauls⬦?

Genitive
of
Description

Objective
Genitive

1ST DECLENSION GENITIVES

	M./F.
Sing.	-ae
Pl.	-ārum

2ND DECLENSION GENITIVES

	M.	N.
Sing.	-ī	-ī
Pl.	-ōrum	-ōrum

3RD DECLENSION GENITIVES

	M./F.	N.
Sing.	-is	-is
Pl.	-um	-um

GENITIVE OF POSSESSION

GENITIVE OF POSSESSION

Genitive case can
indicate ownership.

↓

"OF" or "'S"

Vōcem **Antōniae** agnōscō.

I recognize ⋄Antonia's⋄ voice.

I recognize the voice ⋄of Antonia⋄.

APOSTROPHE RULES

When the possessive noun
is plural, the apostrophe
goes after the "s."

Singular	Plural
's	s'

Meārum amīcārum vōcēs agnōscō.
I recognize ⋄my friends'⋄ voices.

Marcus possesses the friend,
not the food.

Genitives are
generally placed
close to to the
nouns they
possess.

Marcī amīcus cibum devōrat.

👍 ⋄Marcus'⋄ friend devours the food.
✗ A friend devours ⋄Marcus'⋄ food.

PARTITIVE GENITIVE

PART
OF
THE
WHOLE

PARTITIVE GENITIVE

Multī, nēmō, pars, quis, and numbers represent a "part" (or quantity).

A noun in the genitive represents the "whole" that the "part" belongs to.

↓

"OF"

NUMBERS

ūnus (1)
quīnque (5)
decem (10)
centum (100)

PARTITIVE GENITIVE TRIGGERS

multī, multae, multa (many)
nēmō, nēminis, m. (no one)
pars, partis, f. (part)
quis (who?)

Part   Whole

↓   ↓

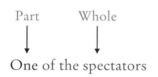

One of the spectators

Multōs **equōrum** laudāmus.
We praise many ⬧of the horses⬧.

Nēmō **agricolārum** tē timet.
None (no one) ⬧of the farmers⬧ fears you.

Partem **urbis** vīdī.
I saw part ⬧of the city⬧.

Quis **poētārum** Rōmam amat?
Who/Which ⬧of the poets⬧ loves Rome?

Quīnque **equōrum** effūgērunt.
Five ⬧of the horses⬧ fled.

PARTITIVE GENITIVE

PART
OF
THE
WHOLE

PARTITIVE GENITIVE

Nihil, aliquid, satis, etc. (see below) represent a "part" (or quantity).

A noun in the genitive represents the "whole" that the "part" belongs to.

"OF" is not neeeded.

PARTITIVE GENITIVE TRIGGERS

nihil (nothing)
aliquid (something)
satis (enough)
tantum (so much)
quantum (how much?)
nimis (too much)
parum (too little)
plūs (more)
minus (less)

NOTE:

These forms are all neuter nominative or accusative.

tantum **aquae**
so much ⋄water⋄

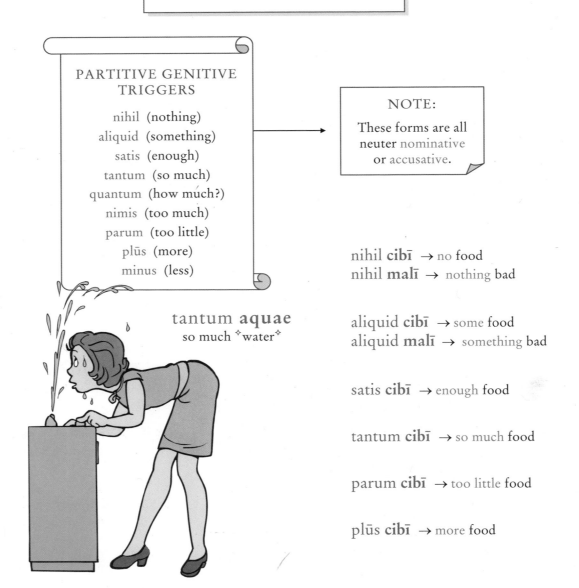

nihil **cibī** → no food
nihil **malī** → nothing bad

aliquid **cibī** → some food
aliquid **malī** → something bad

satis **cibī** → enough food

tantum **cibī** → so much food

parum **cibī** → too little food

plūs **cibī** → more food

OBJECTIVE GENITIVE

With Action or Emotion noun

> ## OBJECTIVE GENITIVE
>
> An action or emotion noun can trigger a noun in the genitive case.
>
> That genitive noun is the recipient of the action or emotion expressed by the trigger noun.
> ↓
> "OF" or "FOR" or "'S"

"OBJECT"
↓
Noun that receives action.

COMMON NOUNS THAT IMPLY EMOTION

amor, amōris, m. (love)

cūra, cūrae, f. (concern, care)

spēs, speī, f. (hope)

studium, studiī, n. (zeal, enthusiasm)

metus, metūs, m. (fear)

timor, timōris, m. (fear)

odium, odiī, n. (hatred)

COMMON NOUNS THAT IMPLY ACTION

auxilium, auxiliī, n. (help)

causa, causae, f. (cause, reason)

iniūria, iniūriae, f. (injury, insult)

dux, ducis, m. (leader)

imperātor, imperātōris, m. (commander)

magister, magistrī, m. (teacher)

custōs, custōdis, m./f. (guardian)

Metum **fābulārum horrendārum** habeō.
I have a fear ⁺of scary stories⁺.

"Scary stories" are the direct object of the implied verb "to fear."

Quis erit custōs **līberōrum**?
Who will be the ⁺children's⁺ guardian?

"Children" are the direct object of the implied verb "to guard."

Studium **salūtis** mē rēgit.
Enthusiasm ⁺for safety⁺ guides me.

Fābula erat causa **timōris**.
The story was the reason ⁺for my fear⁺.

SUBJECTIVE GENITIVE

SUBJECTIVE GENITIVE

An action or emotion noun can trigger
a noun in the genitive case.

That genitive noun represents the subject
of the action or emotion expressed
by the trigger noun.

↓

"OF" or "'S"

"SUBJECT"
↓
Noun that
performs action.

Huius virī adventus nōs terruit.
The arrival ✧of this man✧ frightened us.

↓

"This man" is
the subject of
the implied verb
"to arrive."

Studium **huius virī** malum est.
✧This man's✧ enthusiasm is sinister.

↓

"This man" is
the subject of
the implied verb
"to hope."

COMMON NOUNS
THAT IMPLY EMOTION

amor, amōris, m. (love)
cūra, cūrae, f. (concern, care)
spēs, speī, f. (hope)
studium, studiī, n. (zeal, enthusiasm)
metus, metūs, m. (fear)
timor, timōris, m. (fear)
odium, odiī, n. (hatred)

COMMON NOUNS
THAT IMPLY ACTION

auxilium, auxiliī, n. (help)
iniūria, iniūriae, f. (injury, insult)
adventus, adventūs, m. (arrival)
exitus, exitūs, m. (departure)
impetus, impetūs, m. (attack)
ductus, ductūs, m. (leadership)
mandātum, mandātī, n. (order)

GENITIVE OF DESCRIPTION

GENITIVE OF
DESCRIPTION

Genitive Noun + Adjective pair
↓
Indicates a characteristic of
some other noun in the sentence.
↓
"OF" or "WITH"

Descriptions
can give physical
or personality
information.

NOUN
&
ADJECTIVE

Hominem **fortis animī** dēsīderāmus.
We need a person ⬦with a courageous heart⬦.

EIUS MODĪ
↓
"of that sort"

Vir **eius modī** es.
You are a man ⬦of that sort⬦.

GENITIVE & ABLATIVE
Both cases can convey
descriptions (see p. 73).

The genitive is used when
the description involves
definite measurements.
This use of the genitive of
description is sometimes
called the "Genitive of
Measurement."

Vir **tantae prūdentiae** es!
You are a man ⬦of such great wisdom⬦!

(Genitive)

Vir **tantā prūdentiā** es!
You are a man ⬦of such great wisdom⬦!

(Ablative)

Ignem vīcistī post proelium **trium hōrārum**.
You conquered the fire after a battle ⬦of three hours⬦.

GENITIVE OF MATERIAL

> **GENITIVE OF MATERIAL**
>
> Genitive noun indicates the material
> of which something is composed.
>
> ↓
>
> "OF"

COMMON MATERIALS

aes, aeris, n. (bronze)
argentum, argentī, n. (silver)
aurum, aurī, n. (gold)
lignum, lignī, n. (wood)
marmor, marmoris, n. (marble)
saxum, saxī, n. (stone)

Haec domus **lignī** ā tē aedificāta est.
This house ⋄of wood⋄ was built by you.

The house
was composed
of wood.

Ingentem acervum **vestīmentōrum** portābās.
You were carrying a huge pile ⋄of clothes⋄.

The pile
was composed
of clothes.

Genitive of Material
is not limited to
construction
materials!

GENITIVE OF VALUE

GENITIVE OF VALUE

A verb of buying, selling, esteeming or a linking verb can trigger a genitive noun indicating value/importance.

to **sell** for a high price

Note the special meaning these verbs take on when combined with a genitive of value.

BUYING, SELLING, ESTEEMING

emō, emere, ēmī, emptus (to buy)
vendō, vendere, vendidī, venditus (to sell)

{ faciō, facere, fēcī, factus (to value)
habeō, habēre, habuī, habitus (to value)
aestimō, aestimāre, aestimāvī, aestimātus (to value)

LINKING

sum, esse, fuī, futūrus (to be)
fīō, fīerī, factus sum (to become)

to **value** highly

to **be** of great value

Quantī venditur cibus?
⬧For how much⬧ is the food sold?

Hunc lūdum **maximī** facis.
You value this game ⬧very highly⬧.

Quid **plūris** est quam victōria?
What is ⬧of greater value⬧ than victory?

GENITIVES OF VALUE

magnī - high
plūris - higher
maximī - highest

parvī - little
minōris - less
minimī - the least

tantī - so much
quantī - how much?

nihilī - unimportant

GENITIVE AS AN APPOSITIVE

Genitive acts as an Appositive.

APPOSITIONAL GENITIVE

Genitive noun can rename/explain another noun.

e.g. the burden **of fear**
("Of fear" explains what the burden is.)
↓
"OF"

NOTE:

The appositional genitive is not used for phrases like:
"the city of Troy"
or
"the island of Sardinia"
↓
A simple appositive is used instead:

urbs Trōia
īnsula Sardinia

Promētheus dōnum **flammae** hominibus dedit.
Prometheus gave the gift ⬦of fire⬦ to mankind.
↓
"Of fire" explains what the gift is.

Promētheus poenam **exsiliī** pependit.
Prometheus paid the penalty ⬦of exile⬦.
↓
"Of exile" explains what the penalty is.

GENITIVE OF THE CHARGE

> **GENITIVE OF THE CHARGE**
>
> Genitive noun indicates the charge of which someone has been accused, convicted, or acquitted.
>
> ↓
>
> "OF" or "FOR"

Pecūniae publicae accūsātus es.
You were accused ⋄of embezzlement⋄.

CHARGES

ambitus, ambitūs, m. (bribery)
avāritia, avāritiae, f. (greed)
fūrtum, fūrtī, m. (theft)
impietās, impietātis, f. (blasphemy)
pecūnia pūblica, -ae, f. (embezzlement)

ACCUSING, CONVICTING, ACQUITTING

accūsō, -āre, -āvī, -ātus (to accuse)
arguō, arguere, arguī, argūtus (to accuse)
condemnō, -āre, -āvī, -ātus (to condemn)
damnō, -āre, -āvī, -ātus (to condemn)
absolvō, -solvere, -solvī, -solūtus (to acquit)

NON-GENITIVE CHARGES

dē vī - "of assault"
dē venēficiīs - "of poisoning"
dē caede - "of murder"
inter sīcāriōs - "of murder"

Lūcium fūrtī damnāvērunt.
They condemned Lucius ⋄for theft⋄.

Lūcium dē vī absolvētur.
Lucius will be acquitted ⋄of assault⋄.

GENITIVE WITH SPECIAL ADJECTIVES

GENITIVE WITH ADJECTIVES

Some adjectives
can trigger a genitive noun.

↓

"OF" or "FOR"

NOTE:

Adjectives that trigger a
genitive tend to express desire,
memory, knowledge, fullness,
power, and sharing.

Cupida **cibī** sum!
I am eager ✧for food✧.

COMMON ADJECTIVES THAT
TRIGGER A GENITIVE

avidus, avida, avidum (greedy)

cupidus, cupida, cupidum (desirous, eager)

memor, memōris (mindful)

perītus, perīta, perītum (skilled [in])

imperītus, imperīta, imperītum (ignorant)

plēnus, plēna, plēnum (full)

expers, expertis (devoid)

potēns, potentis (powerful [over])

particeps, participis (sharing [in])

affīnis, affīne (involved [with])

Sometimes words other
than "of" and "for"
may be necessary.

Perīta **artium coquīnāriārum** sum.
I am skilled ✧in the culinary arts✧.

GENITIVE WITH SPECIAL VERBS

GENITIVE WITH SPECIAL VERBS

Some verbs take their direct object
in the genitive case.

Virī vulnerātī miserētur.
She pities ⬦the wounded man⬦.

VERBS WITH GENITIVE OBJECTS

misereor, miserērī, miseritus sum (to pity, feel sorry for)

meminī, meminisse (to remember)

oblīvīscor, oblīvīscī, oblītus sum (to forget)

potior, potīrī, potītus sum (to get control of, get possession of)

Meminī and oblīvīscor
sometimes take
accusative objects.

Potior can also
take an ablative
object, and in fact
it usually does so.

(See p. 87)

MEMINĪ, MEMINISSE

DEFECTIVE:
Only has perfect, pluperfect, future perfect forms

↓

Translate as present, perfect, and future

meministī	You remember
meminerās	You remembered
memineris	You will remember

GENITIVE WITH IMPERSONAL VERBS

WITH THE GENITIVE

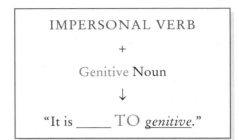

IMPERSONAL VERB

+

Genitive **Noun**

↓

"It is _____ TO *genitive*."

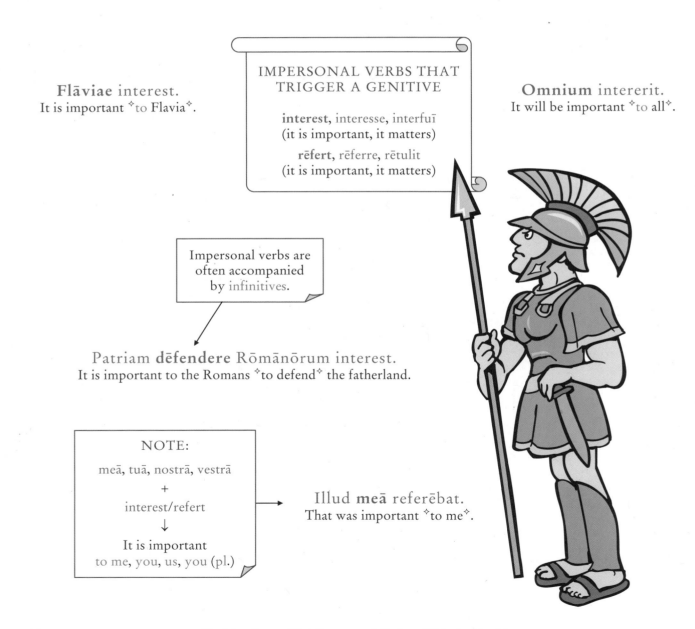

Flāviae interest.
It is important ⬩to Flavia⬩.

IMPERSONAL VERBS THAT TRIGGER A GENITIVE

interest, interesse, interfuī
(it is important, it matters)

rēfert, rēferre, rētulit
(it is important, it matters)

Omnium intererit.
It will be important ⬩to all⬩.

Impersonal verbs are often accompanied by infinitives.

Patriam **dēfendere** Rōmānōrum interest.
It is important to the Romans ⬩to defend⬩ the fatherland.

NOTE:

meā, tuā, nostrā, vestrā
+
interest/refert
↓
It is important
to me, you, us, you (pl.)

Illud **meā** referēbat.
That was important ⬩to me⬩.

GENITIVE WITH IMPERSONAL VERBS

WITH THE GENITIVE AND THE ACCUSATIVE

ACCUSATIVE
↓
Person
affected

**IMPERSONAL VERBS THAT TRIGGER
GENITIVE & ACCUSATIVE**

miseret, miserēre, miseruīt (<u>*acc.*</u> pities <u>*gen.*</u>)

piget, pigēre, piguit (<u>*acc.*</u> dislikes <u>*gen.*</u>)

pudet, pudēre, puduit (<u>*acc.*</u> is ashamed of <u>*gen.*</u>)

taedet, taedēre, taeduit (<u>*acc.*</u> is weary of <u>*gen.*</u>)

paenitet, paenitēre, paenituit (<u>*acc.*</u> feels sorrow about <u>*gen.*</u>)

GENITIVE
↓
Cause of
accusative's
feeling

Cornēliam piget diērum frīgidōrum.
⬦Cornelia⬦ dislikes ⬦cold days⬦.

Labōrum Cornēliam taedēbat.
⬦Cornelia⬦ was weary of ⬦her chores⬦.

Urbānōrum miseret Cornēliam.
⬦Cornelia⬦ pities ⬦city folk⬦.

Vītae Cornēliam nōn paenitēbit.
⬦Cornelia⬦ will not feel regret about ⬦her life⬦.

INTRODUCTION TO THE DATIVE CASE

> ## DATIVE CASE
>
> Often translated
> into English
> by adding
> "TO" or "FOR."

Mīlitibus auxilium dabimus.
We will give help ⋄to the soldiers⋄.

> Dative
> of
> Indirect
> Object

Locum **castrīs** petimus.
We look for a place ⋄for our camp⋄.

Tentōrium **vulnerātīs** ponēs.
You will set up a tent ⋄for the wounded⋄.

> Dative
> of
> Purpose

> Dative
> of
> Reference

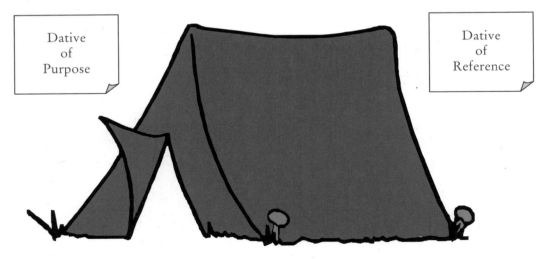

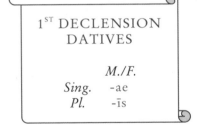

1ST DECLENSION DATIVES

	M./F.
Sing.	-ae
Pl.	-īs

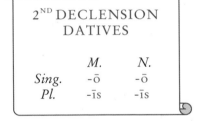

2ND DECLENSION DATIVES

	M.	*N.*
Sing.	-ō	-ō
Pl.	-īs	-īs

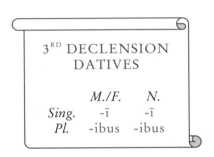

3RD DECLENSION DATIVES

	M./F.	*N.*
Sing.	-ī	-ī
Pl.	-ibus	-ibus

DATIVE OF INDIRECT OBJECT

GIVE
SHOW
TELL

DATIVE OF INDIRECT OBJECT

INDIRECT OBJECT:
Noun to which something
is given, shown, or said.

I give *noun* a gift.
I give a gift to *noun*.
↓
"TO"

INDIRECT OBJECT TRIGGERS

dō, dare, dedī, datus
(to give)

mōnstrō, -āre, -āvī, -ātus
(to show)

nārrō, -āre, -āvī, -ātus
(to tell)

dīcō, dīcere, dīxī, dictus
(to say, speak)

Fābulam **fīliae** nārrābō dē itineribus meīs.
I will tell a story about my travels ✧to my daughter✧.
I will tell ✧my daughter✧ a story about my travels.

Mihi, nautae, virtūtem monstrāte.
Show your courage ✧to me✧, sailors.
Show ✧me✧ your courage, sailors.

Deī **linteīs** ventum dant.
The gods give wind ✧to the sails✧.
The gods give ✧the sails✧ wind.

DIRECT OBJECT
The noun that is
given, shown, or told.

Pauca verba dīcam.
I will speak ✧a few words✧.

INDIRECT OBJECT
The noun that something is
given, shown, or told *to*.

Nautae dīcam.
I will speak ✧to the sailor✧.

DATIVE OF REFERENCE

ADVANTAGE AND DISADVANTAGE

DATIVE OF REFERENCE

Dative noun indicates the person/thing
"for whom" the verb is performed:

can indicate that the verb happens to the
. advantage or disadvantage of the dative noun.

↓

"FOR"

ADVANTAGE

Rēgnum **tibi** condam.
I will found a kingdom ⋄for you⋄.

DISADVANTAGE

Calamitātem **Graecīs** parāvistī.
You prepared disaster ⋄for the Greeks⋄.

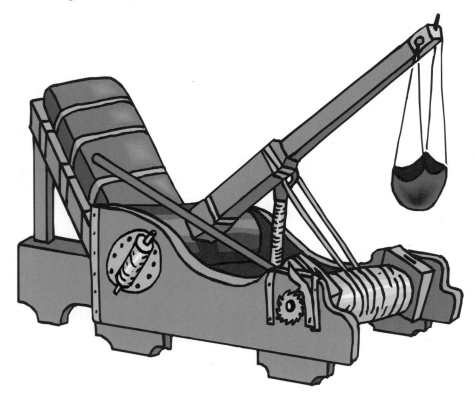

DATIVE OF REFERENCE

DATIVE OF REFERENCE
WITH GENITIVE FORCE

Sometimes a dative of reference is best translated as if it were a possessive genitive. When this occurs, we use the term:

"Dative of Reference with Genitive Force."

Amor animum **tibi** flammāvit.
Love inflamed ⋄your⋄ heart.

(Love inflamed the heart ⋄for you⋄.)

When the dative seems to indicate who is being affected by some action but "to" or "for" sound ridiculous, try "of".

Crīnēs **puerō** tondēbās.
You were cutting ⋄the boy's⋄ hair.

(You were cutting the hair ⋄for the boy⋄.)

DATIVE OF POSSESSION

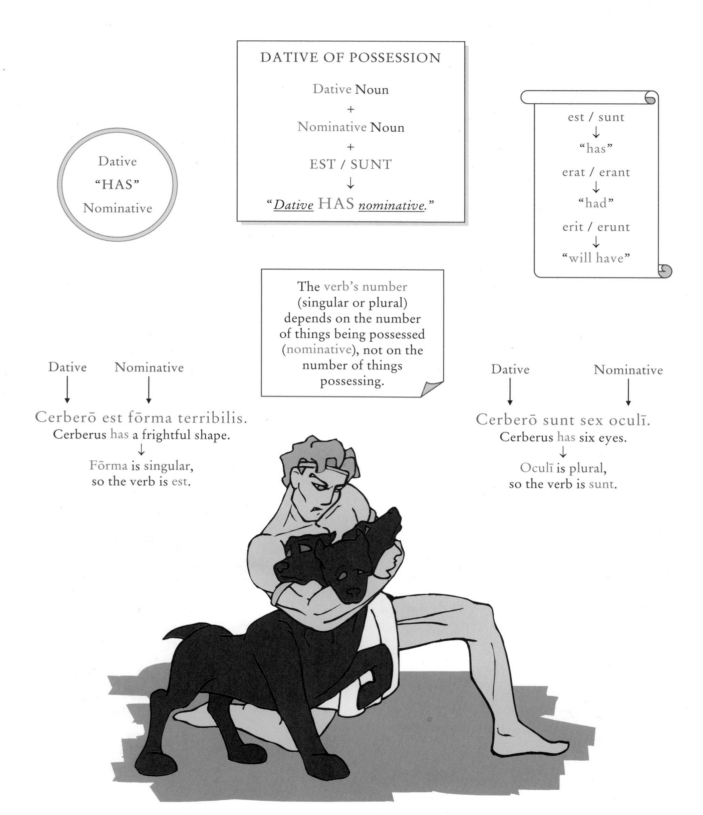

DATIVE OF POSSESSION

Dative Noun
+
Nominative Noun
+
EST / SUNT
↓
"*Dative* HAS *nominative*."

Dative
"HAS"
Nominative

est / sunt
↓
"has"
erat / erant
↓
"had"
erit / erunt
↓
"will have"

The verb's number
(singular or plural)
depends on the number
of things being possessed
(nominative), not on the
number of things
possessing.

Dative   Nominative
↓   ↓
Cerberō est fōrma terribilis.
Cerberus has a frightful shape.
↓
Fōrma is singular,
so the verb is est.

Dative   Nominative
↓   ↓
Cerberō sunt sex oculī.
Cerberus has six eyes.
↓
Oculī is plural,
so the verb is sunt.

DATIVE OF PURPOSE

> ### DATIVE OF PURPOSE (OR END)
>
> Dative noun indicates the purpose or the effect of some noun or action.
>
> ↓
>
> "AS" or "FOR"

Cornēlia **auxiliō** veniet.
Cornelia will come ⁺as a help⁺.

↓

Auxiliō indicates the purpose of Cornelia coming.

Haec sella **dolōrī** est!
This chair is ⁺as a source of pain⁺!

↓

Dolōrī indicates the effect of the chair.

Malum locum **sellae** dēlēgī.
I picked a bad place ⁺for my chair⁺!

↓

Sellae indicates the purpose of picking a place.

> ### IMPORTANT DATIVES OF PURPOSE
>
> auxiliō - as a help
> subsidiō - as a help
> praesidiō - as protection
> salūtī - as a salvation
> ūsuī - as an advantage
> impedīmentō - as a hindrance
> dōnō - as a gift
> mūnerī - as a gift/service
> cūrae - as a source of concern
> dolōrī - as a source of sorrow
> odiō - as a source of hatred

> ### AWKWARD TRANSLATIONS
>
> Literal translations with "as" sometimes sound awkward, so you may wish to rephrase in more natural terms.

Cornēlia auxiliō veniet.
Cornelia will come to help.

Haec sella dolōrī est.
This chair is causing pain.

DOUBLE DATIVE

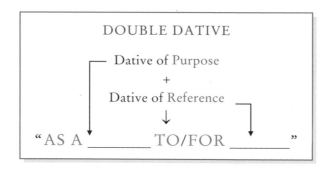

> **DOUBLE DATIVE**
>
> ┌─ Dative of Purpose
> │   +
> │ Dative of Reference
> │   ↓
> "AS A _____ TO/FOR _____ "

Milités **subsidiō tibi** vēnērunt.
The soldiers came ⟡as a help for you⟡.

Vōbisne cūrae est bellum?
Is war ⟡as a source of concern to you (pl.)⟡?

> ### IMPORTANT DATIVES OF PURPOSE
>
> auxiliō - as a help
> subsidiō - as a help
> praesidiō - as protection
> salūtī - as a salvation
> ūsuī - as an advantage
> impedīmentō - as a hindrance
> dōnō - as a gift
> mūnerī - as a gift/service
> cūrae - as a source of concern
> dolōrī - as a source of sorrow
> odiō - as a source of hatred

> ### AWKWARD TRANSLATIONS
>
> Literal translations with "as" sometimes sound awkward, so you may wish to rephrase in more natural terms.

Milités subsidiō tibi vēnērunt.
The soldiers came to help you.

Vōbisne cūrae est bellum?
Does war worry you (pl.)?

DATIVE OF AGENT

DATIVE OF AGENT

Typically appears with the passive periphrastic.
(See pp. 258-262)

↓

"*Nominative*
must be *verb*ed
BY *dative*."

**PASSIVE
PERIPHRASTIC
PHRASINGS**

"*Nominative*
must be *verb*ed
by *dative*."

OR

"*Dative*
must *verb*
nominative."

Scōpae **nōbis** agendae sunt.

↓

The brooms must be driven ⋄by us⋄.

or

⋄We⋄ must drive the brooms.

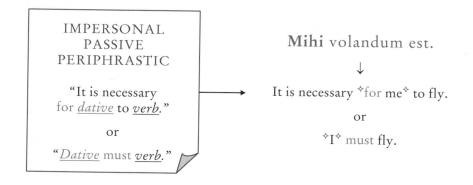

**IMPERSONAL
PASSIVE
PERIPHRASTIC**

"It is necessary
for *dative* to *verb*."

or

"*Dative* must *verb*."

Mihi volandum est.

↓

It is necessary ⋄for me⋄ to fly.

or

⋄I⋄ must fly.

DATIVE WITH SPECIAL ADJECTIVES

> ## DATIVE WITH ADJECTIVES
>
> Some adjectives can trigger
> a dative noun.
> ↓
> "TO" or "FOR"

Flōrēs **āvibus** grātī sunt.
Flowers are pleasing ⬦to birds⬦.

Facile **āvibus** est volāre.
It is easy ⬦for birds⬦ to fly.

> "to"/"for"
> ↓
> sometimes
> unnecessary

In arbore propinquā **viae** habitant.
They live in a tree near ⬦[to] the road⬦.

> ## TRANSLATION TIP
>
> In English, you can put
> the adjective before or after
> the noun it modifies. Use
> whichever order sounds
> more natural to you.

terra idōnea tibi
↓
a ⬦land suitable⬦ for you
a ⬦suitable land⬦ for you

> ## COMMON ADJECTIVES
> ## THAT TRIGGER A DATIVE
>
> fidēlis, fidēle (loyal)
> īnfestus, īnfesta, īnfestum (hostile)
> amīcus, amīca, amīcum (friendly)
> inimīcus, inimīca, inimīcum (unfriendly)
>
> facilis, facile (easy)
> difficilis, difficile (difficult)
>
> pār, paris (equal)
> similis, simile (similar)
> dissimilis, dissimile (unlike)
>
> fīnitimus, fīnitima, fīnitimum (neighboring)
> propinquus, propinqua, propinquum (near)
> vīcīnus, vīcīna, vīcīnum (near)
>
> cārus, cāra, cārum (dear)
> grātus, grāta, grātum (pleasing)
> idōneus, idōnea, idōneum (suitable)
> molestus, molesta, molestum (troublesome)
> nōtus, nōta, nōtum (well-known)
> ūtilis, ūtile (useful)

> ## SIMILIS
> ↓
> Often goes with the
> genitive instead of
> the dative when a
> person is involved.

→ similis **Corinthō**
similar ⬦to Corinth⬦

(Standard use of similis with dative)

→ similis **Marcī**
similar ⬦to Marcus⬦

(Special use of similis with genitive
because Marcus is a person)

DATIVE WITH SPECIAL VERBS

> ### DATIVE WITH SPECIAL VERBS
> Some verbs take their direct object
> in the dative case.

Appius **Līviae** favet.
Appius favors ⋄Livia⋄.

VERBS WITH DATIVE OBJECTS†

cēdō, cēdere, cessī, cessus (to give way, yield to)

cōnfīdō, cōnfīdere, cōnfīsus sum (to rely on, trust)

crēdō, crēdere, crēdidī, crēditus (to believe, trust)

diffīdō, diffīdere, diffīsus sum (to distrust, not trust)

faveō, favēre, fāvī, fautus (to favor)

ignōscō, ignōscere, ignōvī, ignōtus (to pardon)

imperō, imperāre, imperāvī, imperātus (to order)

noceō, nocēre, nocuī, nocitus (to harm)

nūbō, nūbere, nūpsī, nūptus (to marry)

parcō, parcere, pepercī, parsus (to spare)

pāreō, pārēre, pāruī, pāritus (to obey)

persuādeō, persuādēre, persuāsī, persuāsus (to persuade)

placeō, placēre, placuī, placitus (to please)

serviō, servīre, servīvī, servītus (to serve)

studeō, studēre, studuī (to study, be enthusiastic about)

†Different books list the principle parts of these verbs in a number of different ways. For example, you may
see *cessūrus* or *cessum* as the fourth principle parts of *cēdō* instead of *cessus*.

DATIVE WITH SPECIAL VERBS

PASSIVE VOICE OF SPECIAL VERB CONSTRUCTION

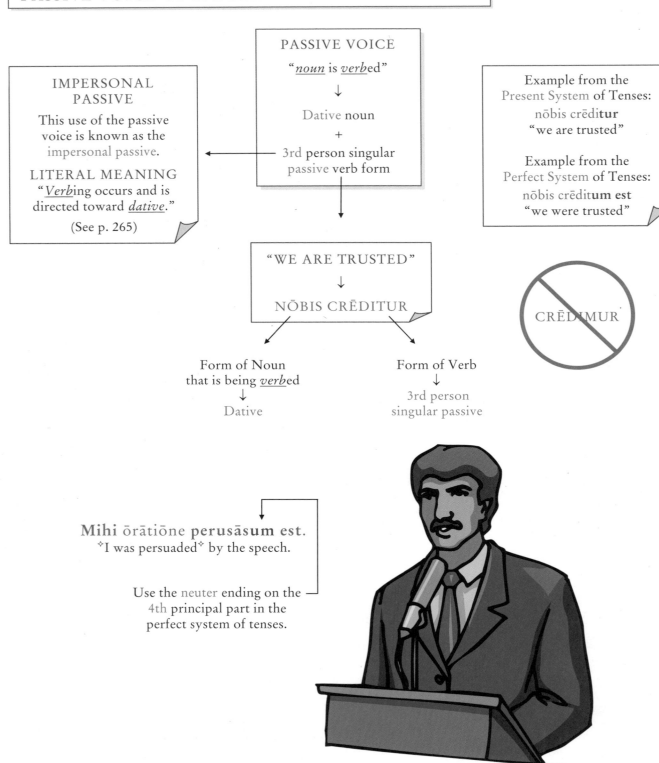

IMPERSONAL PASSIVE

This use of the passive voice is known as the impersonal passive.

LITERAL MEANING
"*Verb*ing occurs and is directed toward *dative*."

(See p. 265)

PASSIVE VOICE
"*noun* is *verb*ed"
↓
Dative noun
+
3rd person singular passive verb form

Example from the Present System of Tenses:
nōbis crēdi**tur**
"we are trusted"

Example from the Perfect System of Tenses:
nōbis crēdit**um est**
"we were trusted"

"WE ARE TRUSTED"
↓
NŌBIS CRĒDITUR

Form of Noun that is being *verb*ed
↓
Dative

Form of Verb
↓
3rd person singular passive

CRĒDIMUR

Mihi ōrātiōne **perusāsum est.**
⬦I was persuaded⬦ by the speech.

Use the neuter ending on the 4th principal part in the perfect system of tenses.

DATIVE WITH COMPOUND VERBS

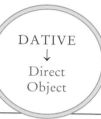

DATIVE
↓
Direct
Object

If the root verb is intransitive (cannot take a direct object), the compound verb can take a dative noun as its direct object instead of the usual accusative.

DATIVE WITH COMPOUND VERBS

Many verbs with the following prefixes can trigger a noun in the dative case:

ad-	in-	prae-
ante-	inter-	prō-
circum-	ob-	sub-
con-	post-	super-

DATIVE
↓
Finishes the
thought

If the root verb is transitive (can take a direct object), the compound verb takes an accusative direct object and uses a dative to finish the thought.

Puerī **Marcō** īnstant.
The boys pursue ⋄Marcus⋄.

Root Verb:
stō, stāre, stetī, stātus (to stand)
↓
Intransitive

Corōnam Marcī **capitī** impōnēmus.
We will place a garland on Marcus' ⋄head⋄.

Root Verb:
pōnō, pōnere, posuī, positus (to put)
↓
Transitive

NOTE:

Some letters in these prefixes tend to change when they are placed next to certain letters.

in + p = **imp**-
ad + p = **app**-
etc.

DATIVE WITH IMPERSONAL VERBS

IMPERSONAL VERB

+

Dative Noun

↓

"It is ____ TO/FOR *dative*."

Tibi necesse est.
It is necessary ⬦for you⬦.

IMPERSONAL VERBS THAT TRIGGER A DATIVE

accidit, accidere, accidit (it happens)
cōnstat, cōnstāre, cōnstitit (it is clear)
libet, libēre, libuit (it is pleasing)
licet, licēre, licuit (it is necessary)
necesse est, esse, fuit (it is necessary)
placet, placēre, placuit (it seems good)
praestat, praestāre, praestitit (it is better)

Claudiō libet.
It is pleasing ⬦to Claudius⬦.

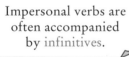

Impersonal verbs are often accompanied by infinitives.

Virīs necesse est **festīnāre**.
It is necessary for the men ⬦to hurry⬦.

Claudiō libet **clāmāre**.
It is pleasing to Claudius ⬦to shout⬦.

INTRODUCTION TO THE ACCUSATIVE CASE

> ### ACCUSATIVE CASE
>
> Usually acts as the direct object of the verb.
>
> OR
>
> Appears after a preposition.

Accusative
Direct
Object

Aemulōs vincēs.
You will defeat your ✧competitors✧.

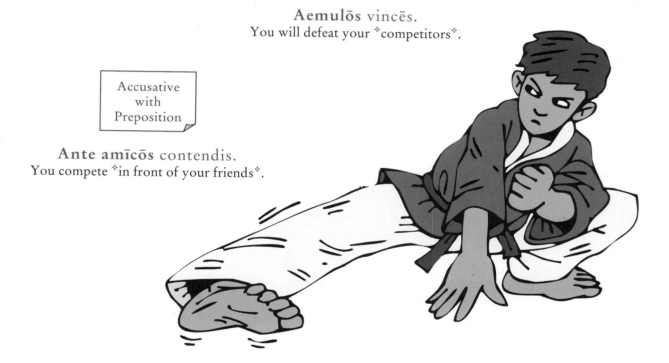

Accusative
with
Preposition

Ante amīcōs contendis.
You compete ✧in front of your friends✧.

1ST DECLENSION ACCUSATIVES		
		M./F.
Sing.		-am
Pl.		-ās

2ND DECLENSION ACCUSATIVES		
	M.	*N.*
Sing.	-um	-um
Pl.	-ōs	-a

3RD DECLENSION ACCUSATIVES		
	M./F.	*N.*
Sing.	-em	-varies-
Pl.	-ēs	-a

ACCUSATIVE OF PLACE TO WHICH

> ### ACCUSATIVE OF PLACE TO WHICH
>
> AD or IN or SUB
>
> +
>
> Accusative **Noun**
>
> ↓
>
> Indicates place to which.

> ad, prep. + acc. (to, toward)
>
> in, prep. + acc. (into, onto, against)
>
> sub, prep. + acc. ([to] under, up to, to the foot of)

Ad terram siccam properāmus.
We hurry ⬦to dry land⬦.

Caelum pluviam **in umbrāculum** fundit.
The sky pours rain ⬦onto the umbrella⬦.

Aqua **in fenestram** cadit.
Rain falls ⬦against the window⬦.

Sub umbrāculum venī!
Come ⬦[to] under the umbrella!⬦

Sub montem currimus et antrum petimus.
We run ⬦to the foot of the mountain⬦ and look for a cave.

ACCUSATIVE DIRECT OBJECT

> ### ACCUSATIVE DIRECT OBJECT
>
> #### DIRECT OBJECT:
> Noun that receives the action of the verb.
>
> | I | call | you. |
> |:---:|:---:|:---:|
> | ↓ | ↓ | ↓ |
> | Subject | Verb | Direct Object |
> | (nom.) | | (acc.) |

Claudia **Aureliam** salūtat.
Claudia greets ✧Aurelia✧.

Accusative case
indicates that
Aurelia is the
direct object
of salutat.

Claudiam Aurelia salūtat.
Aurelia greets ✧Claudia✧.

Accusative case
indicates that
Claudia is the
direct object
of salutat.

> Although the direct object
> comes after the verb in English,
> it may appear anywhere in
> a Latin sentence.

Puer **aviam** iuvat.

Aviam iuvat puer.

Puer iuvat **aviam**.

↓

The boy helps his ✧grandmother✧.

ACCUSATIVE OF DURATION OF TIME

ACCUSATIVE OF
DURATION OF TIME

Accusative noun indicates
how long some situation lasts.

↓

"FOR"

TIME VOCABULARY

hōra, hōrae, f. (hour)

diēs, diēī, m. (day)

nox, noctis, f. (night)

mēnsis, mēnsis, m. (month)

annus, annī, m. (year)

tempus, temporis, n. (time)

vēr, vēris, n. (spring)

aestās, aestātis, f. (summer)

autumnus, autumnī, m. (fall)

hiems, hiemis, f. (winter)

saeculum, saeculī, n. (century, age)

Duās hōrās exspectāvimus.
We waited ⋄for two hours⋄.

Tōtam aestātem rūrī mānsimus.
We stayed in the country ⋄for the whole summer⋄.

ACCUSATIVE OF EXTENT OF SPACE

ACCUSATIVE OF
EXTENT OF SPACE

Accusative noun indicates
how far something goes or
how far away something is.
↓
I walked three miles.
I live three miles away.

Centum pedēs in caelum ferimur.
We are carried ✧100 feet✧ into the air.

(How far)

Nunc ab urbe **mille passūs** absumus.
Now we are ✧one mile✧ away from the city.

(How far away)

SPATIAL VERBS

eō, īre, īvī or iī, itus (to go)†
absum, abesse, āfuī, āfutūrus (to be away)
ambulō, -āre, -āvī, -ātus (to walk)
currō, currere, cucurrī, cursus (to run)†
nāvigō, -āre, -āvī, -ātus (to sail)
volō, -āre, -āvī, -ātus (to fly)

SPATIAL UNITS

pēs, pedis, m. (foot)
passus, passūs, m. (pace)
mille passūs (mile)
mīlia passuum (miles)
spatium, spatiī, n. (space, distance)

MILEAGE

1 mile → mille passūs
2 miles → duo mīlia passuum
3 miles → tria mīlia passuum
4 miles → quattuor mīlia passuum
5 miles → quīnque mīlia passuum
etc.

†Different books list the principle parts of these verbs in a number of different ways. You may see
itūrus and *cursūrus* or *itum* and *cursum* as fourth principle parts instead of *itus* and *cursus*.

PREDICATE ACCUSATIVE

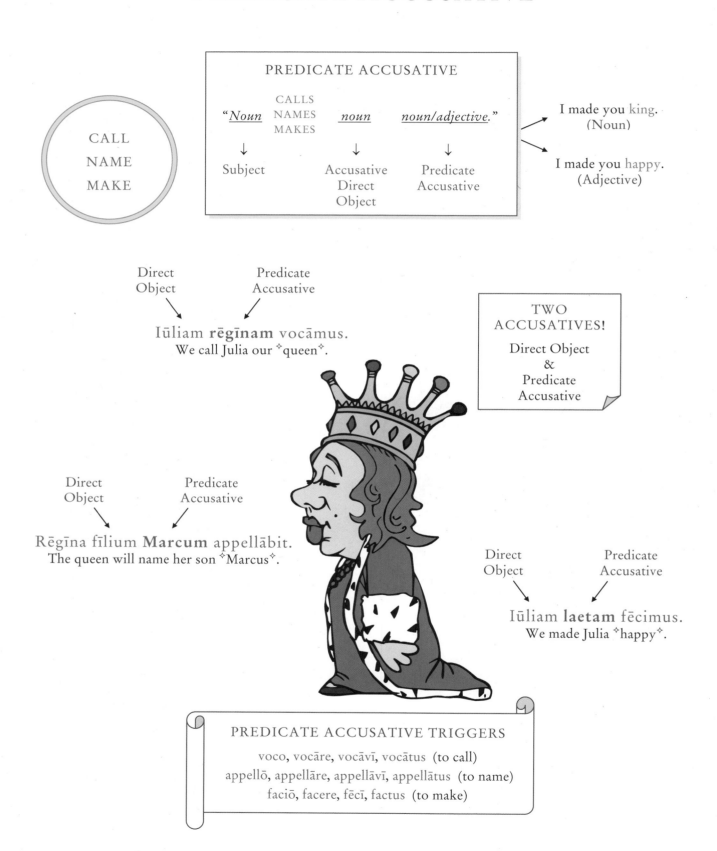

CALL
NAME
MAKE

PREDICATE ACCUSATIVE

	CALLS		
"Noun	NAMES	*noun*	*noun/adjective."*
	MAKES		
↓		↓	↓
Subject		Accusative Direct Object	Predicate Accusative

I made you king.
(Noun)

I made you happy.
(Adjective)

Direct Object   Predicate Accusative

Iūliam **rēgīnam** vocāmus.
We call Julia our ⬧queen⬧.

TWO ACCUSATIVES!
Direct Object
&
Predicate Accusative

Direct Object   Predicate Accusative

Rēgīna fīlium **Marcum** appellābit.
The queen will name her son ⬧Marcus⬧.

Direct Object   Predicate Accusative

Iūliam **laetam** fēcimus.
We made Julia ⬧happy⬧.

PREDICATE ACCUSATIVE TRIGGERS
voco, vocāre, vocāvī, vocātus (to call)
appellō, appellāre, appellāvī, appellātus (to name)
faciō, facere, fēcī, factus (to make)

ACCUSATIVE IN EXCLAMATIONS

ACCUSATIVE IN EXCLAMATIONS

Accusative Noun + Adjective

↓

Expresses an exclamation.

Fēlīcem diem nātālem!
Happy Birthday!

Ō pulcherrimum crustum!
Oh most beautiful cake!

Exclamatory
accusatives are not
a complete sentence.
There is no verb.
The accusative
stands alone.

Tē fēlīcem!
Lucky you!

ACCUSATIVE WITH IMPERSONAL VERBS

IMPERSONAL VERB
+
Accusative Noun
↓
"It is ____ FOR *accusative*."

IMPERSONAL VERBS THAT TRIGGER AN ACCUSATIVE

decet, decēre, decuit (it is fitting)
dēdecet, dēdecēre, dēdecuit (it is unsuitable)
oportet, oportēre, oportuit (it is necessary/proper)

Mē oportet.
It is proper ⋄for me⋄.

Iūliam decet.
It is fitting ⋄for Julia⋄.

Impersonal verbs are often accompanied by infinitives.

Mē oportet hortum **colere**.
It is necessary for me ⋄to take care of⋄ the garden.

INTRODUCTION TO THE ABLATIVE CASE

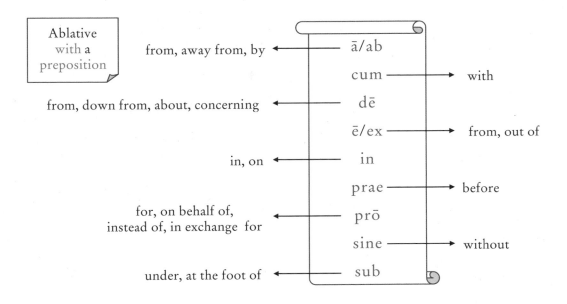

Ablative with a preposition

from, away from, by ←	ā/ab
	cum → with
from, down from, about, concerning ←	dē
	ē/ex → from, out of
in, on ←	in
	prae → before
for, on behalf of, instead of, in exchange for ←	prō
	sine → without
under, at the foot of ←	sub

Ablative without a preposition

Many uses of the ablative without a preposition will require you to add words in your English translation that are not actually present in the Latin.

↓

"by means of *noun*"
"because of *noun*"
"in respect to *noun*"
"than *noun*"

Piscem **magnitūdine** īnsignem capiēmus.
We will catch a fish remarkable ◇in respect to its size◇.

1ST DECLENSION ABLATIVES

	M./F.
Sing.	-ā
Pl.	-īs

2ND DECLENSION ABLATIVES

	M.	N.
Sing.	-ō	-ō
Pl.	-īs	-īs

3RD DECLENSION ABLATIVES

	M./F.	N.
Sing.	-e	-e
Pl.	-ibus	-ibus

ABLATIVE OF PLACE WHERE

> ABLATIVE OF PLACE WHERE
>
> IN or SUB
>
> +
>
> Ablative **Noun**
>
> ↓
>
> Indicates location.

> in, prep. + abl. (in, on)
>
> sub, prep. + abl. (under, at the foot of)

Mōns **in Ītaliā** est.
The mountain is ⋄in Italy⋄.

Vir **in summō monte** stat.
The man stands ⋄on the top of the mountain⋄.

Sub sōle labōrat.
He toils ⋄under the sun⋄.

Sub monte stāmus.
We stand ⋄at the foot of the mountain⋄.

ABLATIVE OF PLACE FROM WHICH

ā/ab
dē
ē/ex

-Ā/AB

Ā can be used when the next word starts with a consonant (except for *h*).

Ab can be used in any situation.

ABLATIVE OF PLACE FROM WHICH

Ā/AB or DĒ or Ē/EX

+E

Ablative **Noun**

↓

Indicates place from which.

Ē/EX

Ē can be used when the next word starts with a consonant (except for *h*).

Ex can be used in any situation.

> ā/ab, prep. + abl. (from, away from)
>
> dē, prep. + abl. (from, down from)
>
> ē/ex, prep. + abl. (from, out of)

Lux **dē lucernā** fulget.
Light shines ⋄down from the lamp⋄.

Trabs **ēx terrā** surgit.
A pole rises ⋄out of the ground⋄.

Via **ā vīllā meā** dūcit.
The path leads ⋄away from my house⋄.

PARTITIVE ABLATIVE

dē
ē/ex

> **PARTITIVE ABLATIVE**
>
> Multī, paucī, quis, numbers
> +
> DĒ / ĒX
> +
> Ablative noun
> ↓
> "many/few/who/1, 2, 3
> OF the *nouns*"

PART
OF
THE
WHOLE

> **NUMBERS**
>
> ūnus (1)
> quīnque (5)
> decem (10)
> centum (100)

> **PARTITIVE ABLATIVE TRIGGERS**
>
> multī, multae, multa (many)
> paucī, paucae, pauca (few, a few)
> quis (who?)

Multī ex amīcīs tuīs cantāre et salīre amant.
Many ⬧of your friends⬧ like to sing and dance.

Ūnam dē amīcīs tuīs laudāmus.
We praise one ⬧of your friends⬧.

Quis ē vōbis cantābat?
Who ⬧of you⬧ was singing?
(Which of you was singing?)

> **PARTITIVE
> GENITIVE & ABLATIVE**
>
> Most of these partitive ablative
> triggers can also be used with a
> partitive genitive. (See p. 31)
>
> Paucī is used only
> with the ablative.

ABLATIVE OF AGENT

ā/ab

ABLATIVE OF AGENT

Ā/AB

+

Ablative Noun

↓

Indicates the person by whom
some action is accomplished.

↓

"BY"

"AGENT"

↓

The noun by which an
action is performed.

Ablative of agent
is only for people.

"By *thing*"
is expressed without a
preposition using the
Ablative of Means.

(See p. 71)

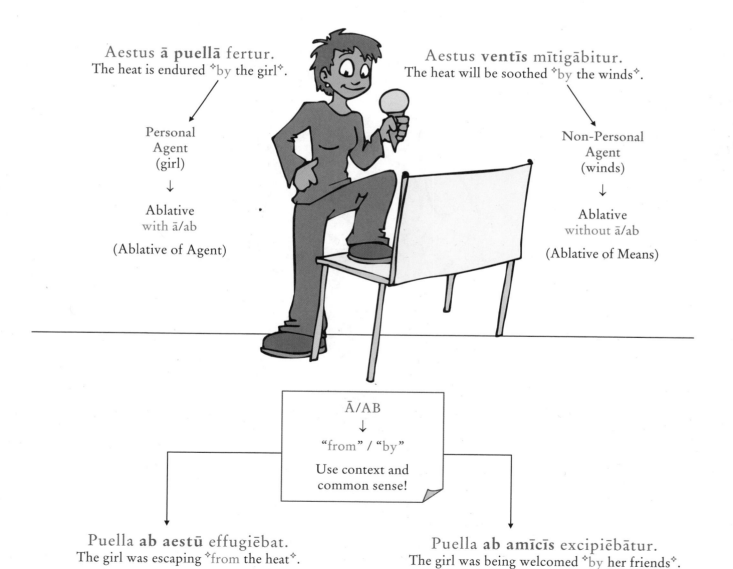

Aestus **ā puellā** fertur.
The heat is endured ⁺by the girl⁺.

Aestus **ventīs** mītigābitur.
The heat will be soothed ⁺by the winds⁺.

Personal
Agent
(girl)

↓

Ablative
with ā/ab

(Ablative of Agent)

Non-Personal
Agent
(winds)

↓

Ablative
without ā/ab

(Ablative of Means)

Ā/AB

↓

"from" / "by"

Use context and
common sense!

Puella **ab aestū** effugiēbat.
The girl was escaping ⁺from the heat⁺.

Puella **ab amīcīs** excipiēbātur.
The girl was being welcomed ⁺by her friends⁺.

ABLATIVE OF ACCOMPANIMENT

cum

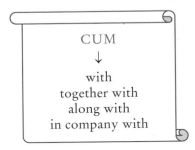

CUM
↓
with
together with
along with
in company with

ABLATIVE OF
ACCOMPANIMENT

CUM
+
Ablative Noun
↓
Indicates companionship.
↓
"WITH"

SPECIAL FORMS

mēcum   nōbiscum
with me   with us

tēcum   vōbiscum
with you   with you (pl.)

Quīntus **cum aliīs cīvibus** gaudet.
Quintus rejoices ✧with the other citizens✧.

Cum gladiō ante portās stat.
He stands in front of the gates ✧with his sword✧.

ABLATIVE OF MEANS

> ### ABLATIVE OF MEANS
>
> Indicates the means or instrument (*tool*) with which something is accomplished.
>
> (No Preposition)
> ↓
> "BY MEANS OF"
> "WITH"
> "BY"

Pēnicillō pingis.
You paint ✧with a brush✧.

Deōs **dōnīs** plācābis.
You will appease the gods ✧by means of gifts✧.

Nāve ad patriam tuam venīmus.
We are coming to your country ✧by boat✧.

> IN and ON
> are sometimes
> appropriate translations
> for the ablative
> of means.

Equīs ad urbem ībimus.
We will go to the city ✧on horses✧.

Meā linguā dīcēbās.
You were speaking ✧in my language✧.

> "BY <u>THING</u>" VS. "BY <u>PERSON</u>"
>
> "The picture was painted by hand."
> ↓
> Ablative of Means (no preposition)
>
> "The picture was painted by Paul."
> ↓
> Ablative of Agent (ā/ab + ablative: see p. 69)

ABLATIVE OF MANNER

With or without cum

ABLATIVE OF MANNER		
CUM + Ablative **noun**	CUM + Ablative noun/adjective pair	No Preposition + Ablative noun/adjective pair

Indicates the manner/style in which
some action is accomplished.
↓
"WITH"

Magnō gaudiō vītam agit.
She lives life ⬥with great joy⬥.

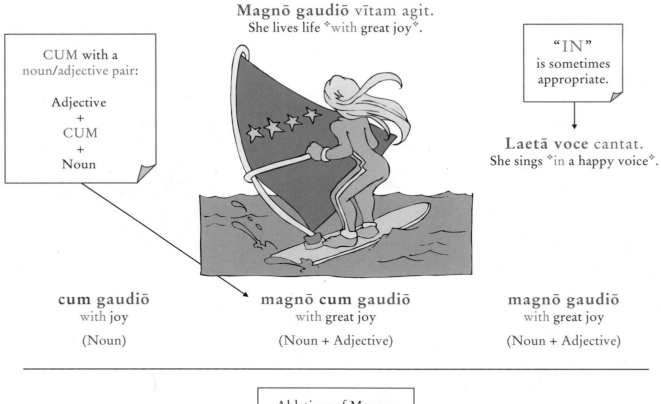

CUM with a
noun/adjective pair:

Adjective
+
CUM
+
Noun

"IN"
is sometimes
appropriate.

↓

Laetā voce cantat.
She sings ⬥in a happy voice⬥.

cum gaudiō
with joy

(Noun)

magnō cum gaudiō
with great joy

(Noun + Adjective)

magnō gaudiō
with great joy

(Noun + Adjective)

Ablatives of Manner
can describe physical
as well as emtional
styles.

Citīs gradibus currit.
She runs ⬥with quick steps⬥.
(Physical)

Cum gaudiō currit.
She runs ⬥with joy⬥.
(Emotional)

ABLATIVE OF DESCRIPTION

No Preposition

> ### ABLATIVE OF DESCRIPTION
>
> Ablative **Noun** + Adjective pair
> ↓
> Indicates a characteristic of
> some other noun in the sentence.
> ↓
> "OF" or "WITH"

Descriptions can give physical or personality information.

NOUN
&
ADJECTIVE

Bēstia **magnā saevitiā** in antrō cōnspecta est.
A beast ⬦of great ferocity⬦ was seen in the cave.

Cruentīs faucibus dracō domum meam incendit.
A dragon ⬦with gory jaws⬦ burned my house.

GENITIVE & ABLATIVE
Both cases can convey
descriptions (see p. 35).

Vir **tantae prūdentiae** es!
You are a man ⬦of such great wisdom⬦!

(Genitive)

Vir **tantā prūdentiā** es!
You are a man ⬦of such great wisdom⬦!

(Ablative)

ABLATIVE OF TIME WHEN

No Preposition

> ### ABLATIVE OF TIME WHEN
>
> Ablative **noun** indicates when some situation takes place.
>
> (No Preposition)
>
> ↓
>
> "IN" or "ON" or "AT"

Aestāte male dormiō.
⁺In the summer⁺, I sleep poorly.

TIME VOCABULARY

hōra, hōrae, f. (hour)

diēs, diēī, m. (day)

nox, noctis, f. (night)

mēnsis, mēnsis, m. (month)

annus, annī, m. (year)

tempus, temporis, n. (time)

vēr, vēris, n. (spring)

aestās, aestātis, f. (summer)

autumnus, autumnī, m. (fall)

hiems, hiemis, f. (winter)

saeculum, saeculī, n. (century, age)

Illō diē maximē dēfessus fuī.
⁺On that day⁺, I was extremely tired.

Nocte dormiō et aliquando ambulō.
⁺At night⁺ I sleep and sometimes I walk.

ABLATIVE OF TIME WITHIN WHICH

> ### ABLATIVE OF TIME WITHIN WHICH
>
> Ablative noun indicates the time span within which some situation takes place.
>
> (No Preposition)
>
> ↓
>
> "IN" or "WITHIN" or "DURING"

Tribus hōrīs aurum inveniēmus.
✦Within three hours✦, we will find the gold.

Ūnō diē aurum cōnsūmēs.
You will spend the gold ✦in one day✦.

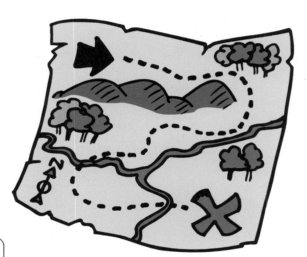

TIME VOCABULARY

hōra, hōrae, f. (hour)

diēs, diēī, m. (day)

nox, noctis, f. (night)

mēnsis, mēnsis, m. (month)

annus, annī, m. (year)

tempus, temporis, n. (time)

vēr, vēris, n. (spring)

aestās, aestātis, f. (summer)

autumnus, autumnī, m. (fall)

hiems, hiemis, f. (winter)

saeculum, saeculī, n. (century, age)

> ### "DURING"
>
> ↓
>
> Be careful not to associate this word with "duration" of time.
>
> "During" indicates time when!
>
> (During the spring
> =
> In the spring)

ABLATIVE OF SPECIFICATION

ABLATIVE OF SPECIFICATION

Ablative noun can indicate the specific area
involved in some action or description.

(No Preposition)

↓

"IN RESPECT TO" or "IN"

Quīntus **sapientiā** praecēdit.
Quintus excels ✦in respect to wisdom✦.

In what specific area
does Quintus excel?
In wisdom.

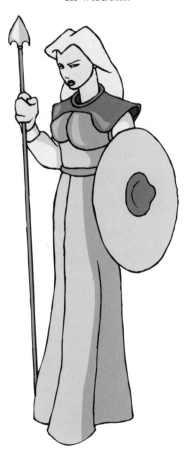

ABLATIVE OF SPECIFICATION TRIGGERS

praestāns, praestantis (outstanding)
splendidus, splendida, splendidum (outstanding, brilliant)
ēgregius, ēgregia, ēgregium (excellent, distinguished)
saucius, saucia, saucium (wounded)
integer, integra, integrum (healthy, sound)

excellō, excellere (to excel)
praecēdō, praecēdere, praecessī, praecessus (to excel)
praestō, praestāre, praestitī, praestitus (to excel)
superō, superāre, superāvī, superātus (to excel, surpass)

Valida **corpore et animō** est.
She is strong ✦in respect to her body and her mind✦.

In what specific area
is she strong?
In body and mind.

Minerva **virtūte** praecēdit.
Minerva excels ✦in courage✦.

ABLATIVE OF CAUSE

No Preposition

> ### ABLATIVE OF CAUSE
>
> Ablative noun indicates
> the cause of some situation.
>
> (No Preposition)
> ↓
> "BECAUSE OF"

Sōle gaudēmus.
We rejoice ⁺because of the sunshine⁺.

Aestū dēfessī estis.
You (pl.) are tired ⁺because of the heat⁺.

> meā/tuā/nostrā/vestrā
> +
> causā
> ↓
> because of
> me/you/us/you (pl.)

> GENITIVE NOUN
> +
> causā
> ↓
> because of
> *genitive*

Tuā causā hīc manēbimus.
⁺Because of you⁺, we will stay here.

Brūtī causā hīc manēbimus.
⁺Because of Brutus⁺, we will stay here.

ABLATIVE OF SEPARATION

With or without ā/ab

ABLATIVE OF SEPARATION

Verbs or adjectives of
freeing, depriving, lacking, prohibiting
can trigger an ablative with Ā/AB
or without a preposition.

↓

"OF" or "FROM"

LĪBERŌ & LĪBER

In general, ā/ab
is used only to express
freedom from a person.

Otherwise, no
preposition is used.

**PROHIBEŌ,
VACŌ & VACUUS**

Sometimes ā/ab is used,
and sometimes it is not.
There is no general
pattern.

ABLATIVE OF SEPARATION TRIGGERS

prohibeō, -ēre, -uī, -itus (to prohibit, to keep away)
vacō, vacāre, vacāvī, vacātus (to be without, to be empty)
vacuus, vacua, vacum (empty, without)

careō, carēre, caruī, caritus (to be without, to lack)
prīvō, prīvāre, prīvāvī, prīvātus (to deprive)

līberō, līberāre, līberāvī, līberātus (to set free)
līber, lībera, līberum (free)

dēfendō, dēfendere, dēfendī, dēfensus (defend)

CAREŌ & PRĪVŌ

No preposition
is used.

DĒFENDŌ

ā/ab is
always used.

Ab hortō meō prohibēberis.
You will be kept away ⬦from my garden⬦.

Ager flōribus nunc vacuus est.
The field is now empty ⬦of flowers⬦.

Sextus dolōre līber est!
Sextus is free ⬦of sorrow⬦!

"Of" and "from"
are sometimes
unnecessary.

Sextus cūrīs vacat!
Sextus is without ⬦worries⬦!

Terram ā rēge malō līberāvimus.
We freed the land ⬦from the evil king⬦.

ABLATIVE OF COMPARISON

No Preposition

> ### ABLATIVE OF COMPARISON
>
> After a comparative,
> the ablative case indicates the noun
> to which some previously mentioned noun
> is being compared.
>
> (No Preposition)
>
> ↓
>
> "THAN"
>
> *noun #1* ... THAN *noun #2*
> ↓
> Ablative

Flāvia celerior **Lūciō** est.
Flavia is swifter *than Lucius*.

Flāvia celerius **Lūciō** currit.
Flavia runs more swiftly *than Lucius*.

> The ablative of comparison
> can be used only when
> Noun #1 is nominative
> or accusative.
>
> Otherwise, quam must
> be used for "than."

> ### QUAM
>
> Can also mean "than."
>
> ↓
>
> The noun that comes after quam
> must agree with the noun to which
> it is being compared in case.

Flāvia celerius **quam Lūcius** currit.
Flavia runs more swiftly *than Lucius*. ⟶

Flāvia = Subject Nominative

Lūcius must match Flāvia → Nominative

ABLATIVE OF DEGREE OF DIFFERENCE

No Preposition

ABLATIVE OF DEGREE OF DIFFERENCE

Ablative noun can express how much
____er one thing is than another.

(No Preposition)
↓
"BY"

is sometimes a useful way of translating.

"I am two inches shorter than you."
"I am shorter than you by two inches."

Appears most frequently after a comparative or with ante and post.

Ūnō pede altior es quam ego.
You are ✧one foot✧ taller than I.
You are taller than I ✧by one foot✧.

(How much taller? One foot.)

Multō altior amīcīs es.
You are ✧much✧ taller than your friends.
You are taller than your friends ✧by a lot✧.

(How much taller? Much.)

ABLATIVE OF DEGREE VOCABULARY

multō (much, by a lot)
paulō (a little, by a little)

multīs ante annīs
(many years earlier/ago)

multīs post annīs
(many years later)

ANTE and POST
↓
Can act as the prepositions "before" and "after," but this construction uses them as the adverbs "earlier/ago" and "later."

ADJECTIVE ante/post *NOUN*
└— Ablative —┘

Paucīs ante hōrīs, puellam in hortō vīdī.
✧A few hours ago✧, I saw the girl in the garden.

ABLATIVE ABSOLUTE

No
Preposition

WITH PERFECT PASSIVE PARTICIPLE

[with]
noun
having been
verbed

ABLATIVE ABSOLUTE

Ablative **Noun**

+

Perfect Passive **Participle**

↓

"[with] <u>*noun*</u> having been <u>*verb*</u>ed"

4th Principal
Part
(See p. 216)

Urbe captā maerēbam.
⬥[With] the city having been captured⬥, I was grieving.

Ablative absolutes
may contain extra
words like adverbs
and prepositional
phrases.

Urbe **ab hostibus** captā. . .
The city having been captured ⬥by the enemies⬥. . .

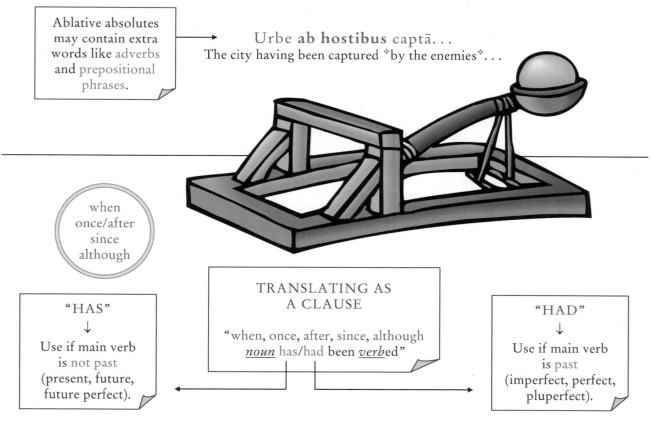

when
once/after
since
although

TRANSLATING AS
A CLAUSE

"when, once, after, since, although
<u>*noun*</u> has/had been <u>*verb*</u>ed"

"HAS"
↓
Use if main verb
is not past
(present, future,
future perfect).

"HAD"
↓
Use if main verb
is past
(imperfect, perfect,
pluperfect).

Urbe captā, hostēs gaudent.
⬥Since the city has been captured⬥,
the enemies rejoice.

Urbe captā, spem tamen habēbam.
⬥Although the city had been captured⬥,
I still had hope.

ABLATIVE ABSOLUTE

No Preposition

WITH PRESENT ACTIVE PARTICIPLE

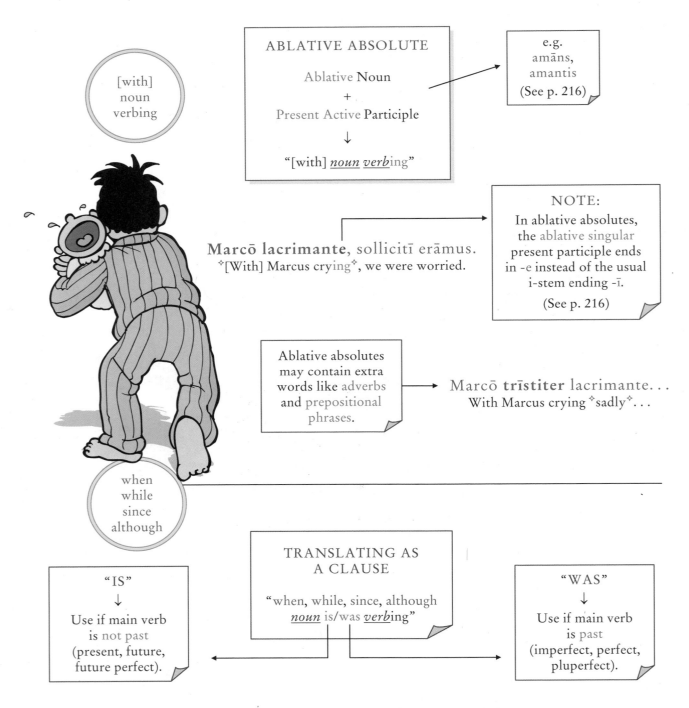

[with]
noun
verbing

ABLATIVE ABSOLUTE

Ablative **Noun**

+

Present Active **Participle**

↓

"[with] *noun verb*ing"

e.g.
amāns,
amantis
(See p. 216)

Marcō lacrimante, sollicitī erāmus.
⬧[With] Marcus crying⬧, we were worried.

NOTE:
In ablative absolutes,
the ablative singular
present participle ends
in -e instead of the usual
i-stem ending -ī.

(See p. 216)

Ablative absolutes
may contain extra
words like adverbs
and prepositional
phrases.

Marcō **trīstiter** lacrimante...
With Marcus crying ⬧sadly⬧...

when
while
since
although

"IS"

↓

Use if main verb
is not past
(present, future,
future perfect).

TRANSLATING AS
A CLAUSE

"when, while, since, although
noun is/was *verb*ing"

"WAS"

↓

Use if main verb
is past
(imperfect, perfect,
pluperfect).

Marcō lacrimante, cantāmus.
⬧While Marcus is crying⬧, we sing.

Marcō lacrimante, dormīre nōn poterāmus.
⬧Since Marcus was crying⬧, we were not able to sleep.

ABLATIVE ABSOLUTE

No Preposition

[with]
noun
as/being

ABLATIVE ABSOLUTE

Ablative **Noun**

+

Ablative **Noun** or Adjective

↓

"[with] *noun* as/being *noun/adjective*"

NOUN

Tulliā magistrā gaudēmus.
✦With Tullia as the teacher✦, we rejoice.
✦With Tullia being the teacher✦, we rejoice.

ADJECTIVE

Tulliā miserā dolēmus.
✦With Tullia sad✦, we are sad.
✦With Tullia being sad✦, we are sad.

when
while
since
although

"IS"
↓
Use if main verb
is not past
(present, future,
future perfect).

TRANSLATING AS
A CLAUSE

"when, while, since, although
noun is/was *noun/adjective*"

"WAS"
↓
Use if main verb
is past
(imperfect, perfect,
pluperfect).

Gāiō laetō, trīstēs tamen sumus.
✦Although Gaius is happy✦, we are nevertheless sad.

Gāiō magistrō, bene didicistis.
✦While Gaius was your teacher✦, you learned well.

ABLATIVE OF PRICE

No Preposition

> ## ABLATIVE OF PRICE
>
> Ablative noun can indicate the price
> for which something is bought or sold.
>
> (No Preposition)
> ↓
> "FOR" or "AT"

BUYING AND SELLING VOCABULARY

emō, emere, ēmī, emptus (to buy)
vendō, vendere, vendidī, venditus (to sell)

pretium, pretiī, n. (price)
aureus, aureī, m. (gold coin)
dēnārius, dēnāriī, m. (silver coin)
sestertius, sestertiī, m. (silver coin)
as, assis, m. (copper coin)

Vestēs novās **parvō prētiō** emēmus.
We will buy new clothes ⬦at a small price⬦.

1 Aureus = 25 Denarii

4 Sestertii = 1 Denarius

16 Asses = 1 Denarius

A well-paid Roman might earn several
hundred denarii per year.

Vigintī sestertiīs venditus est petasus.
A hat was sold ⬦for 20 sestertii⬦.

ABLATIVE OF SOURCE

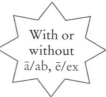

With or without
ā/ab, ē/ex

ABLATIVE OF SOURCE

Ablative noun with or without
Ā/AB or Ē/EX indicates ancestry.

↓

"OF" or "FROM"

ANCESTRY VOCABULARY

nascor, nascī, nātus sum (to be born)
nātus, -a, -um (born, descended)

orior, orīrī, ortus sum (to rise, be born)
ortus, -a, -um (born, descended)

genus, generis, n. (descent, origin, stock)

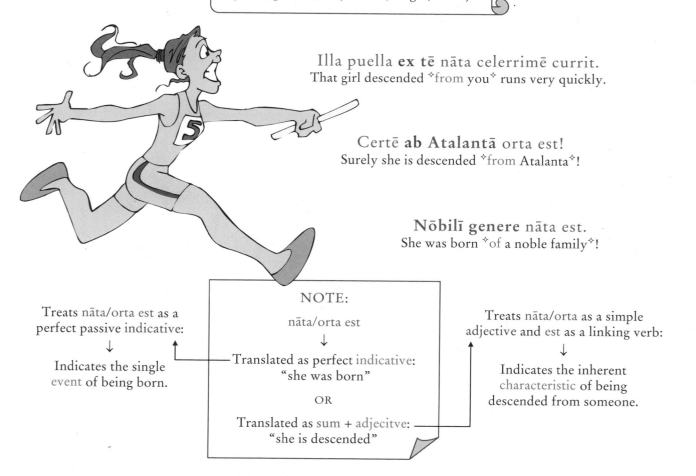

Illa puella **ex tē** nāta celerrimē currit.
That girl descended ⬦from you⬦ runs very quickly.

Certē **ab Atalantā** orta est!
Surely she is descended ⬦from Atalanta⬦!

Nōbilī genere nāta est.
She was born ⬦of a noble family⬦!

Treats nāta/orta est as a
perfect passive indicative:

↓

Indicates the single
event of being born.

NOTE:

nāta/orta est

↓

Translated as perfect indicative:
"she was born"

OR

Translated as sum + adjecitve:
"she is descended"

Treats nāta/orta as a simple
adjective and est as a linking verb:

↓

Indicates the inherent
characteristic of being
descended from someone.

ABLATIVE WITH SPECIAL ADJECTIVES

No Preposition

> ### ABLATIVE WITH SPECIAL ADJECTIVES
>
> Some adjectives can trigger an ablative noun.
>
> ↓
>
> Supply whatever extra words seem logical.

COMMON ADJECTIVES THAT TRIGGER AN ABLATIVE

creber, crebra, crebrum (crowded [with])

dignus, digna, dignum (worthy [of])

indigus, indigna, indignum (unworthy [of])

dīves, dīvitis (rich [in])

frētus, frēta, frētum (relying [on])

līber, lībera, līberum (free [from])

vacuus, vacua, vacuum (empty [of])

Artibus suīs frētus, ursus cēnam capiet.
Relying ⋄on his skills⋄, the bear will catch dinner.

Aqua crebra **piscibus** erat.
The water was crowded ⋄with fish⋄.

Hic ursus dignus **praemiō** est.
This bear is worthy ⋄of a prize⋄.

ABLATIVE WITH DEPONENT VERBS

No
Preposition

> ### ABLATIVE WITH DEPONENT VERBS
> Some deponent verbs take their direct object
> in the ablative case.

Artibus meīs ūtar ut ignem concipiam.
I will use ⁺my skills⁺ to make a fire.

VERBS WITH ABLATIVE OBJECTS

fruor, fruī, frūctus sum (to enjoy, have the benefit of)

fungor, fungī, fūnctus sum (to perform)

potior, potīrī, potītus sum (to get possession of, obtain)

ūtor, ūtī, ūsus sum (to use, make use of)

vēscor, vēscī (to eat)

Note that potior can also take
a genitive object, though the
ablative is more common.

(See p. 41)

VOCATIVE OF DIRECT ADDRESS

DIRECT ADDRESS

Vocative nouns
do not usually appear
first in a Latin sentence,
but they can be placed
anywhere in your
English translation.

VOCATIVE CASE

Used for direct address
(calling someone by name)

↓

"*Noun*, what time is it?"

"What time is it, *noun*?"

Vocative nouns
are often set off
by commas from
the rest of the
sentence.

VOCATIVE   NOMINATIVE
Singular   =   Singular
& Plural   & Plural

EXCEPT

Vocative singular of
2nd declension -us and -ius nouns

-US
↓
-E

-IUS
↓
-Ī

-US	SINGULAR	-IUS
Marcus	*Nominative*	Lūcius
↓		↓
Marce	*Vocative*	Lūcī

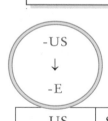

Patriamne amās, **Auguste**?
Do you love the fatherland,
✧Augustus✧?

(Vocative Singular of Augustus)

SECOND DECLENSION
VOCATIVE PHRASES

mī fīlī
"my son, . . ."
(vocative of meus fīlius)

servē
"slave, . . ."
(vocative of servus)

Patriam, **Rōmānī**, amō.
I do love the fatherland,
✧Romans✧.

(Vocative Plural of Rōmānus)

TRANSLATING NOUN PHRASES

POSSESSIVE GENITIVE

Genitive noun possesses
some other noun.

Hostēs **patriae** crūdēlēs sunt.
The enemies ⬥of the fatherland⬥ are cruel.

↓

"The fatherland"
possesses
"the enemies."

GENITIVE OF DESCRIPTION

Genitive noun is a characteristic.

Virī **magnae pietātis** patriam amant.
Men ⬥of great devotion⬥ love the fatherland.

↓

"Great devotion"
is a characteristic.

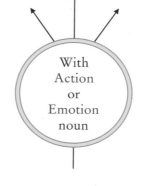

SUBJECTIVE GENITIVE

Genitive noun is the subject
of some action/emotion.

Timorēs **patriae** multī sunt.
The fears ⬥of the fatherland⬥ are many.

↓

"The fatherland"
is the subject of the
implied verb "to fear."

OBJECTIVE GENITIVE

Genitive noun is the direct object
of some action/emotion.

Noster amor **patriae** magnus est.
Our love ⬥of the fatherland⬥ is great.

↓

"The fatherland"
is the direct object of the
implied verb "to love."

With
Action
or
Emotion
noun

TRANSLATING NOUN PHRASES

"TO" PHRASES

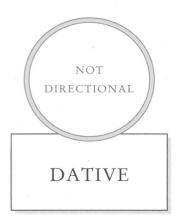

NOT
DIRECTIONAL

DATIVE

DIRECTIONAL

AD
+
ACCUSATIVE

Musae **Lūciō** nōtae sunt.
The Muses are well known ⁺to Lucius⁺.

Lūciō libet cantāre.
It is pleasing ⁺to Lucius⁺ to sing.

Laudem **Lūciō** damus.
We give praise ⁺to Lucius⁺.

Admīrantēs **ad Lūcium** currunt.
Admirers run ⁺to Lucius⁺.

Oculōs **ad Lūcium** vertō.
I turn my eyes ⁺to Lucius⁺.

TRANSLATING NOUN PHRASES

> ABLATIVE OF ACCOMPANIMENT,
> MEANS, MANNER, DESCRIPTION
>
> ↓
>
> "With" is used in the English translation
> of all four grammatical constructions,
> but the constructions have very
> different meanings.

ACCOMPANIMENT

"Companion"

The man stands with the girl.

Always
with
cum

MEANS

"Tool"

The man points with his finger.

No
Preposition

MANNER

"Style"

The man talks with great concern.

Cum
is optional

DESCRIPTION

"Characteristic"

The man with grey hair talks.

No
Preposition

PREPOSITIONAL PHRASES

COMMON PREPOSITIONS

about	before	through
across	by	to
after	from	toward
around	near	under
at	out of	with
because of	over	without

OBJECT OF THE PREPOSITION
↓
Noun that goes with the preposition.

PREPOSITIONAL PHRASE
↓
Combination of Preposition + Object.

PREPOSITION: "in"   OBJECT: "road"

In viā stābat.
She was standing ⋄in the road⋄.

PREPOSITIONAL PHRASE

In viā stābat.
She was standing ⋄in the road⋄.

WORD ORDER OF PREPOSITIONAL PHRASES

Prepositional phrases are usually written as follows:

in multīs terrīs
(in many lands)

However, word order is flexible and rearrangement is possible:

multīs in terrīs
(in many lands)

GENITIVES IN PREPOSITIONAL PHRASES

Note that genitives often appear inside prepositional phrases:

in Rōmānōrum terrīs
(in the lands of the Romans)

PREPOSITIONAL PHRASES

ACCUSATIVE

ABLATIVE

ad iānuam
to the door

ab iānuā
away from the door

in aquam
into the water

in aquā
in the water

sub umbrāculum
under the umbrella
(to under)

sub umbrāculō
under the umbrella
(at under)

SPECIAL PLACE CONSTRUCTIONS

Cities
Towns
Small Islands
domus
rūs
humus

CITIES, TOWNS, SMALL ISLANDS,
DOMUS, RŪS, HUMUS

Place	Place	Place
Where	to Which	from Which
↓	↓	↓
Locative	Accusative	Ablative

NO PREPOSITIONS

Rōmae habitō.
I live ⋄in Rome⋄.
(Locative)

Rōmam eō.
I go ⋄to Rome⋄.
(Accusative)

Rōmā discēdō.
I depart ⋄from Rome⋄.
(Ablative)

Humum cecidistī.
You fell ⋄to the ground⋄.

NAMES OF CERTAIN CITIES, TOWNS, & SMALL ISLANDS

domus, domūs, f. (home)
rūs, rūris, n. (country, countryside)
humus, humī, f. (the ground)

Rōma, Rōmae, f. - Rome
Pharus, Pharī, f. - small island near Egypt
Carthāgō, Carthāginis, f. - city in Africa
Sirmiō, Sirmiōnis, f. - town in N. Italy

Athēnae, Athēnārum, f. - Athens
Delphī, Delphōrum, m. - town in Greece
Gādēs, Gādium, f. - a city in Spain

Some place names
are plural.

domus:
Belongs to the 4th declension, but
can use some 2nd declension forms.

	Singular	Plural
Nom.	domus	domūs
Gen.	domī	domōrum
Dat.	domō	domibus
Acc.	domum	domōs
Abl.	domō	domibus

SPECIAL PLACE CONSTRUCTIONS

PLACE TO WHICH

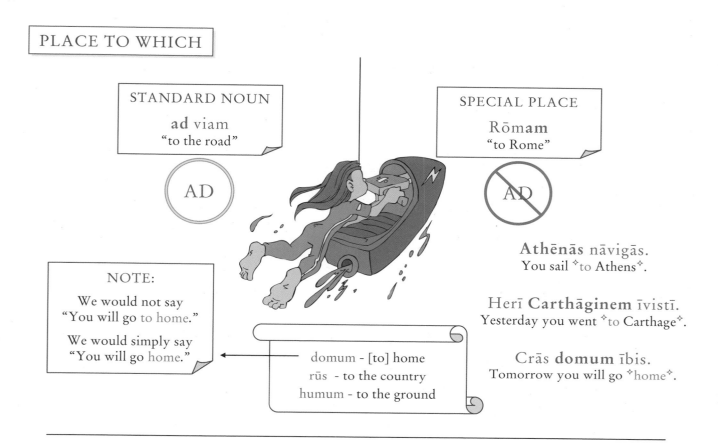

STANDARD NOUN

ad viam
"to the road"

AD

SPECIAL PLACE

Rōm**am**
"to Rome"

~~AD~~

NOTE:

We would not say
"You will go to home."

We would simply say
"You will go home."

domum - [to] home
rūs - to the country
humum - to the ground

Athēnās nāvigās.
You sail ⬧to Athens⬧.

Herī **Carthāginem** īvistī.
Yesterday you went ⬧to Carthage⬧.

Crās **domum** ībis.
Tomorrow you will go ⬧home⬧.

PLACE FROM WHICH

STANDARD NOUN

ā viā
"from the road"

AB

SPECIAL PLACE

Rōm**ā**
"from Rome"

~~AB~~

domō - from home
rūre - from the country
humō - from the ground

Mercūrius **domō** discēdit.
Mercury departs ⬧from his home⬧.

Tertiō diē **Gādibus** redībit.
He will return ⬧from Gades⬧ on the third day.

SPECIAL PLACE CONSTRUCTIONS

PLACE WHERE: LOCATIVE

STANDARD NOUN

in viā
"in the road"

IN

LOCATIVE CASE
↓
Generally looks like the ablative

except

1st & 2nd declension singular:
Locative looks like genitive.

SPECIAL PLACE

Rōmae
"in Rome"

Rūrī erās.
You were ⬥in the countryside⬥.

LOCATIVE CASE		
	<u>Sing.</u>	<u>Pl.</u>
1st	-ae	-īs
2nd	-ī	-īs
3rd	-e	-ibus

domī - at home
rūrī - in the country
humī - on the ground

NOTE:
Carthāginī or Carthāgine –
at Carthage

Note that rūs and
Carthāgō belong to
the third declension
but use -ī in the
locative.

Sirmiōne prope aquam manēbis.
You will stay ⬥at Sirmio⬥ near the water.

ABLATIVE VS. LOCATIVE

Since these cases frequently
look the same, you have to use
context to choose between a
"place from which" and a
"place where" translation.

Delphīs nāvigāvimus.
We sailed ⬥from Delphi⬥.

(Ablative of Place from Which)

Delphīs mānsimus.
We stayed ⬥at Delphi⬥.

(Locative of Place Where)

APPOSITIVES

APPOSITIVE
↓
Noun that renames some previously mentioned noun.

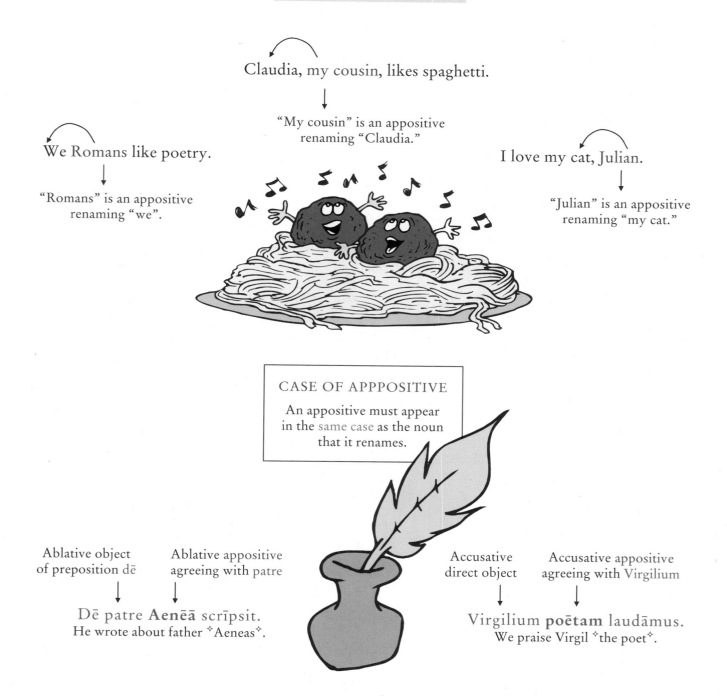

Claudia, my cousin, likes spaghetti.
↓
"My cousin" is an appositive renaming "Claudia."

We Romans like poetry.
↓
"Romans" is an appositive renaming "we".

I love my cat, Julian.
↓
"Julian" is an appositive renaming "my cat."

CASE OF APPPOSITIVE

An appositive must appear in the same case as the noun that it renames.

Ablative object of preposition dē

Ablative appositive agreeing with patre
↓
Dē patre **Aenēā** scrīpsit.
He wrote about father ⟡Aeneas⟡.

Accusative direct object

Accusative appositive agreeing with Virgilium
↓
Virgilium **poētam** laudāmus.
We praise Virgil ⟡the poet⟡.

APPOSITIVES

RENAMING UNEXPRESSED NOMINATIVES

APPOSITIVES OF UNEXPRESSED NOMINATIVES

Sometimes, the subject of the verb is not directly stated.

↓

A sentence might have a nominative appositive that points back to this type of unexpressed subject.

Patrēs quoque carrulīs lūdimus.
We ⬧fathers⬧ also play with mini-cars.

Patrēs is an appositive that renames nōs, the unexpressed subject of lūdimus.

ALTERNATE TRANSLATIONS

Sometimes it helps to add the word "AS" when translating appositives.

Sometimes (especially with place names), "OF" can be used to translate appositives.

Patrōnus in fōrum vēnistī.
You came ⬧as an advocate⬧ into the forum.

Urbs **Rōma** multās causās vīdit.
The city ⬧of Rome⬧ saw many trials.

POSSESSION

GENITIVE OF POSSESSION VS. POSSESSIVE ADJECTIVES

GENITIVE OF POSSESSION
↓

Used by most nouns
to indicate ownership.

The farmer's sons work hard.

POSSESSIVE ADJECTIVES
↓

Used by I, You, We, You (pl.)
to indicate ownership.

My sons work hard.

Fīlia **Iūliī** es.
You are ⋄Julius'⋄ daughter.

↓

Possessive
Genitive

Fīlia **mea** es.
You are ⋄my⋄ daughter.

↓

Possessive Adjective

The genitives of
"I," "You,"
"We," "You (pl.)"
are never used
for possession.

Possessive adjectives
do not take on the
gender and number
of the possessor.

↓

In the sentence above,
mea is feminine because
"daughter" is feminine.
It does not matter whether
"my" represents a male
or a female possessor.

POSSESSIVE ADJECTIVES

meus, mea, meum (my, mine)
tuus, tua, tuum (your, yours)
noster, nostra, nostrum (our, ours)
vester, vestra, vestrum (your, yours)

POSSESSION

THIRD PERSON POSSESSION: *SUUS* VS. *EIUS*

EIUS / EŌRUM / EĀRUM

"his" "her" "its"	"their" (masculine or neuter possessor)	"their" (feminine possessor)

(Genitive of Possession of Is, Ea, Id)

"His," "Her," "Its," "Their"
↓
Used when the possessor is not the subject of the main verb.

SUUS, SUA, SUUM

Gender/Number of possessor is irrelevant - suus agrees with the noun it modifies.

(Possessive Adjective)

"His," "Her," "Its," "Their"
↓
Used when the possessor is also the subject of the main verb.

Octāvia **eius crīnēs** compōnit.
Octavia arranges ✧her hair✧.

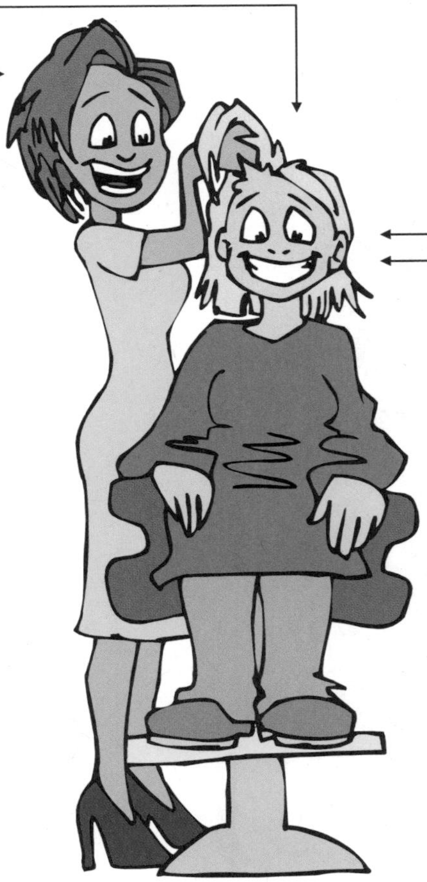

Aurēlia **crīnēs suōs** amat.
Aurelia likes ✧her hair✧.

Possessor

Subject

Subject

Possessor

Possessor & Subject are not the same person.

Possessor & Subject are the same person.

OVERVIEW OF ADJECTIVES

INTRODUCTION

ATTRIBUTIVE
↓
Noun
+
Adjective

"the tall trees"

ADJECTIVE
↓
Word that describes a noun.
↓
We say that adjectives
"modify" (go with) nouns.

PREDICATE
↓
Noun
+
Linking Verb
+
Adjective

"The trees are tall."

DICTIONARY ENTRY

bonus,	bona,	bonum	(good)
↓	↓	↓	↓
MASCULINE	FEMININE	NEUTER	MEANING

-----NOMINATIVE SINGULARS-----

FORMS

Like nouns, adjectives have
a full set of singular and
plural case forms.

Unlike nouns, adjectives
can take on any gender.

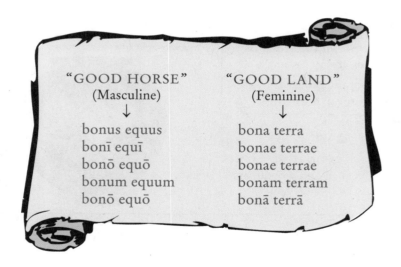

"GOOD HORSE"
(Masculine)
↓
bonus equus
bonī equī
bonō equō
bonum equum
bonō equō

"GOOD LAND"
(Feminine)
↓
bona terra
bonae terrae
bonae terrae
bonam terram
bonā terrā

STEM

Adjective stems are
generally obtained
by removing the
feminine nominative
singular ending.

(See pp. 103-104, 106)

GLOSSARY ENTRY		STEM
bonus, bon a, bonum (good)	→	bon-
celer, celer is, celere (swift)	→	celer-
fort is, forte (brave)	→	fort-
audāx, audāc is (bold)	→	audāc- →

For some adjectives,
the stem is obtained
by removing the
genitive singular
ending.

(See p. 106)

AGREEMENT OF ADJECTIVES

CASE
NUMBER
GENDER

Adjectives in Latin must agree with the nouns they modify in case, number, and gender.

↓

Adjectives must have the same case, number, and gender as the nouns they modify.

Adjectives may appear before or after the nouns they modify.

Puella **parva** fēminam spectat.
The ⋄small⋄ girl watches the woman.

Puella **parvam** fēminam spectat.
The girl watches the ⋄small⋄ woman.

Parva is
nominative singular feminine:

↓

modifies puella
(also nominative singular feminine).

To translate an adjective in a sentence, you must identify the noun with which it agrees.

Parvam is
accusative singular feminine:

↓

modifies fēminam
(also accusative singular feminine).

PREDICATE
ADJECTIVES

↓

Masculine if the group of nouns are living beings.

Neuter if the group of nouns are not living beings.

ADJECTIVES MODIFYING
A GROUP OF NOUNS
OF MIXED GENDER

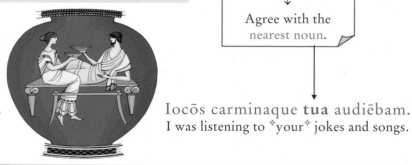

ATTRIBUTIVE
ADJECTIVES

↓

Agree with the nearest noun.

Vir fēminaque **Graecī** sunt.
The man and woman are ⋄Greek⋄.

Iocōs carminaque **tua** audiēbam.
I was listening to ⋄your⋄ jokes and songs.

Nominative Plural

3rd Decl.
Noun

2-1-2
Adjective

↓   ↓

Canēs īrātī lātrant.
⋄The angry dogs⋄ are barking.

The adjective ending does not have to look the same as the noun ending as long as it has the right case, number, and gender.

Accusative Singular

1st Decl.
Noun

3rd Decl.
Adjective

↓   ↓

Rēgīnam potentem vīdīstī.
You saw ⋄the powerful queen⋄.

BONUS NAUTA

2-1-2 Adjective
Nominative Singular
Masculine ————————

———— 1st Decl. Noun
Nominative Singular
Masculine

2-1-2 Adjectives

ADJECTIVES IN -*US*, -*A*, -*UM*

> ### 2-1-2 ADJECTIVES IN -*US*, -*A*, -*UM*
>
> Use 1st and 2nd declension endings.
>
> Typical:
> bonus, bona, bonum (good)
>
> These are called 2-1-2 adjectives because they use 2nd declension forms when they are masculine, 1st declension forms when they are feminine, and 2nd declension forms when they are neuter.

2nd Declension Masculine Endings → Masculine Adjective

1st Declension Endings → Feminine Adjective

2nd Declension Neuter Endings → Neuter Adjective

2-1-2 ADJECTIVE
bonus, bona, bonum (good)

	Singular			Plural		
	Masculine	*Feminine*	*Neuter*	*Masculine*	*Feminine*	*Neuter*
Nom.	bonus	bona	bonum	bonī	bonae	bona
Gen.	bonī	bonae	bonī	bonōrum	bonārum	bonōrum
Dat.	bonō	bonae	bonō	bonīs	bonīs	bonīs
Acc.	bonum	bonam	bonum	bonōs	bonās	bona
Abl.	bonō	bonā	bonō	bonīs	bonīs	bonīs

Montēs **altōs** ascenditis.
You (pl.) climb ⬥high⬥ mountains.

STEM
↓
Cut off -A from feminine nominative singular.

STEM:
bonus, **bona**, bonum
↓
BONA → BON-

2-1-2 ADJECTIVES

-r, -a, -um

ADJECTIVES IN -R, -A, -UM

NOTE:

pulcher, pulchra, pulchrum
drops the "e"
from its stem.

2-1-2 ADJECTIVES IN -R, -A, -UM

Use 1st and 2nd declension endings.

Typical:
pulcher, pulchra, pulchrum (beautiful)
līber, lībera, līberum (free)

NOTE:

līber, lībera, līberum
keeps the "e"
in its stem.

2-1-2 ADJECTIVE
pulcher, pulchra, pulchrum (beautiful) → drops its "e"

	Singular			Plural		
Nom.	pulcher	pulchra	pulchrum	pulchrī	pulchrae	pulchra
Gen.	pulchrī	pulchrae	pulchrī	pulchrōrum	pulchrārum	pulchrōrum
Dat.	pulchrō	pulchrae	pulchrō	pulchrīs	pulchrīs	pulchrīs
Acc.	pulchrum	pulchram	pulchrum	pulchrōs	pulchrās	pulchra
Abl.	pulchrō	pulchrā	pulchrō	pulchrīs	pulchrīs	pulchrīs

2-1-2 ADJECTIVE
līber, lībera, līberum (free) → keeps its "e"

	Singular			Plural		
	Masculine	*Feminine*	*Neuter*	*Masculine*	*Feminine*	*Neuter*
Nom.	līber	lībera	līberum	līberī	līberae	lībera
Gen.	līberī	līberae	līberī	līberōrum	līberārum	līberōrum
Dat.	līberō	līberae	līberō	līberīs	līberīs	līberīs
Acc.	līberum	līberam	līberum	līberōs	līberās	lībera
Abl.	līberō	līberā	līberō	līberīs	līberīs	līberīs

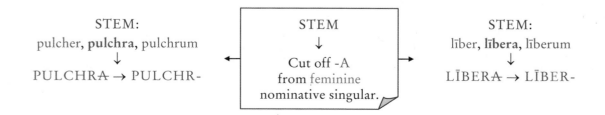

STEM:
pulcher, **pulchra**, pulchrum
↓
PULCHR~~A~~ → PULCHR-

STEM
↓
Cut off -A
from feminine
nominative singular.

STEM:
līber, **lībera**, līberum
↓
LĪBER~~A~~ → LĪBER-

THIRD DECLENSION ADJECTIVES

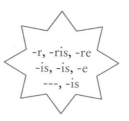

-r, -ris, -re
-is, -is, -e
---, -is

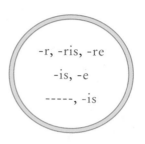

-r, -ris, -re
-is, -e
-----, -is

THIRD DECLENSION ADJECTIVES

Use 3rd declension endings.

Glossary entry is distinctly different from that of a 2-1-2 Adjective.

celer, celeris, celere (swift)
ācer, ācris, ācre (sharp, fierce)
dulcis, dulce (sweet)
clēmēns, clēmentis (kind, merciful)

2-1-2 ADJECTIVES

-us, -a, -um

or

-r, -a, -um

2-1-2 ADJECTIVES

Use 1st and 2nd declension endings

↓

puellam **bonam** 👍 → acc. sing. fem.

puellam **bonem** ✗ → mismatch:
2-1-2 adjective cannot use 3rd declension endings

THIRD DECLENSION ADJECTIVES

Use 3rd declension endings

↓

puellam **celeram** ✗ → mismatch:
3rd declension adjective cannot use 2-1-2 endings

puellam **celerem** 👍 → acc. sing. fem.

TERMINATION

Three Types of Third Declension Adjectives:

3 Termination: ācer, ācris, ācre
2 Termination: dulcis, dulce
1 Termination: clēmēns, clēmentis

Fēmina **audāx** ad lūnam volābit.
The ◆daring◆ woman will fly to the moon.

Dictionary entry looks similar to a noun dictionary entry, BUT noun entries also list a gender.

clēmēns, clēmentis - adjective
gēns, gentis, **f.** - noun

THIRD DECLENSION ADJECTIVES

-er, -ris, -re
-is, -is, -e
---, -is

| 1, 2, 3 TERMINATION |

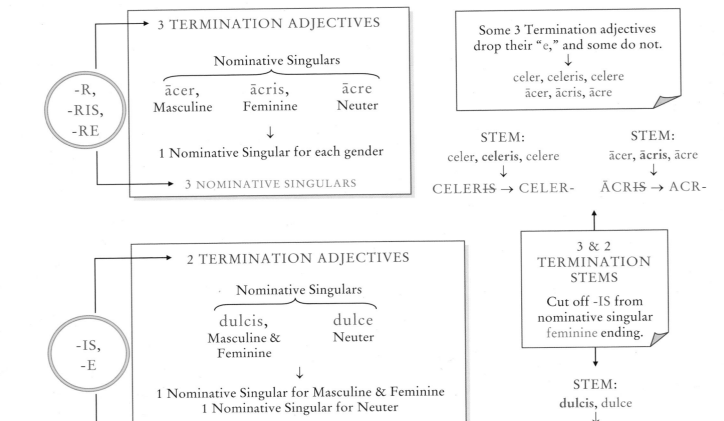

3 TERMINATION ADJECTIVES

Nominative Singulars

ācer,   ācris,   ācre
Masculine   Feminine   Neuter

↓

1 Nominative Singular for each gender

3 NOMINATIVE SINGULARS

-R,
-RIS,
-RE

Some 3 Termination adjectives drop their "e," and some do not.

↓

celer, celeris, celere
ācer, ācris, ācre

STEM: STEM:
celer, **celeris**, celere   ācer, **ācris**, ācre
↓   ↓
CELER~~IS~~ → CELER-   ĀCR~~IS~~ → ACR-

2 TERMINATION ADJECTIVES

Nominative Singulars

dulcis,   dulce
Masculine &   Neuter
Feminine

↓

1 Nominative Singular for Masculine & Feminine
1 Nominative Singular for Neuter

2 NOMINATIVE SINGULARS

-IS,
-E

3 & 2 TERMINATION STEMS

Cut off -IS from nominative singular feminine ending.

↓

STEM:
dulcis, dulce
↓
DULC~~IS~~ → DULC-

1 TERMINATION ADJECTIVES

clēmēns,   clēmentis
Nominative   Genitive
Singular   Singular
Masc./Fem./Neut.

↓

1 Nominative Singular shared by
Masculine, Feminine & Neuter

1 NOMINATIVE SINGULAR

-VARIES-,
-IS

1 TERMINATION STEMS

Cut off -IS from genitive singular ending.

↓

STEM:
clēmēns, **clēmentis**
↓
CLĒMENT~~IS~~ → CLĒMENT-

THIRD DECLENSION ADJECTIVES

-er, -ris, -re
-is, -is, -e
---, -is

ENDINGS

THIRD DECLENSION ADJECTIVE

↓

3rd declension adjective resembles 3rd declension noun but has some extra i's.

NOMINATIVE SINGULAR

The dictionary entry will tell you what nominative singular endings are used by a given adjective.

ABLATIVE SINGULAR

In the 3rd declension, most nouns have "e" in the ablative singular, but adjectives have "i."

THIRD DECLENSION ADJECTIVE ENDINGS

| | SINGULAR | | PLURAL | |
	Masc./Fem.	Neut.	Masc./Fem.	Neut.
Nom.	----	----	-ēs	-ia
Gen.	-is	-is	-ium	-ium
Dat.	-ī	-ī	-ibus	-ibus
Acc.	-em	----	-ēs / -īs	-ia
Abl.	-ī	-ī	-ibus	-ibus

THIRD DECLENSION ADJECTIVE
ingēns, ingentis (huge)

| | SINGULAR | | PLURAL | |
	Masc./Fem.	Neut.	Masc./Fem.	Neut.
Nom.	ingēns	ingēns	ingentēs	ingentia
Gen.	ingentis	ingentis	ingentium	ingentium
Dat.	ingentī	ingentī	ingentibus	ingentibus
Acc.	ingentem	ingēns	ingentēs / -īs	ingentia
Abl.	ingentī	ingentī	ingentibus	ingentibus

An adjective's ending might **not** look the same as the ending of the noun it modifies!

Ingentīs dinosaurōs vīdī.
I saw ⋄huge dinosaurs⋄.

IRREGULAR ADJECTIVES

-IUS
-Ī

IRREGULAR ADJECTIVES

Some 2-1-2 Adjectives are declined with a few unusual forms.

↓

Genitive Singular: -IUS
Dative Singular: -Ī

These adjectives resemble ille in the genitive and the dative.

(See p. 128)

IRREGULAR ADJECTIVES

alius, alia, aliud (other, another)
alter, altera, alterum (the other [of two], second)
neuter, neutra, neutrum (neither)
nūllus, nūlla, nūllum (no, none)
sōlus, sōla, sōlum (only, alone)
tōtus, tōta, tōtum (whole, entire)
ūllus, ūlla, ūllum (any)
uter, utra, utrum (which? [of two])
uterque, utraque, utrumque (each [of two])

Additional irregularity: neuter nominative and accusative end in -ud instead of -um.

Forms of uter with -que on the end.

IDIOMS

alius. . .alius (one. . .another)
aliī. . .aliī (some. . .others)
alter. . .alter (one. . .the other)

Alterī poētae laudem dedī, sed **alter** mē nōn dēlectāvit.
I gave praise to ◆one◆ poet, but ◆the other◆ did not delight me.

	IRREGULAR ADJECTIVES nūllus, nūlla, nūllum (no, none)					
	SINGULAR			PLURAL		
	Masculine	Feminine	Neuter	Masculine	Feminine	Neuter
Nom.	nūllus	nūlla	nūllum	nūllī	nūllae	nūlla
Gen.	nūllius	nūllius	nūllius	nūllōrum	nūllārum	nūllōrum
Dat.	nūllī	nūllī	nūllī	nūllīs	nūllīs	nūllīs
Acc.	nūllum	nūllam	nūllum	nūllōs	nūllās	nūlla
Abl.	nūllō	nūllā	nūllō	nūllīs	nūllīs	nūllīs

NUMBERS

CARDINAL NUMBERS 1, 2, 3, 4, 5...

Most are indeclinable, BUT 1, 2, 3 are declinable.

DECLINABLE:

Adjective has multiple case forms (nominative, genitive, dative, etc.).

INDECLINABLE:

Adjective has only one form representing all cases.

1	I	ūnus, ūna, ūnum	11	XI	ūndecim
2	II	duo, duae, duo	12	XII	duodecim
3	III	trēs, tria	13	XIII	trēdecim
4	IV	quattuor	14	XIV	quattuordecim
5	V	quīnque	15	XV	quīndecim
6	VI	sex	16	XVI	sēdecim
7	VII	septem	17	XVII	septendecim
8	VIII	octō	18	XVIII	duodēvigintī
9	IX	novem	19	XIX	ūndēvigintī
10	X	decem	20	XX	vīgintī

ūna placenta
one cake
(Nominative)

septem candēlae
seven candles
(Nominative)

ūnam placentam
one cake
(Accusative)

septem candēlās
seven candles
(Accusative)

NUMBERS

①　　　　②　　　　③

ŪNUS, ŪNA, ŪNUM			DUO, DUAE, DUO			TRĒS, TRIA	
M.	F.	N.	M.	F.	N.	M. & F.	N.
ūnus	ūna	ūnum	duo	duae	duo	trēs	tria
ūnīus	ūnīus	ūnīus	duōrum	duārum	duōrum	trium	trium
ūnī	ūnī	ūnī	duōbus	duābus	duōbus	tribus	tribus
ūnum	ūnam	ūnum	duōs/duo	duās	duo	trēs/trīs	tria
ūnō	ūnā	ūnō	duōbus	duābus	duōbus	tribus	tribus

duae rotae
two wheels

(Nominative)
_____

ūnus puer
one boy

(Nominative)
_____

ūnum puerum
one boy

(Accusative)

duābus rotīs
two wheels

(Dative/Ablative)

tria astra
three stars

(Nominative)
_____

trium astrōrum
three stars

(Genitive)

NUMBERS

ORDINAL NUMBERS

1ST, 2ND, 3RD, 4TH, 5TH . . .

2-1-2 Adjectives
(-us, -a, -um)

1st	I	prīmus	11th	XI	ūndecimus	
2nd	II	secundus	12th	XII	duodecimus	
3rd	III	tertius	13th	XIII	tertius decimus	⎫
4th	IV	quārtus	14th	XIV	quārtus decimus	
5th	V	quīntus	15th	XV	quīntus decimus	
6th	VI	sextus	16th	XVI	sextus decimus	Both words must be declined to match the noun they modify.
7th	VII	septimus	17th	XVII	septimus decimus	⎭
8th	VIII	octāvus	18th	XVIII	duōdēvīcēsimus	
9th	IX	nōnus	19th	XIX	ūndēvīcēsimus	
10th	X	decimus	20th	XX	vīcēsimus	

Per **tertiam decimam** fenestram spectās.
You look through the ⬧13th⬧ window.

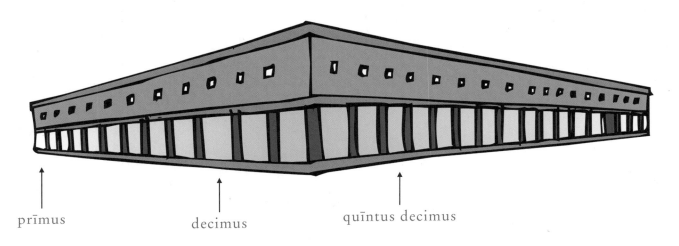

prīmus   decimus   quīntus decimus

NUMBERS

CARDINAL (Indeclinable)			ORDINAL (2-1-2 Adjectives)		
20	XX	vīgintī	20th	XX	vīcēsimus
30	XXX	trīgintā	30th	XXX	trīcēsimus
40	XL	quadrāgintā	40th	XL	quadrāgēsimus
50	L	quīnquāgintā	50th	L	quīnquāgēsimus
60	LX	sexāgintā	60th	LX	sexāgēsimus
70	LXX	septuāgintā	70th	LXX	septuāgēsimus
80	LXXX	octōgintā	80th	LXXX	octōgēsimus
90	XC	nōnāgintā	90th	XC	nōnāgēsimus
100	C	centum	100th	C	centēsimus

21	21ST
↓	↓
vīgintī ūnus or ūnus et vīgintī	vīcēsimus prīmus

In ūnō diē sunt **quattuor et vīgintī** hōrae.
In one day there are ◇24◇ hours.

Trīcēsimō quīntō momentō pervēnistī.
You arrived at the ◇35th◇ minute.

Quadrāgintā mōmenta dormīvī.
I slept for ◇40◇ minutes.

NUMBERS

CARDINAL (Indeclinable & Declinable)			ORDINAL (2-1-2 Adjectives)		
100	C	centum	100th	C	centēsimus
200	CC	ducentī	200th	CC	ducentēsimus
300	CCC	trecentī	300th	CCC	trecentēsimus
400	CCCC	quadringentī	400th	CCCC	quadringentēsimus
500	D	quīngentī	500th	D	quīngentēsimus
600	DC	sescentī	600th	DC	sescentēsimus
700	DCC	septingentī	700th	DCC	septingentēsimus
800	DCCC	octingentī	800th	DCCC	octingentēsimus
900	DCCCC	nongentī	900th	DCCCC	nōngentēsimus
1000	M	mille	1000th	M	millēsimus

Declinable –
plural 2-1-2 adjectives:
ducentī, ducentae, ducenta

101	101ST
↓	↓
centum ūnus	centēsimus
or	prīmus
centum et ūnus	

Familia tua **quīngentōs** annōs patriam rēgnāvit.
Your family ruled the fatherland for ⬧500⬧ years.

Trecentēsimō septuāgēsimō secundō annō rēx fuistī.
You were king in the ⬧372nd⬧ year.

NUMBERS

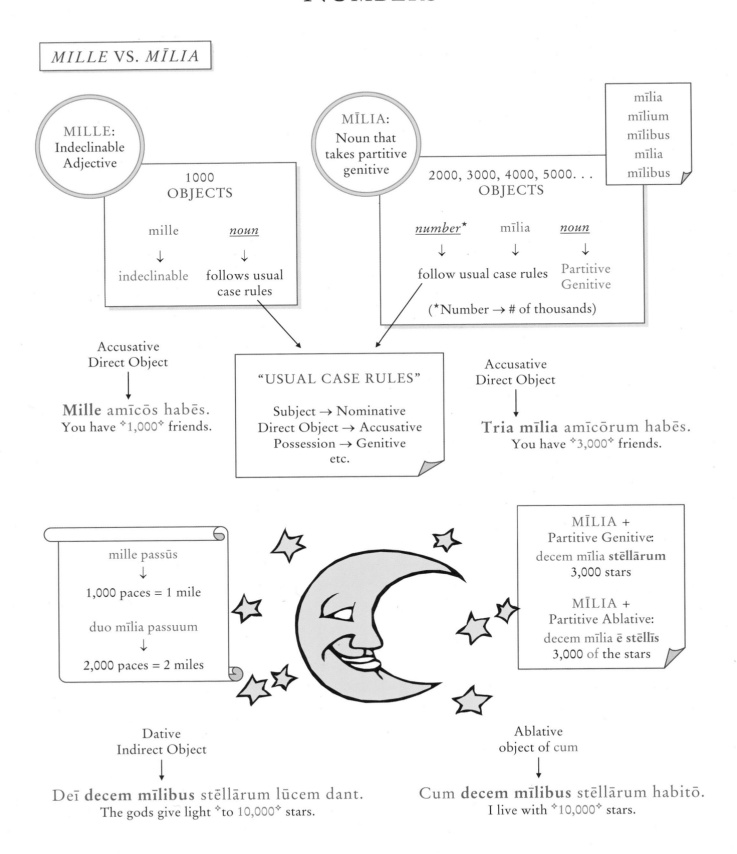

MILLE VS. MĪLIA

MILLE:
Indeclinable
Adjective

1000
OBJECTS

mille   *noun*
↓   ↓
indeclinable   follows usual
case rules

MĪLIA:
Noun that
takes partitive
genitive

mīlia
mīlium
mīlibus
mīlia
mīlibus

2000, 3000, 4000, 5000. . .
OBJECTS

*number**   mīlia   *noun*
↓   ↓   ↓
follow usual case rules   Partitive
Genitive

(*Number → # of thousands)

Accusative
Direct Object
↓

Mille amīcōs habēs.
You have ⬦1,000⬦ friends.

"USUAL CASE RULES"

Subject → Nominative
Direct Object → Accusative
Possession → Genitive
etc.

Accusative
Direct Object
↓

Tria mīlia amīcōrum habēs.
You have ⬦3,000⬦ friends.

mille passūs
↓
1,000 paces = 1 mile

duo mīlia passuum
↓
2,000 paces = 2 miles

MĪLIA +
Partitive Genitive:
decem mīlia **stēllārum**
3,000 stars

MĪLIA +
Partitive Ablative:
decem mīlia ē **stēllīs**
3,000 of the stars

Dative
Indirect Object
↓

Deī **decem mīlibus** stēllārum lūcem dant.
The gods give light ⬦to 10,000⬦ stars.

Ablative
object of cum
↓

Cum **decem mīlibus** stēllārum habitō.
I live with ⬦10,000⬦ stars.

SUBSTANTIVE ADJECTIVES

SUBSTANTIVE ADJECTIVE

When an adjective has no noun to modify,
it acts like a noun itself.
↓
Add "man"/"person," "woman," "thing"
according to the gender of the adjective.

Masculine Accusative Plural
↓
Multōs videō.
I see ⋄many men/people⋄.

Feminine Accusative Plural
↓
Multās videō.
I see ⋄many women⋄.

Neuter Accusative Plural
↓
Multa videō.
I see ⋄many things⋄.

MAN/PERSON
WOMAN
THING

Hī simiī **multīs** nōtī sunt.
These monkeys are well known ⋄to many people⋄.

-A
(e.g. multa)
↓
PROBABLY:
neuter nominative/accusative
plural

OTHERWISE:
feminine nominative
singular

Mala effugite, simiī.
Avoid ⋄bad things⋄, monkeys.

Illa nautam salutāvit.
⋄That woman⋄ greeted the sailor.
⋄She⋄ greeted the sailor.

HIC, ILLE, IS
↓
Substantive
usage indicates
"he," "she," "it," "they."
(See p. 129)

OVERVIEW OF ADVERBS

ADVERBS

Adverbs describe
verbs, adjectives, and other adverbs.

Adverbs tell you when, where, how,
how often, how much.

"NOT"

↓

Adverb that
expresses
negation.

We will go to the Circus Maximus ⋄today⋄.
(When - modifies the verb "we will go")

We will go ⋄there⋄ with our friends.
(Where - modifies the verb "we will go")

We will cheer ⋄loudly⋄ for our favorite charioteers.
(How - modifies the verb "we will cheer")

We ⋄usually⋄ meet people we know at the Circus Maximus.
(How Often - modifies the verb "we meet")

We will cheer ⋄very⋄ loudly.
(How Much - modifies the adverb "loudly")

We selected horses ⋄not⋄ afraid of the crowd.
(Negation - modifies the adjective "afraid")

ENGLISH ADVERBS

In English, many (but not all)
adverbs are formed by adding
-ly to adjectives:

| Quick | → | Quickly |
| Adjective | | Adverb |

LATIN ADVERBS

In Latin, adverbs formed
from adjectives end either
in -Ē or in -TER.

Notice that these adverbs'
stems come from adjectives,
but the endings are not
adjective endings.

Laetē cum face currit.
He runs ⋄happily⋄ with the torch.
↓
Adverb formed from
laetus, laeta, laetum (happy)

Celeriter cum face currit.
He runs ⋄swiftly⋄ with the torch.
↓
Adverb formed from
celer, celeris, celere (swift)

2-1-2 ADVERBS

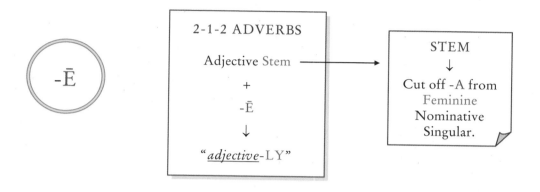

-Ē

2-1-2 ADVERBS

Adjective Stem

+

-Ē

↓

"*adjective*-LY"

STEM
↓
Cut off -A from Feminine Nominative Singular.

Adjectives in -US	laetus, laeta, laetum (happy)	→	laetē (happily)
Adjectives in -ER (e retained)	miser, misera, miserum (wretched)	→	miserē (wretchedly)
Adjectives in -ER (e dropped)	pulcher, pulchra, pulchrum (beautiful)	→	pulchrē (beautifully)

NOTE:

longē lātēque → far and wide
longē → far off, by far

IRREGULAR ADVERBS
(bonus, malus, magnus)

bene → well
male → badly
magnopere → greatly

Caecē ambulābās.
You were walking ⬦blindly⬦.

Bene vidēre nōn poterās.
You were not able to see ⬦well⬦.

THIRD DECLENSION ADVERBS

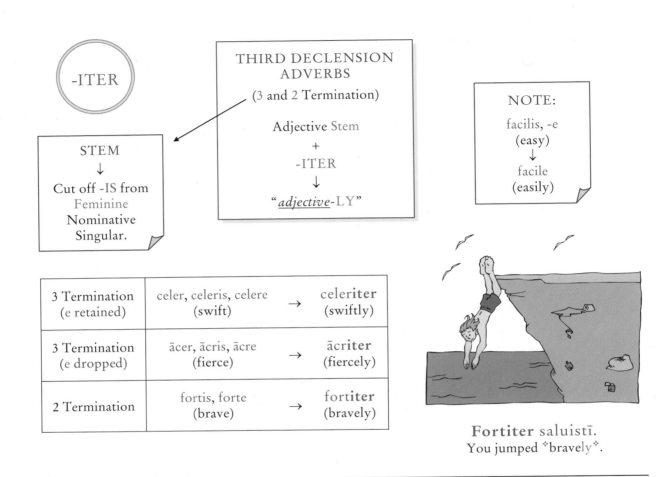

-ITER

THIRD DECLENSION
ADVERBS

(3 and 2 Termination)

Adjective Stem
+
-ITER
↓
"*adjective*-LY"

STEM
↓
Cut off -IS from
Feminine
Nominative
Singular.

NOTE:
facilis, -e
(easy)
↓
facile
(easily)

3 Termination (e retained)	celer, celeris, celere (swift)	→	celer**iter** (swiftly)
3 Termination (e dropped)	ācer, ācris, ācre (fierce)	→	ācr**iter** (fiercely)
2 Termination	fortis, forte (brave)	→	fort**iter** (bravely)

Fortiter saluistī.
You jumped ⁺bravely⁺.

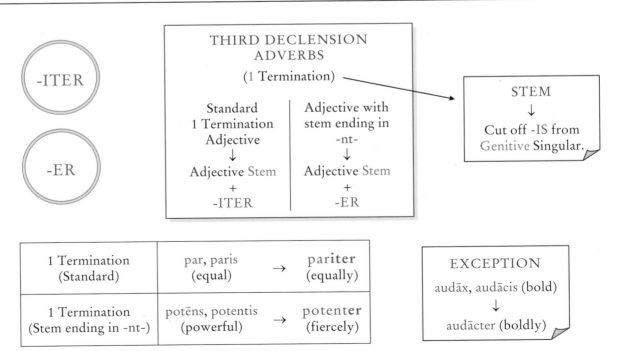

-ITER

-ER

THIRD DECLENSION
ADVERBS

(1 Termination)

Standard 1 Termination Adjective ↓ Adjective Stem + -ITER	Adjective with stem ending in -nt- ↓ Adjective Stem + -ER

STEM
↓
Cut off -IS from
Genitive Singular.

1 Termination (Standard)	par, paris (equal)	→	par**iter** (equally)
1 Termination (Stem ending in -nt-)	potēns, potentis (powerful)	→	potent**er** (fiercely)

EXCEPTION
audāx, audācis (bold)
↓
audācter (boldly)

COMPARISON OF ADJECTIVES

"DEGREE"
Positive
Comparative
Superlative

"big"

ingēns, ingentis

(POSITIVE)

"bigger"

ingentior, ingentius

(COMPARATIVE)

"biggest"

ingentissimus, -a, -um

(SUPERLATIVE)

-IOR
-IUS

COMPARATIVE

Adjective Stem
+
-IOR, -IUS
↓ ↓

| Masc./Fem. Nominative Singular | Neuter Nominative Singular |

"-ER," "MORE," "RATHER," "TOO"

→ 3rd Declension Noun Endings

-ISSIMUS

SUPERLATIVE

Adjective Stem
+
-ISSIMUS, -ISSIMA, -ISSIMUM
↓ ↓ ↓

| Masculine Nominative Singular | Feminine Nominative Singular | Neuter Nominative Singular |

"-EST," "MOST," "VERY"

→ 2-1-2 Adjective Endings

See p. 101 on the formation of adjective stems.

COMPARATIVE DEGREE OF
ingēns, ingentis

	MASCULINE/FEMININE		NEUTER	
	Singular	Plural	Singular	Plural
Nom.	ingentior	ingentiōrēs	ingentius	ingentiōra
Gen.	ingentiōris	ingentiōrum	ingentiōris	ingentiōrum
Dat.	ingentiōrī	ingentiōribus	ingentiōrī	ingentiōribus
Acc.	ingentiōrem	ingentiōrēs	ingentius	ingentiōra
Abl.	ingentiōre	ingentiōribus	ingentiōre	ingentiōribus

DECLINING COMPARATIVES

Comparative Masc./Fem. Nominative Singular (-ior)
+
Endings

(Note -ius in neuter nominative/accusative singular)

COMPARISON OF ADJECTIVES

ADJECTIVES IN -*ILIS* AND -*ER*

Some adjectives in -ilis and -er have regular comparative forms
but special superlative forms.

-LIMUS

-RIMUS

ADJECTIVES IN -ILIS

SUPERLATIVE
↓
STEM + -LIMUS

facillimus, -a, -um

(only for certain adjectives)

ADJECTIVES IN -ER

SUPERLATIVE
↓
Masc. Nom. Sing. + -RIMUS

ācerrimus, -a, -um

(līber, pulcher, celer, ācer, etc.)

ISSIMUS

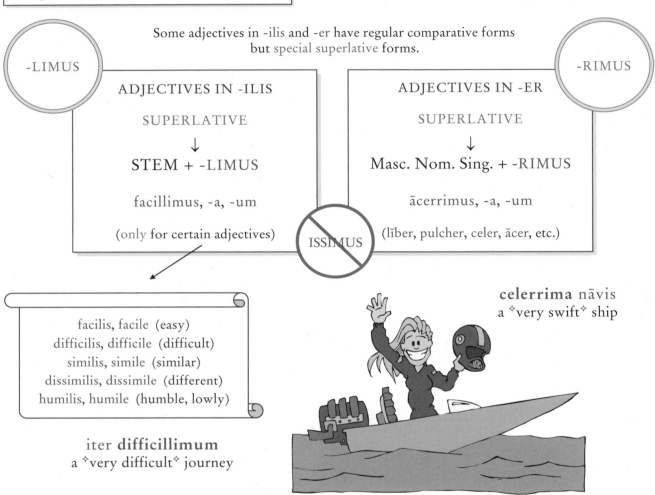

facilis, facile (easy)
difficilis, difficile (difficult)
similis, simile (similar)
dissimilis, dissimile (different)
humilis, humile (humble, lowly)

celerrima nāvis
a ⁺very swift⁺ ship

iter **difficillimum**
a ⁺very difficult⁺ journey

ADJECTIVES IN -*EUS* AND -*IUS*

Adjectives in -eus and -ius have
special comparative and superlative forms.

MĀGIS

MAXIMĒ

COMPARATIVE
↓
MĀGIS + POSITIVE

magis idōneus, -a ,-um
(more suitable)

SUPERLATIVE
↓
MAXIMĒ + POSITIVE

maximē anxius, -a ,-um
(most anxious)

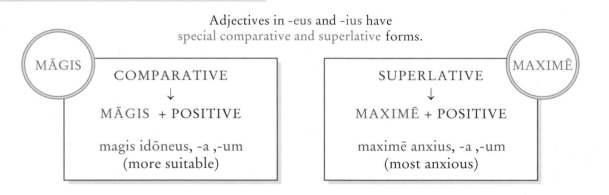

maximē idōnea nāvis
a ⁺very suitable⁺ ship

COMPARISON OF ADJECTIVES

POSITIVE	COMPARATIVE	SUPERLATIVE
bonus, -a, -um good	melior, melius better	optimus, -a, -um best
malus, -a, -um bad	peior, peius worse	pessimus, -a, -um worst
magnus, -a, -um great	maior, maius greater	maximus, -a, -um greatest
parvus, -a, -um small	minor, minus smaller	minimus, -a, -um smallest
multus, -a, -um much	*plūs + genitive more	plūrimus, -a, -um most
multī, -ae, -a many	*plūrēs, plūra more	plūrimī, -ae, -a most

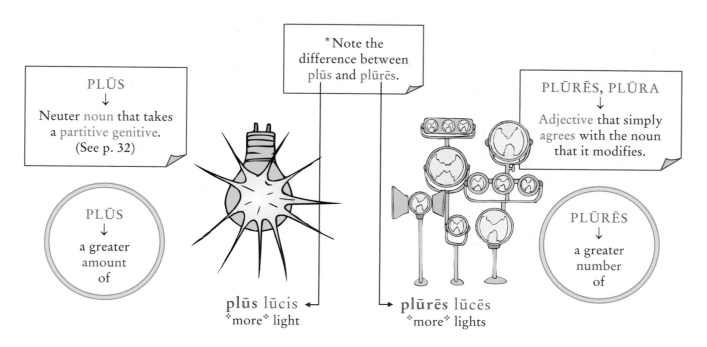

*Note the difference between plūs and plūrēs.

PLŪS
↓
Neuter noun that takes a partitive genitive.
(See p. 32)

PLŪS
↓
a greater amount of

plūs lūcis
◆more◆ light

PLŪRĒS, PLŪRA
↓
Adjective that simply agrees with the noun that it modifies.

PLŪRĒS
↓
a greater number of

plūrēs lūcēs
◆more◆ lights

COMPARISON OF ADJECTIVES

MORE IRREGULAR ADJECTIVES: PART I

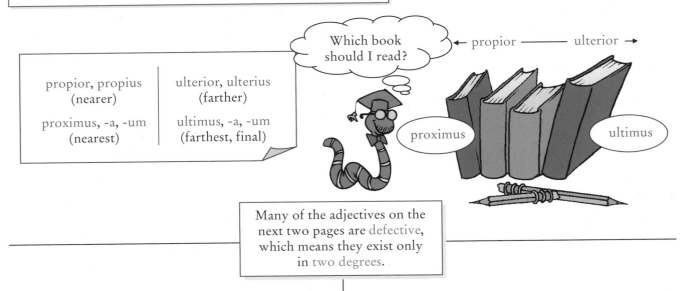

Which book should I read?

← propior ——— ulterior →

propior, propius (nearer)	ulterior, ulterius (farther)
proximus, -a, -um (nearest)	ultimus, -a, -um (farthest, final)

proximus

ultimus

Many of the adjectives on the next two pages are defective, which means they exist only in two degrees.

exterior, exterius (outer)	interior, interius (inner)
extrēmus, -a, -um (outermost, last, farthest, end of)	intimus, -a, -um (inmost)

superior, superius (higher)	īnferior, īnferius (lower)
summus, -a, -um (highest, top of)	īnfimus, -a, -um īmus, -a, -um (lowest, bottom of)

Two different forms of this adjective exist.

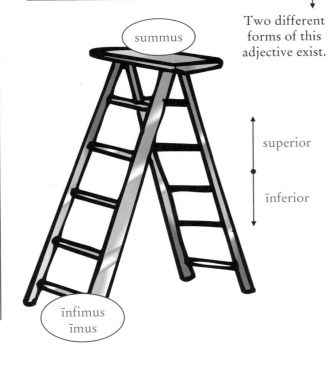

extrēmus

interior

intimus

exterior

summus

superior

īnferior

īnfimus
īmus

COMPARISON OF ADJECTIVES

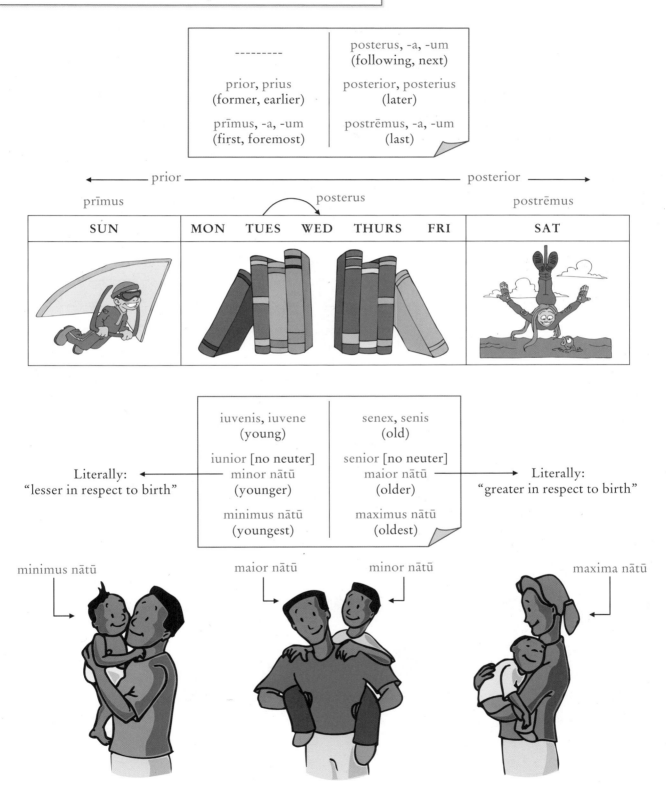

----
posterus, -a, -um
(following, next)

prior, prius
(former, earlier)

posterior, posterius
(later)

prīmus, -a, -um
(first, foremost)

postrēmus, -a, -um
(last)

← prior ——— posterior →

prīmus

posterus

postrēmus

| SUN | MON TUES WED THURS FRI | SAT |

iuvenis, iuvene
(young)

senex, senis
(old)

iunior [no neuter]
minor nātū
(younger)

senior [no neuter]
maior nātū
(older)

minimus nātū
(youngest)

maximus nātū
(oldest)

Literally:
"lesser in respect to birth"

Literally:
"greater in respect to birth"

minimus nātū

maior nātū

minor nātū

maxima nātū

COMPARISON OF ADVERBS

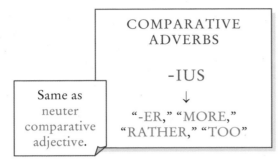

COMPARATIVE
ADVERBS

-IUS

↓

"-ER," "MORE,"
"RATHER," "TOO"

Same as neuter comparative adjective.

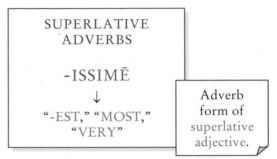

SUPERLATIVE
ADVERBS

-ISSIMĒ

↓

"-EST," "MOST,"
"VERY"

Adverb form of superlative adjective.

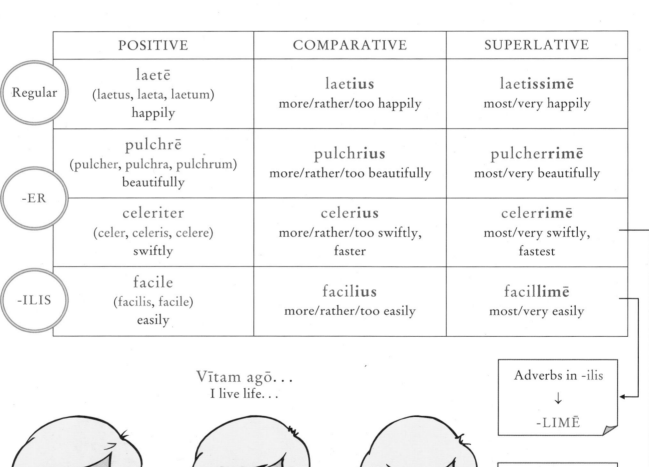

	POSITIVE	COMPARATIVE	SUPERLATIVE
Regular	laetē (laetus, laeta, laetum) happily	laetius more/rather/too happily	laetissimē most/very happily
-ER	pulchrē (pulcher, pulchra, pulchrum) beautifully	pulchrius more/rather/too beautifully	pulcherrimē most/very beautifully
-ER	celeriter (celer, celeris, celere) swiftly	celerius more/rather/too swiftly, faster	celerrimē most/very swiftly, fastest
-ILIS	facile (facilis, facile) easily	facilius more/rather/too easily	facillimē most/very easily

Vītam agō. . .
I live life. . .

laetē

laetius

laetissimē

Adverbs in -ilis
↓
-LIMĒ

Adverbs in -er
↓
-RIMĒ

COMPARISON OF ADVERBS

IRREGULAR ADVERBS

POSITIVE	COMPARATIVE	SUPERLATIVE
bene (bonus, -a, -um) well	melius better, rather/too well	optimē best, very well
male (malus, -a, -um) badly	peius worse, rather/too badly	pessimē best, very badly
magnopere (magnus, -a, -um) greatly	magis more, more greatly	maximē very greatly, especially
parum little, not much	minus less	minimē least, not at all, by no means
multum (multus, -a, -um) much, a lot	plūs more	plūrimum most, very much
diū for a long time	diūtius longer, for a longer time for a rather/too long time	diūtissimē for the longest time for a very long time
saepe often	saepius more/rather/too often	saepissimē very/most often

Diūtissimē exspectābō.
I will wait ⋄for a very long time⋄.

Minimē patiēns sum.
I am ⋄not at all⋄ patient.

QUAM

COMPARATIVE

+

QUAM

↓

"THAN"

Cēna tua **suāvior** erat **quam** cibus frīctus.
Your dinner was ✧tastier than✧ fried food.

Nominative:
Subject

Nominative:
Matches cēna

Noun that comes
after "than" must be
in the same case as
the noun to which it
is being compared.

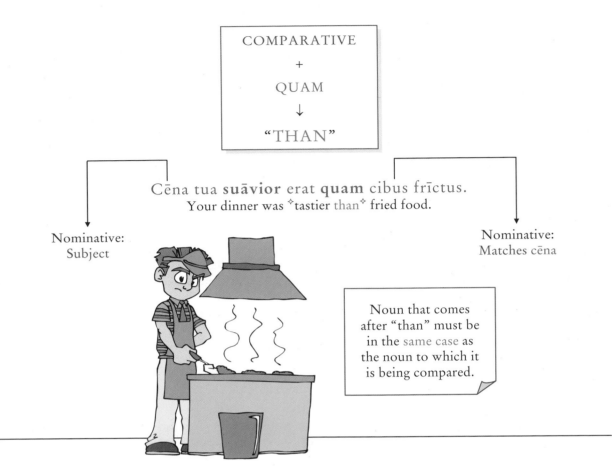

QUAM

+

SUPERLATIVE

↓

"AS _positive_ AS POSSIBLE"

Quam iūstissimās legēs pōnēmus.
We will set up laws ✧as just as possible✧.

Quam iūstissimē regēmus.
We will rule ✧as justly as possible✧.

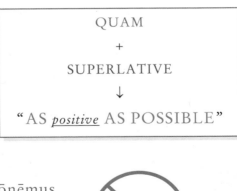

"most"
"very"

DEMONSTRATIVE PRONOUNS/ADJECTIVES

INTRODUCTION

DEMONSTRATIVE
ADJECTIVE
↓
"Pointer Adjectives"

"THIS" / "THAT"

HIC
↓
this
(here by
me)

ILLE
↓
that
(not near me)

IS
↓
this/that
(neutral
demonstrative)

Haec capsula
gravis est,
et illa schola
procul abest!

This bag is heavy,
and that school
is far away.

Eā causā
tē iuvāre volō.

For that reason,
I want to help you.

hic, haec, hoc (this, these; the latter)
ille, illa, illud (that, those; the former)
is, ea, id (this/these, that/those)

"The former"
refers to the first
of two previously
mentioned things,
and "the latter"
refers to the
second.

Rōma et Carthāgō sunt urbēs clārae. Illa in Italiā est, haec in Āfricā est.
Rome and Carthage are famous cities. The former is in Italy, the latter is in Africa.

DEMONSTRATIVE PRONOUNS/ADJECTIVES

FORMS OF *HIC, ILLE, IS*

Note the long marks that distinguish hoc (nom.) from hōc (abl.).

HIC, HAEC, HOC (THIS, THESE)

	SINGULAR			PLURAL		
	Masculine	Feminine	Neuter	Masculine	Feminine	Neuter
Nom.	hic	haec	hoc	hī	hae	haec
Gen.	huius	huius	huius	hōrum	hārum	hōrum
Dat.	huic	huic	huic	hīs	hīs	hīs
Acc.	hunc	hanc	hoc	hōs	hās	haec
Abl.	hōc	hāc	hōc	hīs	hīs	hīs

ILLE, ILLA, ILLUD (THAT, THOSE)

	SINGULAR			PLURAL		
	Masculine	Feminine	Neuter	Masculine	Feminine	Neuter
Nom.	ille	illa	illud	illī	illae	illa
Gen.	illīus	illīus	illīus	illōrum	illārum	illōrum
Dat.	illī	illī	illī	illīs	illīs	illīs
Acc.	illum	illam	illud	illōs	illās	illa
Abl.	illō	illā	illō	illīs	illīs	illīs

IS, EA, ID (THIS, THESE; THAT, THOSE)

	SINGULAR			PLURAL		
	Masculine	Feminine	Neuter	Masculine	Feminine	Neuter
Nom.	is	ea	id	eī	eae	ea
Gen.	eius	eius	eius	eōrum	eārum	eōrum
Dat.	eī	eī	eī	eīs	eīs	eīs
Acc.	eum	eam	id	eōs	eās	ea
Abl.	eō	eā	eō	eīs	eīs	eīs

Genitive and dative singular resemble the forms of ūnus. (See p. 110)

Similarities to 2-1-2 adjectives appear in the accusative and ablative singular.

Plural forms are just like a 2-1-2 adjective (except for the neuter nominative/accusative form haec).

Neuter nominative and accusative plural always look like the feminine nominative singular.

DEMONSTRATIVE PRONOUNS/ADJECTIVES

he/him
she/her
it
they/them

DEMONSTRATIVE PRONOUN

When hic, ille, and is
stand alone with no noun to modify,
they are called demonstrative pronouns.

↓

Add "man"/"person," "woman," "thing"
as for any other substantive adjective.
or
Treat as 3rd person pronoun:
"he," "she," "it," "they."

this/that
man
woman
thing

Eum laudābimus.
We will praise ⁺him⁺.

ANTECEDENTS

When a demonstrative pronoun
refers to some previously
mentioned noun, this noun is
called the antecedent.

The pronoun must agree
in gender and number with
its antecedent.

Eum laudābimus.
We will praise ⁺that man⁺.

Illī sunt ōrātōrēs.
⁺Those people⁺ are orators.

Illī sunt ōrātōrēs.
⁺They⁺ are orators.

Haec audīte!
Hear ⁺these things⁺.

Patria magnopere amātur et **eam** semper laudābimus.
The fatherland is loved greatly, and we will always praise ⁺it⁺.

Eam ("it") is feminine and singular
because it refers to the feminine noun
patria.

NOTE:

"It" is not necessarily
represented by a
neuter pronoun!

GENITIVE PRONOUNS
(e.g. eius, eōrum, eārum)

↓

Literally mean
"*of* him/her/it/them" –
often can be translated as
"his, her, its, their."

(See p. 100)

Gāium et sorōrem **eius** vōcō.
I call Gaius and ⁺his⁺ sister.
(...the sister ⁺of him⁺)

PERSONAL PRONOUNS

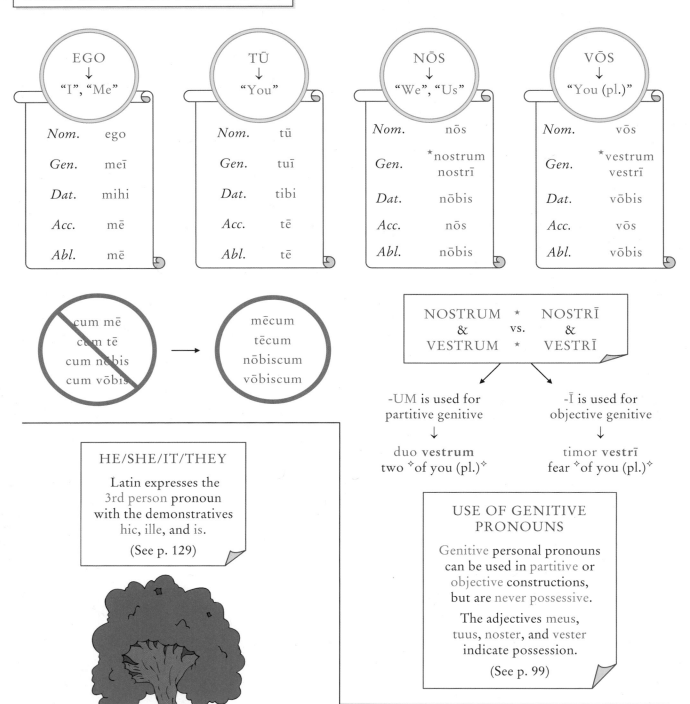

EGO
↓
"I", "Me"

Nom.	ego
Gen.	meī
Dat.	mihi
Acc.	mē
Abl.	mē

TŪ
↓
"You"

Nom.	tū
Gen.	tuī
Dat.	tibi
Acc.	tē
Abl.	tē

NŌS
↓
"We", "Us"

Nom.	nōs
Gen.	*nostrum / nostrī
Dat.	nōbis
Acc.	nōs
Abl.	nōbis

VŌS
↓
"You (pl.)"

Nom.	vōs
Gen.	*vestrum / vestrī
Dat.	vōbis
Acc.	vōs
Abl.	vōbis

cum mē
cum tē
cum nōbis
cum vōbis

→

mēcum
tēcum
nōbiscum
vōbiscum

NOSTRUM ★ NOSTRĪ
& vs. &
VESTRUM ★ VESTRĪ

-UM is used for
partitive genitive
↓
duo **vestrum**
two ⁺of you (pl.)⁺

-Ī is used for
objective genitive
↓
timor **vestrī**
fear ⁺of you (pl.)⁺

HE/SHE/IT/THEY

Latin expresses the
3rd person pronoun
with the demonstratives
hic, ille, and is.

(See p. 129)

USE OF GENITIVE PRONOUNS

Genitive personal pronouns
can be used in partitive or
objective constructions,
but are never possessive.

The adjectives meus,
tuus, noster, and vester
indicate possession.

(See p. 99)

Puerī arborem ascendunt, et rāmī **eōs** sustinent.
The boys climb the tree, and the branches hold ⁺them⁺ up.

REFLEXIVE PRONOUNS

_____ SELF

REFLEXIVE PRONOUNS
↓
Genitive, Dative, Accusative,
or Ablative pronoun that
refers to the subject of the sentence.

REFLEXIVE
PRONOUNS

Myself

Yourself

Himself
Herself
Itself

Ourselves

Yourselves

Themselves

✖ You see ✦you✦ in the mirror.
(Sounds strange!)

👍 You see ✦yourself✦ in the mirror.

"You": accusative direct object
↓
Reflexive pronoun is used
because this direct object is also
the subject of the sentence.

👍 Marcus sees ✦you✦.

✖ Marcus sees ✦yourself✦.
(Sounds strange!)

"You": accusative direct object
↓
Pronoun should not be reflexive
because this direct object is _not_ also
the subject of the sentence.

REFLEXIVE PRONOUNS

FORMS

	MYSELF	OURSELVES	YOURSELF	YOURSELVES	HIM/HER/IT -SELF	THEMSELVES
Nom.	------	------	------	------	------	------
Gen.	meī	nostrum nostrī	tuī	vestrum vestrī	suī	suī
Dat.	mihi	nōbis	tibi	vōbis	sibi	sibi
Acc.	mē	nōs	tē	vōs	sē	sē
Abl.	mē	nōbis	tē	vōbis	sē	sē

1st and 2nd person reflexives look exactly like personal pronouns, but context and common sense will help you determine whether to translate these identical forms as "I," "you," etc. or as "myself," "yourself," etc.

Use context to determine whether suī, sibi, sē, sē means "himself," "herself," "itself", or "themselves."

Claudius cēnam sibi parat.
Claudius prepares dinner ⬦for himself⬦.

(Common sense tells us that sibi must be "himself" and not "herself", "itself", or "themselves.")

USE OF GENITIVE PRONOUNS

Genitive reflexive pronouns can be used in partitive or objective constructions, but are never possessive.

The adjectives meus, tuus, noster, vester, and suus indicate possession.

(See pp. 99-100)

Cūram tuī habēs.
You have concern ⬦for yourself⬦.
(Objective Genitive)

NOTE:

There are no nominative reflexive pronouns because reflexives never act as subjects. It would be nonsense to say: "Myself went to the store."

It is possible to say "I myself went to the store," but this does not involve a reflexive.

(See p. 145)

Pronouns – Reflexive Pronouns – Forms

RELATIVE PRONOUN

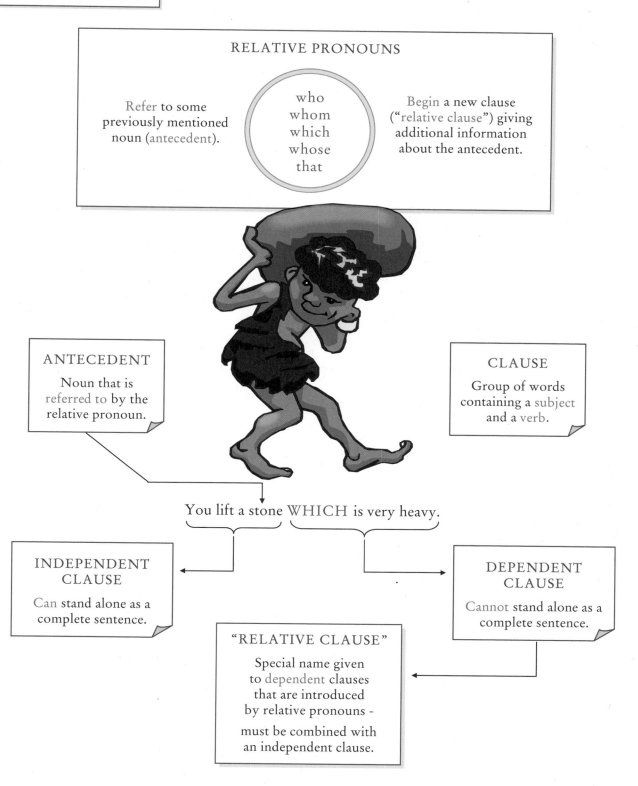

RELATIVE PRONOUNS

Refer to some previously mentioned noun (antecedent).

who
whom
which
whose
that

Begin a new clause ("relative clause") giving additional information about the antecedent.

ANTECEDENT
Noun that is referred to by the relative pronoun.

CLAUSE
Group of words containing a subject and a verb.

You lift a stone WHICH is very heavy.

INDEPENDENT CLAUSE
Can stand alone as a complete sentence.

DEPENDENT CLAUSE
Cannot stand alone as a complete sentence.

"RELATIVE CLAUSE"
Special name given to dependent clauses that are introduced by relative pronouns - must be combined with an independent clause.

RELATIVE PRONOUN

RELATIVE PRONOUN FORMS					
	SINGULAR			PLURAL		
	Masculine	Feminine	Neuter	Masculine	Feminine	Neuter
Nom.	quī	quae	quod	quī	quae	quae
Gen.	cuius	cuius	cuius	quōrum	quārum	quōrum
Dat.	cui	cui	cui	quibus	quibus	quibus
Acc.	quem	quam	quod	quōs	quās	quae
Abl.	quō	quā	quō	quibus	quibus	quibus

TRANSLATING THE RELATIVE PRONOUN

Nominative   who*, which, that

Genitive   whose, of whom, of which

Dative   to/for whom, to/for which

Accusative   whom, which, that

Ablative   (without preposition) by/with/because of/than/etc. which
(with preposition) *preposition* whom, which

> *"WHO"
> ↓
> Only appropriate
> when the pronoun is
> nominative.

Cornēlia est puella **quae** cōmam flāvam habet.
Cornēlia is a girl ⋄who⋄ has blond hair.

Cornēliam, **cuius** cōma flāva est, salūtō.
I greet Cornelia, ⋄whose⋄ hair is blond.

Cornēliam salūtō **cui** numquam anteā dīxī.
I greet Cornelia, ⋄to whom⋄ I never spoke before.

Cornēlia, **quam** hōdie salūtāvī, tua soror est.
Cornelia, ⋄whom⋄ I greeted today, is your sister.

Cornēlia, dē **quā** saepe dīcō, mūsicam amat.
Cornelia, about ⋄whom⋄ I speak often, loves music.

Cornēlia mūsicam facit **quā** dēlectāmur.
Cornelia makes music ⋄by which⋄ we are delighted.

RELATIVE PRONOUN

CASE, NUMBER, GENDER RULE

Case
Agreement

DECLINING THE RELATIVE PRONOUN

Gender & Number	→	Must match the antecedent.
Case	→	Must reflect the grammatical role of the relative pronoun in its own half of the sentence.

Gender & Number Agreement

The grammatical role of the antecedent is irrelevant to the case of the relative pronoun.

DETERMINING THE CASE OF THE RELATIVE PRONOUN

1. Break the sentence into two separate sentences.

2. Identify the role of the word that is inserted when you take out the relative pronoun.

3. Use the case that reflects this grammatical function.

The gender and number of the relative pronoun help us identify the antecedent.

①

You lift a stone
which is very heavy.

↓

You lift a stone.
~~which~~ The stone is very heavy.

①

You called the dogs
whose faces were happy.

↓

You called the dogs.
~~whose~~ The dogs' faces were happy.

②

You lift a stone.
The stone is very heavy.

→

SUBJECT
NOMINATIVE

②

You called the dogs.
The dogs' faces were happy.

→

POSSESSIVE
GENITIVE

③

Saxum tollis **quod** gravissimum est.
You lift a stone ⟡which⟡ is very heavy.

↓

Nominative: subject of est
Neuter Singular: agrees with saxum

③

Canēs vocāvistī **quōrum** vultūs erant laetī.
You called the dogs ⟡whose⟡ faces were happy.

↓

Genitive: possessive
Masculine Plural: agrees with canēs

RELATIVE PRONOUN

IMPLIED DEMONSTRATIVE

MISSING
ANTECEDENT
↓
"he who"

IMPLIED DEMONSTRATIVE

QUĪ, QUAE, QUOD
sometimes appears without an antecedent.
Supply an imaginary is, ea, id.

↓

quī clāmat = **[is] quī** clāmat
⧫he who⧫ is shouting. . .

↓

If the antecedent seems to be missing, try
"HE/SHE WHO," "THAT WHICH,"
"THOSE WHO," etc.

Quī tē iūvit nunc laudātur.
⧫He who⧫ helped you is now being praised.
(is quī)

Dedit **quod** petīverās.
He gave ⧫that which⧫ you had requested.
(id quod)

NOTE:

You can generally
assume that the implied
demonstrative would be
in the same case as the
relative pronoun.

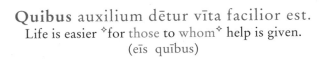

Quibus auxilium dētur vīta facilior est.
Life is easier ⧫for those to whom⧫ help is given.
(eīs quibus)

RELATIVE PRONOUN

MISSING
ANTECEDENT
↓
"he," "she," "it,"
"they"

ACTING AS A DEMONSTRATIVE

QUĪ, QUAE, QUOD
may sometimes be translated
as if it were the pronoun is, ea, id:

↓

Quī nunc in agrīs labōrat.
✧He✧ now works in the fields.

↓

If the antecedent seems to be missing, try:
"HE," "SHE," "IT," "THEY"

In this situation, the
relative pronoun does
not begin a relative
clause. There is no
"who," "which,"
"that," etc.

Frāter meus est medicus. **Quī** in Ītaliā habitat cum familiā suā.
My brother is a doctor. ✧He✧ lives in Italy with his family.

Māter frātrem meum dēsīderat. **Quam** quoque dēsīderat ille.
My mother misses my brother. He also misses ✧her✧.

INTERROGATIVE ADJECTIVE

WHAT
&
WHICH
are
interchangeable.

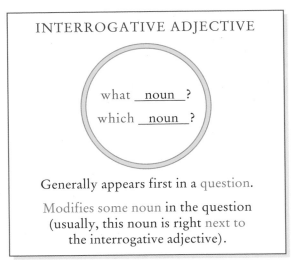

INTERROGATIVE ADJECTIVE

what __noun__ ?

which __noun__ ?

Generally appears first in a question.

Modifies some noun in the question
(usually, this noun is right next to
the interrogative adjective).

Quae hiēms erat peior hāc?
◊Which winter◊ was worse than this one?

Quās terrās vexat nix?
◊What lands◊ does the snow harrass?

Cuius deī manus nivem mittit?
◊What god's◊ hand sends the snow?

PREPOSITIONS
↓
Placed before the
interrogative
adjective.

Questions may begin
in the middle of a
sentence.

The interrogative
adjective may not be
the first word of the
sentence, but it will
generally be the
first word of the
question part.

Ē quā tempestāte effūgistis?
◊From what storm◊ did you (pl.) flee?

Mē rogās, "Quibus cīvibus libet per nivem ambulāre?"
You ask me, "◊To which citizens◊ is it pleasing to walk through the snow?"

INTERROGATIVE ADJECTIVE

INTERROGATIVE ADJECTIVE FORMS					
SINGULAR			PLURAL		
Masculine	Feminine	Neuter	Masculine	Feminine	Neuter
Nom. quī	quae	quod	quī	quae	quae
Gen. cuius	cuius	cuius	quōrum	quārum	quōrum
Dat. cui	cui	cui	quibus	quibus	quibus
Acc. quem	quam	quod	quōs	quās	quae
Abl. quō	quā	quō	quibus	quibus	quibus

Exactly the same as the relative pronoun.

RELATIVE PRONOUN
vs.
INTERROGATIVE
ADJECTIVE

Let context and your instincts guide you in telling these identical forms apart. If you are dealing with a relative, the rest of the sentence will make it very clear that you need to say "who/which/whose/etc."

Suntne animālia **quae** ibi habitant?
Are there creatures ⬧who⬧ live there?
(Relative Pronoun)

Quae animālia ibi habitant?
⬧What creatures⬧ live there?
(Interrogative Adjective)

TRANSLATING THE INTERROGATIVE ADJECTIVE
("which" can be substituted for "what" below)

Nominative   what <u>noun</u>?

Genitive   what <u>noun</u>'s?
of what <u>noun</u>?

Dative   to/for what <u>noun</u>?

Accusative   what <u>noun</u>?

Ablative   (without preposition) by/with/because of/than/etc. what <u>noun</u>?
(with preposition) <u>preposition</u> what <u>noun</u>?

INTERROGATIVE PRONOUN

INTRODUCTION

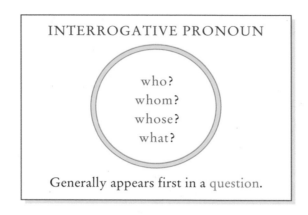

INTERROGATIVE PRONOUN

who?
whom?
whose?
what?

Generally appears first in a question.

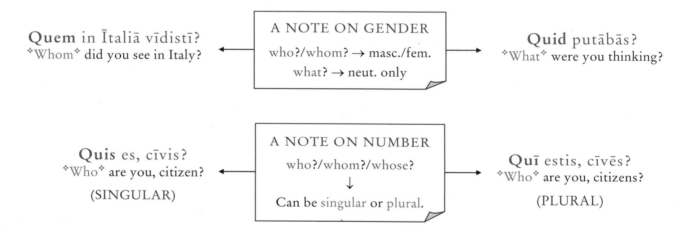

Quem in Ītaliā vīdistī?
◆Whom◆ did you see in Italy?

A NOTE ON GENDER

who?/whom? → masc./fem.

what? → neut. only

Quid putābās?
◆What◆ were you thinking?

Quis es, cīvis?
◆Who◆ are you, citizen?
(SINGULAR)

A NOTE ON NUMBER

who?/whom?/whose?
↓
Can be singular or plural.

Quī estis, cīvēs?
◆Who◆ are you, citizens?
(PLURAL)

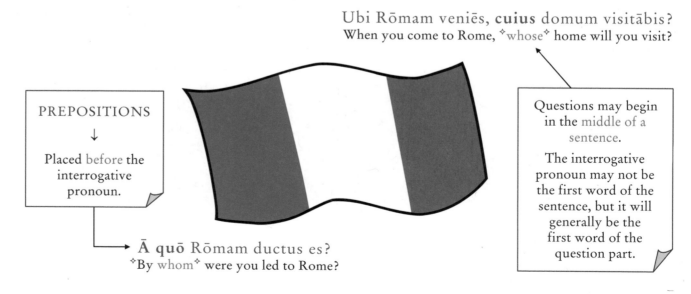

Ubi Rōmam veniēs, **cuius** domum visitābis?
When you come to Rome, ◆whose◆ home will you visit?

PREPOSITIONS
↓
Placed before the interrogative pronoun.

Questions may begin in the middle of a sentence.

The interrogative pronoun may not be the first word of the sentence, but it will generally be the first word of the question part.

Ā quō Rōmam ductus es?
◆By whom◆ were you led to Rome?

INTERROGATIVE PRONOUN

INTERROGATIVE PRONOUN FORMS					
	SINGULAR		PLURAL		
	Masc. & Fem.	Neuter	Masculine	Feminine	Neuter
Nom.	quis	quid	quī	quae	quae
Gen.	cuius	cuius	quōrum	quārum	quōrum
Dat.	cui	cui	quibus	quibus	quibus
Acc.	quem	quid	quōs	quās	quae
Abl.	quō	quō	quibus	quibus	quibus

↓
Masculine & Feminine
are the same.

Plural is exactly like the relative pronoun
and interrogative adjective.

Take care not to confuse the
nominative singular forms of the
relative and interrogative pronouns:

	Relative	Interrog.
Masc. Nom. Sing.	quī	quis
Fem. Nom. Sing.	quae	quis
Neut. Nom./Acc. Sing.	quod	quid

Quis hanc domum aedificāvit?
✦Who✦ built this house?

TRANSLATING THE INTERROGATIVE PRONOUN

Nominative   who? *, what?

Genitive   whose?, of whom?, of what?

Dative   to/for whom?, to/for what?

Accusative   whom?, what?

Ablative   (without preposition) by/with/because of/than/etc. whom/what?
(with preposition) *preposition* whom?/what?

*✦"WHO"
↓
Only appropriate
when the pronoun
is nominative.

INTERROGATIVE PRONOUN VS. ADJECTIVE

INTERROGATIVE PRONOUN	INTERROGATIVE ADJECTIVE
↓	↓
Stands alone.	Modifies some nearby noun.

who?

whom?

whose?

what?

what _noun_ ?

which _noun_ ?

Who goes there?

Whom did you see?

Whose shoes are those?

What are you doing?

What stranger goes there?

What friend did you see?

What child's shoes are those?

What task are you doing?

Quī mē spectant?
⬥Who⬥ are watching me?
(Pronoun)

Quī spectātōrēs mē spectant?
⬥What spectators⬥ are watching me?
(Adjective)

INTERROGATIVE PARTICLES

INTERROGATIVE PARTICLES

Indicate that a question is being asked.

Nōnne and num indicate that the speaker
expects a certain type of response.

NŌNNE

First word
of the question

↓

Indicates that the speaker
expects a "yes" response.

Nōnne nāvigābis ad Ītaliam?
You will sail to Italy, won't you?

NUM

First word
of the question

↓

Indicates that the speaker
expects a "no" response.

Num nāvigābis ad Ītaliam?
You won't sail to Italy, will you?

-NE

Attached to the first word
of the question.

↓

Speaker anticipates a "yes" or "no" response,
but has no expectation as to which of these
two possible answers will be given.

Enclitic:
Can't stand alone -
must be attached
to another word.

Nāvigābis**ne** ad Ītaliam?
Will you sail to Italy?

INTERROGATIVE ADVERBS

> ### INTERROGATIVE ADVERBS
>
> Some questions begin
> with interrogative adverbs,
> in which case there is no need
> for -ne, nōnne, or num.

Cūr Quīntus volāre vult?
◊Why◊ does Quintus want to fly?

Unde vēnit Quīntus?
◊Where◊ did Quintus come ◊from◊?

Quandō redībit Quīntus?
◊When◊ will Quintus return?

Quomodō volat Quīntus sine ālīs?
◊How◊ does Quintus fly without wings?

> ### COMMON INTERROGATIVE ADVERBS
>
> cūr (why?)
>
> ubi (where [at]?)
>
> unde (where from?)
>
> quō (where [to]?)
>
> quandō (when?)
>
> quomodō (how?)

> ### NOTE:
>
> Be careful to
> differentiate between
> ubi and quō, both of
> which mean "where?"

Ubi est Līvia?
◊Where◊ is Livia?
↓
(Location)

Quō volat Līvia?
◊Where◊ is Livia flying?
↓
(Destination)

IPSE, IPSA, IPSUM

-SELF
VERY

IPSE, IPSA, IPSUM

"Intensive Pronoun"
↓
Intensifies the emphasis
on the noun it modifies.

"-SELF," "VERY"

Resembles a 2-1-2
adjective except for the
genitive & dative singular,
which resemble hic and ille.

(See p. 128)

Rēgīnam **ipsam** vīdimus!
We saw the queen ⋄herself⋄!

Illō **ipsō** tempore, rēgīna mē cōnspēxit.
At that ⋄very⋄ time, the queen caught sight of me.

IPSE, IPSA, IPSUM (-SELF, VERY)					
	SINGULAR			PLURAL		
	Masculine	_Feminine_	_Neuter_	_Masculine_	_Feminine_	_Neuter_
Nom.	ipse	ipsa	ipsum	ipsī	ipsae	ipsa
Gen.	ipsīus	ipsīus	ipsīus	ipsōrum	ipsārum	ipsōrum
Dat.	ipsī	ipsī	ipsī	ipsīs	ipsīs	ipsīs
Acc.	ipsum	ipsam	ipsum	ipsōs	ipsās	ipsa
Abl.	ipsō	ipsā	ipsō	ipsīs	ipsīs	ipsīs

Ego **ipse** hunc deum timeō!
I ⋄myself⋄ fear this god!

↓

If "-self" acts as an adjective,
you are dealing with the
INTENSIVE PRONOUN.

("Myself" modifies "I.")

Be careful not to
confuse ipse with the
reflexive pronoun!
Both involve "-self."
(See pp. 131-132)

Mē contrā deum dēfendō.
I protect ⋄myself⋄ against the god.

↓

If "-self" acts like a noun,
you are dealing with a
REFLEXIVE PRONOUN.

("Myself" is simply the direct object
of "protect.")

ALIQUIS, ALIQUID

ALIQUIS, ALIQUID

ali-

+

quis, quid

↓

"SOMEONE/THING"
"ANYONE/THING"

Aliquid in hortō āmīsistī.
You lost ⋄something⋄ in the garden.

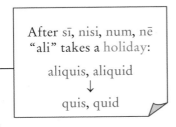

After sī, nisi, num, nē
"ali" takes a holiday:

aliquis, aliquid

↓

quis, quid

Aliquemne in hortō conspexistī?
Did you see ⋄anyone⋄ in the garden?

Num **quid** in hortō āmīsistī?
You didn't lose ⋄anything⋄ in the garden, did you?

ALIQUIS, ALIQUID (SOMEONE, SOMETHING; ANYONE, ANYTHING)					
	SINGULAR		PLURAL		
	Masc. & Fem.	Neuter	Masculine	Feminine	Neuter
Nom.	aliquis	aliquid	aliquī	aliquae	aliquae
Gen.	alicuius	alicuius	aliquōrum	aliquārum	aliquōrum
Dat.	alicui	alicui	aliquibus	aliquibus	aliquibus
Acc.	aliquem	aliquid	aliquōs	aliquās	aliquae
Abl.	aliquō	aliquō	aliquibus	aliquibus	aliquibus

ADJECTIVE VERSION

aliquī, aliqua, aliquod
(some, any)

The adjective is somewhat different
from the pronoun.

Feminine Singular:
aliqua
alicuius
alicui
aliquam
aliquā

Neuter Plural:
aliqua
aliquōrum
aliquibus
aliqua
aliquibus

aliquī deus
⋄some⋄ god

aliqua dea
⋄some⋄ goddess

ĪDEM, EADEM, IDEM

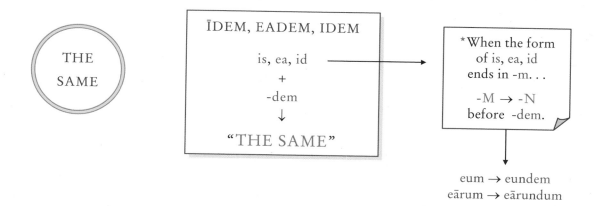

THE SAME

ĪDEM, EADEM, IDEM

is, ea, id
+
-dem
↓
"THE SAME"

*When the form
of is, ea, id
ends in -m. . .

-M → -N
before -dem.

eum → eundem
eārum → eārundum

ĪDEM, EADEM, IDEM (THE SAME)					
	SINGULAR			PLURAL		
	Masculine	Feminine	Neuter	Masculine	Feminine	Neuter
Nom.	īdem	eadem	idem	eīdem	eaedem	eadem
Gen.	eiusdem	eiusdem	eiusdem	eōrundem*	eārundem*	eōrundem*
Dat.	eīdem	eīdem	eīdem	eīsdem	eīsdem	eīsdem
Acc.	eundem*	eandem*	idem	eōsdem	eāsdem	eadem
Abl.	eōdem	eādem	eōdem	eīsdem	eīsdem	eīsdem

LONG MARK

īdem
↓
Masculine
Nominative
Singular

idem
↓
Neuter
Nominative
Singular

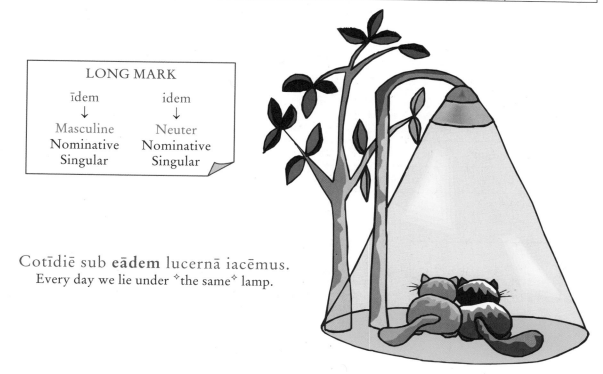

Cotīdiē sub **eādem** lucernā iacēmus.
Every day we lie under ⁺the same⁺ lamp.

Quīdam, Quaedam, Quoddam

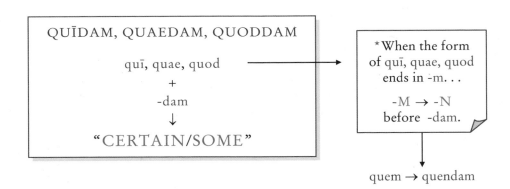

QUĪDAM, QUAEDAM, QUODDAM

quī, quae, quod

+

-dam

↓

"CERTAIN/SOME"

*When the form of quī, quae, quod ends in -m. . .

-M → -N before -dam.

quem → quendam

Quaedam animālia mē terrent.
◇Some◇ animals scare me.

(Used as ADJECTIVE)

Quīdam rānās timent.
◇Some people◇ fear frogs.

(Used as PRONOUN)

Quandam rānam invēnī.
I found ◇a certain◇ frog.

Rāna **quibusdam** inimīca est.
The frog is hostile ◇to certain people◇.

QUĪDAM, QUAEDAM, QUODDAM (CERTAIN, SOME)					
	SINGULAR			PLURAL		
	Masculine	Feminine	Neuter	Masculine	Feminine	Neuter
Nom.	quīdam	quaedam	quoddam	quīdam	quaedam	quaedam
Gen.	cuiusdam	cuiusdam	cuiusdam	quōrundam*	quārundam*	quōrundam*
Dat.	cuidam	cuidam	cuidam	quibusdam	quibusdam	quibusdam
Acc.	quendam*	quandam*	quoddam	quōsdam	quāsdam	quaedam
Abl.	quōdam	quādam	quōdam	quibusdam	quibusdam	quibusdam

Quoddam astrum vidēs.
You see ◇a certain star◇.

(Adjective)

PRONOUN VERSION

quīdam, quaedam, quiddam
(a certain/some person or thing)

The only difference between the adjective and the pronoun is in the neuter nom./acc. singular.

Quiddam in caelō vidēs.
You see ◇a certain thing◇ in the sky.

(Pronoun)

VERB TERMINOLOGY

PERSON & NUMBER

Indicate what kind of subject
is performing the verb.

You can tell
what kind of subject
is performing a Latin
verb by examining
the verb ending.

Īnsulam **amō**.
↓
✧I✧ love the island.
(1st person singular)

Īnsulam **amās**.
↓
✧You✧ love the island.
(2nd person singular)

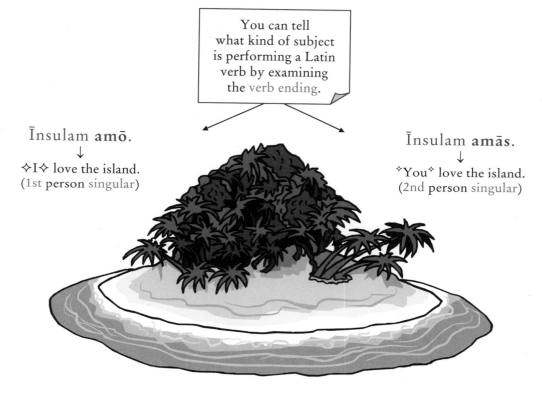

Subject

You and I rest on the shore.

"you and I" = *we*
↓
1st person plural

SUBJECT of verb	PERSON of verb	NUMBER of verb
I	1st	Singular
You	2nd	Singular
He/She/It	3rd	Singular
We	1st	Plural
You (pl.)	2nd	Plural
They	3rd	Plural

Subject
↓
The raft rests on the shore.

"the raft" = *it*
↓
3rd person singular

Verb Terminology

TENSE

TENSE

Indicates when
the verb takes place.

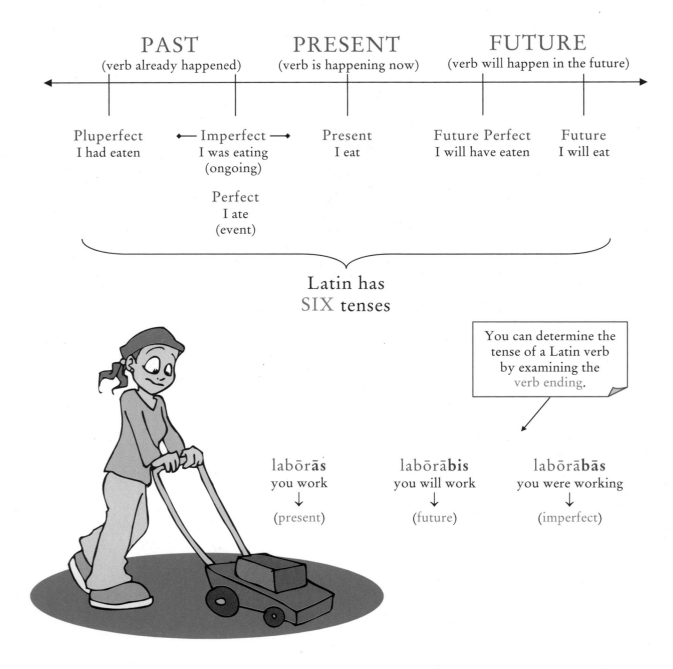

PAST
(verb already happened)

PRESENT
(verb is happening now)

FUTURE
(verb will happen in the future)

Pluperfect
I had eaten

←— Imperfect —→
I was eating
(ongoing)

Present
I eat

Future Perfect
I will have eaten

Future
I will eat

Perfect
I ate
(event)

Latin has
SIX tenses

You can determine the
tense of a Latin verb
by examining the
verb ending.

labōrās
you work
↓
(present)

labōrabis
you will work
↓
(future)

labōrabās
you were working
↓
(imperfect)

VERB TERMINOLOGY

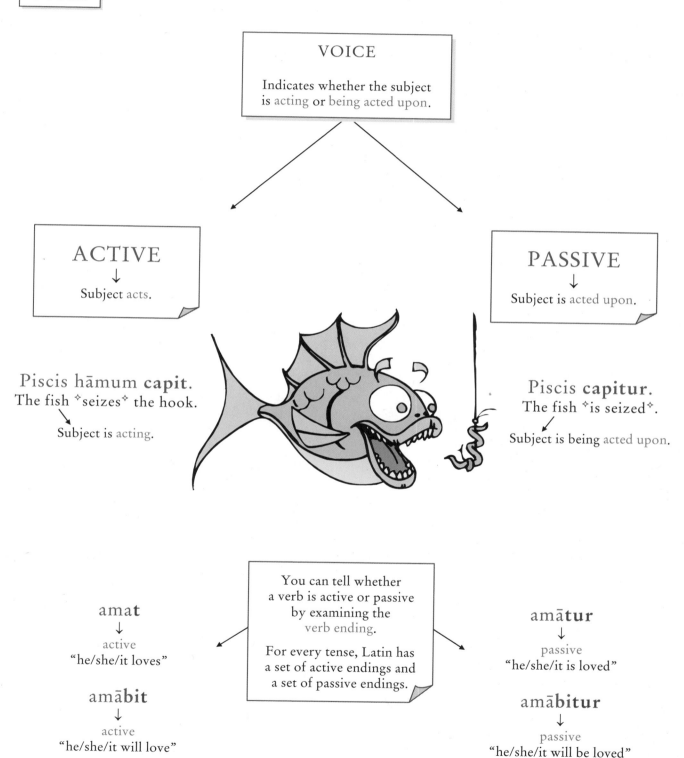

VOICE

Indicates whether the subject is acting or being acted upon.

ACTIVE
↓
Subject acts.

PASSIVE
↓
Subject is acted upon.

Piscis hāmum **capit**.
The fish ⋄seizes⋄ the hook.

Subject is acting.

Piscis **capitur**.
The fish ⋄is seized⋄.

Subject is being acted upon.

ama**t**
↓
active
"he/she/it loves"

amā**bit**
↓
active
"he/she/it will love"

You can tell whether a verb is active or passive by examining the verb ending.

For every tense, Latin has a set of active endings and a set of passive endings.

amā**tur**
↓
passive
"he/she/it is loved"

amā**bitur**
↓
passive
"he/she/it will be loved"

VERB TERMINOLOGY

MOOD

MOOD

Verbs can refer to factual action with a specific subject (indicative mood), generalized action without a specific subject (infinitive mood), commanded action (imperative mood), and more.

The mood of a verb indicates which of these functions is intended.

INDICATIVE
↓
"*Subject* hurries"
"Does *subject* hurry?"

INFINITIVE
↓
"to hurry"

IMPERATIVE
↓
"hurry!"

PARTICIPLE
↓
"hurrying"

SUBJUNCTIVE
↓
(See pp. 226–250, 252)

Different moods use
different endings.

festin**at**
he hurries
↓
(Indicative)

festin**āre**
to hurry
↓
(Infinitive)

festin**ā**
hurry!
↓
(Imperative)

festin**āns**
hurrying
↓
(Participle)

festin**et**

↓
(Subjunctive)

VERB TERMINOLOGY

CONJUGATION

CONJUGATION

"Conjugation" is simply a word that means "Verb Type."

There are 4 main types of verbs in the Latin language, and there are slight differences between the endings that each one uses.

IDENTIFYING A VERB'S CONJUGATION

Every conjugation has an infinitive form that is different from the infinitive forms of other conjugations.

Look at a verb's dictionary entry to find its infinitive form.

Typical Verb Dictionary Entries
↓

rogō, rogāre, rogāvī, rogātus (to ask)

audiō, audīre, audīvī, audītus (to hear)

INFINITIVE ENDINGS

-āre → 1st Conjugation

-ēre → 2nd Conjugation

-ere → 3rd Conjugation

-īre → 4th Conjugation

docēs:
2nd Conjugation
↓
Present

CONJUGATION MATTERS!

It will be difficult to interpret verb endings correctly if you do not know the verb's conjugation.

mittēs:
3rd Conjugation
↓
Future

SECOND CONJUGATION

Present	Imperfect	Future
doceō	docēbam	docēbō
docēs	docēbās	docēbis
docet	docēbat	docēbit
docēmus	docēbāmus	docēbimus
docētis	docēbātis	docēbitis
docent	docēbant	docēbunt

THIRD CONJUGATION

Present	Imperfect	Future
mittō	mittēbam	mittam
mittis	mittēbās	mittēs
mittit	mittēbat	mittet
mittimus	mittēbāmus	mittēmus
mittitis	mittēbātis	mittētis
mittunt	mittēbant	mittent

VERB TERMINOLOGY

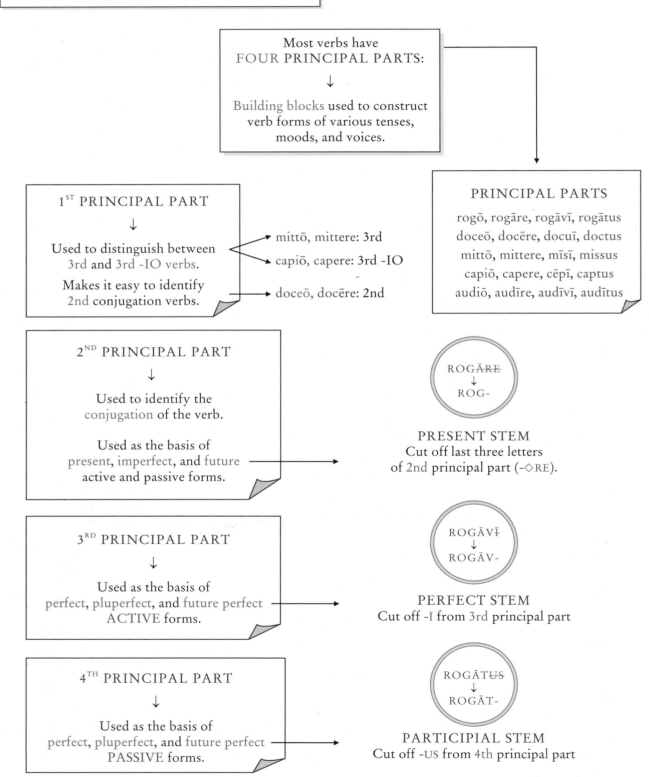

Most verbs have
FOUR PRINCIPAL PARTS:
↓
Building blocks used to construct
verb forms of various tenses,
moods, and voices.

PRINCIPAL PARTS

rogō, rogāre, rogāvī, rogātus
doceō, docēre, docuī, doctus
mittō, mittere, mīsī, missus
capiō, capere, cēpī, captus
audiō, audīre, audīvī, audītus

1ST PRINCIPAL PART
↓
Used to distinguish between
3rd and 3rd -IO verbs.

Makes it easy to identify
2nd conjugation verbs.

mittō, mittere: 3rd
capiō, capere: 3rd -IO
doceō, docēre: 2nd

2ND PRINCIPAL PART
↓
Used to identify the
conjugation of the verb.

Used as the basis of
present, imperfect, and future
active and passive forms.

ROGĀRE
↓
ROG-

PRESENT STEM
Cut off last three letters
of 2nd principal part (-◇RE).

3RD PRINCIPAL PART
↓
Used as the basis of
perfect, pluperfect, and future perfect
ACTIVE forms.

ROGĀVĪ
↓
ROGĀV-

PERFECT STEM
Cut off -ī from 3rd principal part

4TH PRINCIPAL PART
↓
Used as the basis of
perfect, pluperfect, and future perfect
PASSIVE forms.

ROGĀTUS
↓
ROGĀT-

PARTICIPIAL STEM
Cut off -US from 4th principal part

VERB TERMINOLOGY

SUMMARY

PERSON & NUMBER	Indicates who is doing the verb.	1st, 2nd, 3rd person singular or plural
TENSE	Indicates when the verb occurs.	Present, Imperfect, Future, Perfect, Pluperfect, Future Perfect
VOICE	Indicates whether the subject is acting or is being acted upon.	Active or Passive
MOOD	Indicates whether verb is expression of fact, generalized action, command, etc.	Indicative, Imperative, Infinitive, Participle, Subjunctive
CONJUGATION	Verb type – different conjugations use slightly different endings.	1st, 2nd, 3rd, 4th
STEM	Basic foundation of verb: various tenses, moods, and voices are formed by adding endings to stems.	Present Stem Perfect Stem Participial Stem
DICTIONARY ENTRY	Reveals verb conjugation and stems.	e.g. -ō, -āre, -āvī, -ātus

PERSONAL ENDINGS

ACTIVE

Remember that the subect of an active verb performs some action.

ACTIVE
PERSONAL ENDINGS

You can determine the subject of the verb by examining the verb ending.

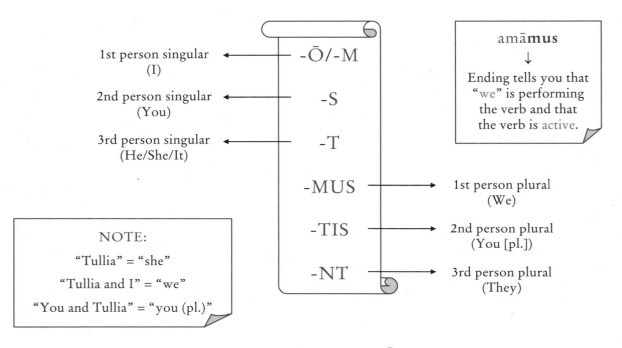

1st person singular (I) ← -Ō/-M

2nd person singular (You) ← -S

3rd person singular (He/She/It) ← -T

-MUS → 1st person plural (We)

-TIS → 2nd person plural (You [pl.])

-NT → 3rd person plural (They)

amā**mus**
↓
Ending tells you that "we" is performing the verb and that the verb is active.

NOTE:

"Tullia" = "she"

"Tullia and I" = "we"

"You and Tullia" = "you (pl.)"

Marcus lūdere **amāt**.
Marcus ⁺loves⁺ to play.

Marcum **spectāmus**.
We ⁺watch⁺ Marcus.

Marcus et Gāius lūdere **amant**.
Marcus and Gaius ⁺love⁺ to play.

PERSONAL ENDINGS

PASSIVE

PASSIVE PERSONAL ENDINGS

You can determine the subject of the verb by examining the verb ending.

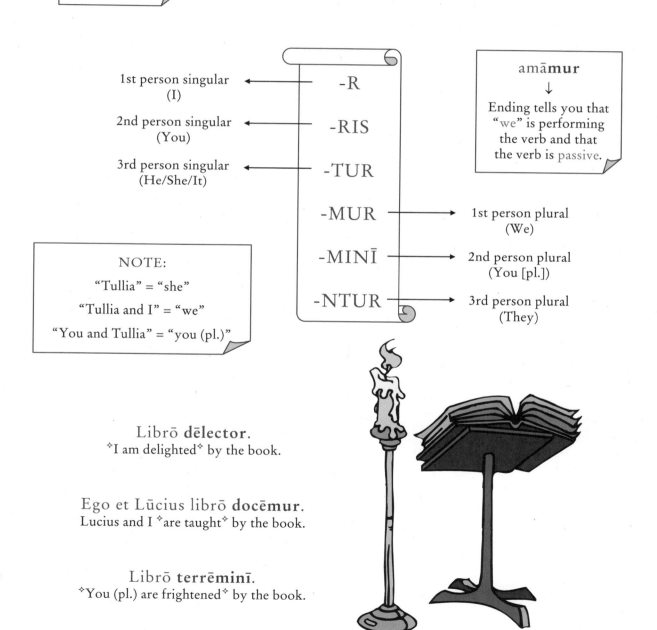

1st person singular (I) ← -R

2nd person singular (You) ← -RIS

3rd person singular (He/She/It) ← -TUR

amāmur
↓
Ending tells you that "we" is performing the verb and that the verb is passive.

-MUR → 1st person plural (We)

-MINĪ → 2nd person plural (You [pl.])

-NTUR → 3rd person plural (They)

NOTE:

"Tullia" = "she"

"Tullia and I" = "we"

"You and Tullia" = "you (pl.)"

Librō **dēlector.**
✧I am delighted✧ by the book.

Ego et Lūcius librō **docēmur.**
Lucius and I ✧are taught✧ by the book.

Librō **terrēminī.**
✧You (pl.) are frightened✧ by the book.

CONNECTOR VOWELS

1ˢᵀ conjugation	2ᴺᴰ conjugation
3ᴿᴰ / 3ᴿᴰ -IO conjugation	4ᵀᴴ conjugation

CONNECTOR VOWELS
(Also called stem vowels)
↓
Vowels attached to the stems
of verbs before adding endings.

Different conjugations
use different connector vowels,
as shown by the charts below.

3ᴿᴰ/3ᴿᴰ -IO

() → something extra
appears in 3rd -IO in
addition to what appears
in 3rd conjugation.

These charts are meant to convey dominant patterns, but some verb endings do deviate from them (e.g. no "i" appears in the 3rd conjugation present form regunt).

It is important to examine all verb forms carefully, and exceptions to these charts are pointed out on the relevant pages.

PRESENT CONNECTOR VOWELS

a	e
1	2
3	4
i	i

IMPERFECT CONNECTOR VOWELS

a	e
1	2
3	4
(i)e	ie

3rd → "e"
3rd -IO → "ie"

FUTURE CONNECTOR & ENDINGS

ābō	ēbō
1	2
3	4
(i)am	iam

3rd → "am, ēs, et..."
3rd -IO → "iam, iēs, iet.."

PRESENT ACTIVE INFINITIVE

āre	ēre
1	2
3	4
ere	īre

PRESENT PASSIVE INFINITIVE

ārī	ērī
1	2
3	4
ī	īrī

PRESENT PARTICIPLE CONNECTOR VOWELS

a	e
1	2
3	4
(i)e	ie

GERUND(IVE) CONNECTOR VOWELS

a	e
1	2
3	4
(i)e	ie

ACTIVE IMPERATIVE ENDINGS

ā	ē
āte	ēte
1	2
3	4
e	ī
ite	īte

PASSIVE IMPERATIVE ENDINGS

āre	ēre
āminī	ēminī
1	2
3	4
ere	īre
iminī	īminī

VOICE

ACTIVE VS. PASSIVE

ACTIVE VOICE

Role of the Subject:

↓

Performs action.

ENDINGS:

-o, -s, -t, -mus, -tis, -nt

PASSIVE VOICE

Role of the Subject:

↓

Receives action.

ENDINGS:

-r, -ris, -tur, -mur, -minī, -ntur

Vir **iacit**.
The man ⸎throws⸎.
(Active)

Vir **iacitur**.
The man ⸎is thrown⸎.
(Passive)

ACTIVE VOICE

Present: I *verb*, am *verb*ing, do *verb*
Imperfect: I was *verb*ing, kept *verb*ing, used to *verb*
Future: I will *verb*
Perfect: I *verb*ed, have *verb*ed, did *verb*
Pluperfect: I had *verb*ed
Future Perfect: I will have *verb*ed

PASSIVE VOICE

Present: I am *verb*ed, am being *verb*ed
Imperfect: I was being *verb*ed, kept being *verb*ed, used to be *verb*ed
Future: I will be *verb*ed
Perfect: I was *verb*ed, have been *verb*ed
Pluperfect: I had been *verb*ed
Future Perfect: I will have been *verb*ed

SYSTEMS OF TENSES: MEANINGS

 ACTIVE (2nd)

 PASSIVE (2nd)

PRESENT SYSTEM

PRESENT INDICATIVE

Action happens now,
in the present time.

SHE IS PREPARING
↓
No extra "helping" verb is
needed in Latin!

parat

~~EST parat~~

ACTIVE

rogat
↓
"asks"
"AM/IS/ARE asking"
"DO/DOES ask"

Strēnuē lūdimus.
⁘We play⁘ energetically.

PASSIVE

rogātur
↓
"AM/IS/ARE asked"
"AM/IS/ARE
being asked"

Ā vōbis laudāmur.
⁘We are praised⁘ by you (pl.).

IMPERFECT INDICATIVE

Action happened in the past
and was ongoing or repeated.

ACTIVE

rogābat
↓
"WAS/WERE asking"
"USED TO ask"
"KEPT asking"

Celeriter currēbam.
⁘I was running⁘ quickly.

(Ongoing)

PASSIVE

rogābātur
↓
"WAS/WERE being asked"
"USED TO be asked"
"KEPT being asked"

Nōmen meum clāmābātur.
My name ⁘kept being shouted⁘.

(Repeated/Ongoing)

FUTURE INDICATIVE

Action will happen
in the future.

ACTIVE

rogābit
↓
"WILL ask"

superābō / vincam
⁘I will win⁘

(1st & 3rd Conjugation)

2 SETS OF ENDINGS	
1st & 2nd Conj.	3rd & 4th Conj.
bō, bis, bit. . .	am, ēs, et. . .

PASSIVE

rogābitur
↓
"WILL be asked"

superābor / vincar
⁘I will be conquered⁘

(1st & 3rd Conjugation)

PERFECT SYSTEM

ACTIVE
rogāvit
↓
"askED"
"HAS/HAVE asked"
"DID ask"

PERFECT INDICATIVE

Action happened in the past, and is seen as completed.

Herī māchinam Stēllam **appellāvī**.
Yesterday ⬥I named⬥ my machine Stella.
↓
Action was completed (not ongoing as in the imperfect).

PASSIVE
rogātus est
↓
"WAS/WERE asked"
"HAS/HAVE been asked"

ACTIVE
rogāverat
↓
"HAD asked"

PLUPERFECT INDICATIVE

Action happened in the past before some other past scenario.

Māchinam tribus ante diēbus **ēmeram**.
⬥I had bought⬥ the machine three days earlier.

PASSIVE
rogātus erat
↓
"HAD been asked"

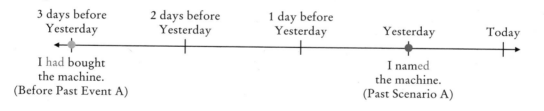

3 days before Yesterday	2 days before Yesterday	1 day before Yesterday	Yesterday	Today

I had bought the machine. (Before Past Event A)

I named the machine. (Past Scenario A)

ACTIVE
rogāverit
↓
"WILL HAVE asked"

FUTURE PERFECT INDICATIVE

Action will be completed in the future before some other future scenario.

Stēlla ante mediam noctem mē **vīcerit**.
Stella ⬥will have conquered⬥ me before midnight.

PASSIVE
rogātus erit
↓
"WILL HAVE been asked"

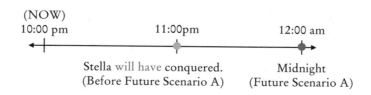

(NOW)
10:00 pm   11:00pm   12:00 am

Stella will have conquered.
(Before Future Scenario A)

Midnight
(Future Scenario A)

PRESENT TENSE

ACTIVE (2nd)

PRESENT ACTIVE INDICATIVE

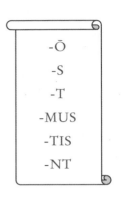

-Ō
-S
-T
-MUS
-TIS
-NT

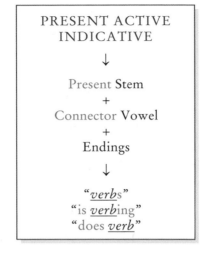

PRESENT ACTIVE
INDICATIVE
↓
Present Stem
+
Connector Vowel
+
Endings
↓
"*verb*s"
"is *verb*ing"
"does *verb*"

*verb*s,
is *verb*ing,
does *verb*

PRESENT
CONNECTOR
VOWELS

a		e
	1 | 2	
	3 | 4	
i		i

Note exceptions to
vowel pattern
in chart below.

Note that the 1st & 3rd
conjugations do not have a
connector vowel before -ō
in the 1st person singular.

Note other important
vowel behavior highlighted
in red below.

PRESENT STEM
Use
2nd principal part.
↓
Cut off -◇RE.

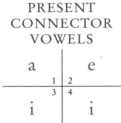

Fulmina **parās**.
◇You prepare◇ thunderbolts.

PRESENT ACTIVE INDICATIVE					
1st Conj.	2nd Conj.	3rd Conj.	3rd -IO Conj.	4th Conj.	Translation
rog**ō**	doce**ō**	mitt**ō**	cap**iō**	aud**iō**	I *verb*, am *verb*ing, do *verb*
rog**ās**	doc**ēs**	mitt**is**	cap**is**	aud**īs**	You *verb*, are *verb*ing, do *verb*
rog**at**	doc**et**	mitt**it**	cap**it**	aud**it**	He/She/It *verb*s, is *verb*ing, does *verb*
rog**āmus**	doc**ēmus**	mitt**imus**	cap**imus**	aud**īmus**	We *verb*, are *verb*ing, do *verb*
rog**ātis**	doc**ētis**	mitt**itis**	cap**itis**	aud**ītis**	You (pl.) *verb*, are *verb*ing, do *verb*
rog**ant**	doc**ent**	mitt**unt**	cap**iunt**	aud**iunt**	They *verb*, are *verb*ing do *verb*

PRESENT TENSE

PRESENT PASSIVE INDICATIVE

-OR
-RIS
-TUR
-MUR
-MINĪ
-NTUR

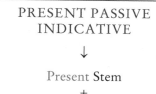

PRESENT PASSIVE
INDICATIVE
↓
Present Stem
+
Connector Vowel
+
Endings

"is *verb*ed"
"is being *verb*ed"

is *verb*ed,
is being
*verb*ed

PRESENT
CONNECTOR
VOWELS

a		e
	1	2
	3	4
i		i

Note exceptions to
vowel pattern
in chart below.

Note that the 1st & 3rd
conjugations do not have a
connector vowel before -or
in the 1st person singular.

Note other important
vowel behavior highlighted
in red below.

Ientāculum **parātur**.
Breakfast ◇is being prepared◇.

PRESENT STEM
Use
2nd principal part.
↓
Cut off -◇RE.

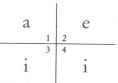

PRESENT PASSIVE INDICATIVE					
1st Conj.	2nd Conj.	3rd Conj.	3rd -IO Conj.	4th Conj.	Translation
rog**or**	doce**or**	mitt**or**	cap**ior**	aud**ior**	I am *verb*ed I am being *verb*ed
rog**ā**ris	doc**ē**ris	mitt**er**is	cap**er**is	aud**ī**ris	You are *verb*ed You are being *verb*ed
rog**ā**tur	doc**ē**tur	mitt**it**ur	cap**it**ur	aud**ī**tur	He/She/It is *verb*ed He/She/It is being *verb*ed
rog**ā**mur	doc**ē**mur	mitt**im**ur	cap**im**ur	aud**ī**mur	We are *verb*ed We are being *verb*ed
rog**ā**minī	doc**ē**minī	mitt**im**inī	cap**im**inī	aud**ī**minī	You (pl.) are *verb*ed You (pl.) are being *verb*ed
rog**an**tur	doce**n**tur	mitt**un**tur	cap**iun**tur	aud**iun**tur	They are *verb*ed They are being *verb*ed

IMPERFECT TENSE

IMPERFECT ACTIVE INDICATIVE

-BAM
-BĀS
-BAT
-BĀMUS
-BĀTIS
-BANT

IMPERFECT ACTIVE INDICATIVE

↓

Present **Stem**
+
Connector **Vowel**
+
Endings

"was *verb*ing"
"used to *verb*"
"kept *verb*ing"

was *verb*ing,
used to *verb*,
kept *verb*ing

IMPERFECT CONNECTOR VOWELS

a	e
1	2
3	4
(i)e	ie

In sellā **sedēbat**.
◇She was sitting◇ in the chair.

PRESENT STEM

Use
2nd principal part.
↓
Cut off -◇RE.

IMPERFECT ACTIVE INDICATIVE

1st Conj.	2nd Conj.	3rd Conj.	3rd -IO Conj.	4th Conj.	Translation
rog**ā**bam	doc**ē**bam	mitt**ē**bam	cap**iē**bam	aud**iē**bam	I was/kept *verb*ing I used to *verb*
rog**ā**bās	doc**ē**bās	mitt**ē**bās	cap**iē**bās	aud**iē**bās	You were/kept *verb*ing You used to *verb*
rog**ā**bat	doc**ē**bat	mitt**ē**bat	cap**iē**bat	aud**iē**bat	He/She/It was/kept *verb*ing He/She/It used to *verb*
rog**ā**bāmus	doc**ē**bāmus	mitt**ē**bāmus	cap**iē**bāmus	aud**iē**bāmus	We were/kept *verb*ing We used to *verb*
rog**ā**bātis	doc**ē**bātis	mitt**ē**bātis	cap**iē**bātis	aud**iē**bātis	You (pl.) were/kept *verb*ing You (pl.) used to *verb*
rog**ā**bant	doc**ē**bant	mitt**ē**bant	cap**iē**bant	aud**iē**bant	They were/kept *verb*ing They used to *verb*

IMPERFECT TENSE

IMPERFECT PASSIVE INDICATIVE

-BAR
-BĀRIS
-BĀTUR
-BĀMUR
-BĀMINĪ
-BANTUR

IMPERFECT PASSIVE INDICATIVE

↓

Present **Stem**
+
Connector **Vowel**
+
Endings

"was being _verb_ed"
"used to be _verb_ed"
"kept being _verb_ed"

was being, used to be, kept being _verb_ed

IMPERFECT CONNECTOR VOWELS

	a	e
	1	2
	3	4
	(i)e	ie

Ūvae **dēvorābantur**.
The grapes ✦were being devoured✦.

PRESENT STEM
Use
2nd principal part.
↓
Cut off -◇RE.

IMPERFECT PASSIVE INDICATIVE					
1st Conj.	2nd Conj.	3rd Conj.	3rd -IO Conj.	4th Conj.	Translation
rogābar	docēbar	mittēbar	capiēbar	audiēbar	I was/kept being _verb_ed I used to be _verb_ed
rogābāris	docēbāris	mittēbāris	capiēbāris	audiēbāris	You were/kept being _verb_ed You used to be _verb_ed
rogābātur	docēbātur	mittēbātur	capiēbātur	audiēbātur	He/She/It was/kept being _verb_ed He/She/It used to be _verb_ed
rogābāmur	docēbāmur	mittēbāmur	capiēbāmur	audiēbāmur	We were/kept being _verb_ed We used to be _verb_ed
rogābāminī	docēbāminī	mittēbāminī	capiēbāminī	audiēbāminī	You (pl.) were/kept being _verb_ed You (pl.) used to be _verb_ed
rogābantur	docēbantur	mittēbantur	capiēbantur	audiēbantur	They were/kept being _verb_ed They used to be _verb_ed

FUTURE TENSE

FUTURE ACTIVE INDICATIVE

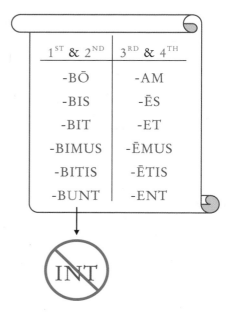

1ˢᵀ & 2ⁿᴰ	3ᴿᴰ & 4ᵀᴴ
-BŌ	-AM
-BIS	-ĒS
-BIT	-ET
-BIMUS	-ĒMUS
-BITIS	-ĒTIS
-BUNT	-ENT

INT

Cēnābis bene!
✦You will dine✦ well!

FUTURE ACTIVE INDICATIVE
↓
Present **Stem**
+
Connector **Vowel**
+
Endings

"will *verb*"

Canis cibum quaeret.
The dog ✦will seek✦ food.

will *verb*

FUTURE CONNECTOR & ENDINGS

ābō	ēbō
1	2
3	4
(i)am	iam

PRESENT STEM
Use
2nd principal part.
↓
Cut off -◇RE.

FUTURE ACTIVE INDICATIVE					
1st Conj.	2nd Conj.	3rd Conj.	3rd -IO Conj.	4th Conj.	Translation
rog**ābō**	doc**ēbō**	mitt**am**	cap**iam**	aud**iam**	I shall (will) *verb*
rog**ābis**	doc**ēbis**	mitt**ēs**	cap**iēs**	aud**iēs**	You will *verb*
rog**ābit**	doc**ēbit**	mitt**et**	cap**iet**	aud**iet**	He/She/It will *verb*
rog**ābimus**	doc**ēbimus**	mitt**ēmus**	cap**iēmus**	aud**iēmus**	We shall (will) *verb*
rog**ābitis**	doc**ēbitis**	mitt**ētis**	cap**iētis**	aud**iētis**	You (pl.) will *verb*
rog**ābunt**	doc**ēbunt**	mitt**ent**	cap**ient**	aud**ient**	They will *verb*

FUTURE TENSE

FUTURE PASSIVE INDICATIVE

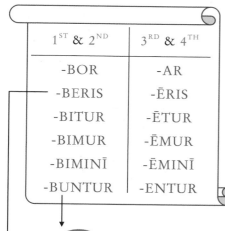

1ST & 2ND	3RD & 4TH
-BOR	-AR
-BERIS	-ĒRIS
-BITUR	-ĒTUR
-BIMUR	-ĒMUR
-BIMINĪ	-ĒMINĪ
-BUNTUR	-ENTUR

ĪRIS
INT

**FUTURE PASSIVE
INDICATIVE**

↓

Present Stem
+
Connector Vowel
+
Endings

"will be *verb*ed"

Ā multīs **spectābitur.**
◇He will be watched◇ by many.

Notable 3rd Conj.
Long Marks:

mitteris   mittēris

↓   ↓

present   future

will
be *verb*ed

**FUTURE
CONNECTOR
& ENDINGS**

ābor	ēbor
1	2
3	4
(i)ar	iar

PRESENT STEM
Use
2nd principal part.

↓

Cut off -◇RE.

Ā tē nōn **cōnspiciētur.**
◇He will not be seen◇ by you.

	FUTURE PASSIVE INDICATIVE				
1st Conj.	2nd Conj.	3rd Conj.	3rd -IO Conj.	4th Conj.	Translation
rog**ābor**	doc**ēbor**	mitt**ar**	cap**iar**	aud**iar**	I shall (will) be *verb*ed
rog**āberis**	doc**ēberis**	mitt**ēris**	cap**iēris**	aud**iēris**	You will be *verb*ed
rog**ābitur**	doc**ēbitur**	mitt**ētur**	cap**iētur**	aud**iētur**	He/She/It will be *verb*ed
rog**ābimur**	doc**ēbimur**	mitt**ēmur**	cap**iēmur**	aud**iēmur**	We shall (will) be *verb*ed
rog**ābiminī**	doc**ēbiminī**	mitt**ēminī**	cap**iēminī**	aud**iēminī**	You (pl.) will be *verb*ed
rog**ābuntur**	doc**ēbuntur**	mitt**entur**	cap**ientur**	aud**ientur**	They will be *verb*ed

PERFECT TENSE

PERFECT ACTIVE INDICATIVE

-Ī
-ISTĪ
-IT
-IMUS
-ISTIS
-ĒRUNT

PERFECT ACTIVE INDICATIVE

Perfect Stem

+

Endings

↓

"*verb*ed"
"has *verb*ed"
"did *verb*"

*verb*ed,
has *verb*ed,
did *verb*

PERFECT STEM

Use
3rd principal part.
↓
Cut off -Ī.

Deī ālās Pēgasō **dedērunt**.
The gods ⋄granted⋄ wings to Pegasus.

PERFECT ACTIVE INDICATIVE		
1st Sing.	rogāv**ī**	I asked, have asked, did ask
2nd Sing.	rogāv**istī**	You asked, have asked, did ask
3rd Sing.	rogāv**it**	He/She/It asked, has asked, did ask
1st Pl.	rogāv**imus**	We asked, have asked, did ask
2nd Pl.	rogāv**istis**	You (pl.) asked, have asked, did ask
3rd Pl.	rogāv**ērunt**	They asked, have asked, did ask

PERFECT TENSE

PASSIVE (4th)

... + SUM
... + ES
... + EST
... + SUMUS
... + ESTIS
... + SUNT

PERFECT PASSIVE INDICATIVE

4th Principal Part
with
Nominative Ending
+
Present of sum
↓
"was *verb*ed"
"has been *verb*ed"

was *verb*ed,
has been *verb*ed

Nominative ending
agrees with subject.

	M.	**F.**	**N.**
Sing.	-us	-a	-um
Pl.	-ī	-ae	-a

When sum, es, est, etc.
stand alone, they are the
present forms of sum.
↓
sum = I am

When sum, es, est, etc. are
attached to a 4th principal part,
they form the perfect passive
of the verb to which they are joined.
↓
rogātus sum = I was asked

Librī **scriptī sunt.**
Books ✦were written✦.
(Masculine plural subject)

Epistulae **scriptae sunt.**
Letters ✦were written✦.
(Feminine plural subject)

Verba **scripta sunt.**
Words ✦were written✦.
(Neuter plural subject)

PERFECT PASSIVE INDICATIVE			
1st Sing.	rogātus **sum**	I was asked, have been asked	[rogātus/rogāta/rogātum sum]
2nd Sing.	rogātus **es**	You were asked, have been asked	[rogātus/rogāta/rogātum es]
3rd Sing.	rogātus **est**	He/She/It was asked, has been asked	[rogātus/rogāta/rogātum est]
1st Pl.	rogātī **sumus**	We were asked, have been asked	[rogātī/rogātae/rogāta sumus]
2nd Pl.	rogātī **estis**	You (pl.) were asked, have been asked	[rogātī/rogātae/rogāta estis]
3rd Pl.	rogātī **sunt**	They were asked, have been asked	[rogātī/rogātae/rogāta sunt]

PLUPERFECT TENSE

ACTIVE (3rd)

PLUPERFECT ACTIVE INDICATIVE

-ERAM

-ERĀS

-ERAT

-ERĀMUS

-ERĀTIS

-ERANT

Looks exactly like the
imperfect of sum!

PLUPERFECT ACTIVE INDICATIVE

Perfect Stem

+

Endings

↓

"had _verb_ed"

had
_verb_ed

PERFECT STEM
Use
3rd principal part.
↓
Cut off -Ī.

When eram, erās, erat, etc.
stand alone, they are the
imperfect forms of sum.
↓
eram = I was

When eram, erās, erat, etc. are
attached to a 3rd principal part,
they form the pluperfect active
of the verb to which they are joined.
↓
rogāveram = I had asked

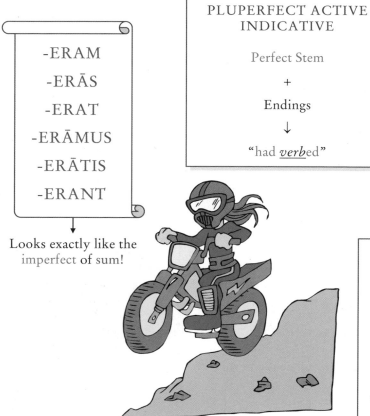

Ad urbem properāvī, sed iam **discesserās**.
I hurried to the city, but ⁺you had left⁺ already.

PLUPERFECT ACTIVE INDICATIVE		
1st Sing.	rogāve**ram**	I had asked
2nd Sing.	rogāve**rās**	You had asked
3rd Sing.	rogāve**rat**	He/She/It had asked
1st Pl.	rogāve**rāmus**	We had asked
2nd Pl.	rogāve**rātis**	You (pl.) had asked
3rd Pl.	rogāve**rant**	They had asked

PLUPERFECT TENSE

PLUPERFECT PASSIVE INDICATIVE

...+ ERAM

...+ ERĀS

...+ ERAT

...+ ERĀMUS

...+ ERĀTIS

...+ ERANT

PLUPERFECT PASSIVE INDICATIVE

4th Principal Part
+
Nominative Ending
+
Imperfect of sum
↓
"had been *verb*ed"

had been *verb*ed

Nominative ending agrees with subject.

	M.	F.	N.
Sing.	-us	-a	-um
Pl.	-ī	-ae	-a

When eram, erās, erat, etc. stand alone, they are the imperfect forms of sum.
↓
eram = I was

When eram, erās, erat, etc. are attached to a 4th principal part, they form the pluperfect passive of the verb to which they are joined.
↓
rogātus eram = I had been asked

Mīles **victus erat.**
The soldier ⁺had been conquered⁺.
(Masculine singular subject)

Patria **victa erat.**
The fatherland ⁺had been conquered⁺.
(Feminine singular subject)

Oppidum **victum erat.**
The town ⁺had been conquered⁺.
(Neuter singular subject)

PLUPERFECT PASSIVE INDICATIVE

1st Sing.	rogātus **eram**	I had been asked	[rogātus/rogāta/rogātum eram]
2nd Sing.	rogātus **erās**	You had been asked	[rogātus/rogāta/rogātum erās]
3rd Sing.	rogātus **erat**	He/She/It had been asked	[rogātus/rogāta/rogātum erat]
1st Pl.	rogātī **erāmus**	We had been asked	[rogātī/rogātae/rogāta erāmus]
2nd Pl.	rogātī **erātis**	You (pl.) had been asked	[rogātī/rogātae/rogāta erātis]
3rd Pl.	rogātī **erant**	They had been asked	[rogātī/rogātae/rogāta erant]

FUTURE PERFECT TENSE

ACTIVE (3rd)

FUTURE PERFECT ACTIVE INDICATIVE

-ERŌ

-ERIS

-ERIT

-ERIMUS

-ERITIS

-ERINT

FUTURE PERFECT ACTIVE INDICATIVE

Perfect Stem

+

Endings

↓

"will have _verb_ed"

will have
_verb_ed

PERFECT STEM

Use
3rd principal part.

↓

Cut off -Ī.

Almost like the future of sum!
(Future of sum has erunt).

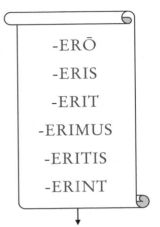

Castra ante noctem **mūnīverimus.**
⁜We will have fortified⁜ our camp before night.

When erō, eris, erit, etc.
stand alone, they are the
future forms of sum.

↓

erō = I will be

When erō, eris, erit, etc. are
attached to a 3rd principal part,
they form the future perfect active
of the verb to which they are joined.

↓

rogāverō = I will have asked

FUTURE PERFECT ACTIVE INDICATIVE		
1st Sing.	rogāver**ō**	I shall (will) have asked
2nd Sing.	rogāve**ris**	You will have asked
3rd Sing.	rogāve**rit**	He/She/It will have asked
1st Pl.	rogāve**rimus**	We shall (will) have asked
2nd Pl.	rogāve**ritis**	You (pl.) will have asked
3rd Pl.	rogāve**rint**	They will have asked

FUTURE PERFECT TENSE

FUTURE PERFECT PASSIVE INDICATIVE

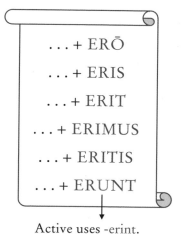

... + ERŌ

... + ERIS

... + ERIT

... + ERIMUS

... + ERITIS

... + ERUNT

Active uses -erint.
Passive uses -erunt.

FUTURE PERFECT PASSIVE
INDICATIVE

4th Principal Part

+

Nominative Ending

+

Future of sum

↓

"will have been _verb_ed"

will have
_verb_ed

Nominative ending
agrees with subject.

	M.	F.	N.
Sing.	-us	-a	-um
Pl.	-ī	-ae	-a

Vestēs **indūtae erunt**.
Clothes ⁺will have been put on⁺.
(Feminine plural subject)

Coma **composita erit**.
Her hair ⁺will have been arranged⁺.
(Feminine singular subject)

Multa **facta erunt**.
Many things ⁺will have been done⁺.
(Neuter plural subject)

When erō, eris, erit, etc.
stand alone, they are the
future forms of sum.
↓
erō = I will be

When erō, eris, erit, etc. are
attached to a 4th principal part,
they form the future perfect passive
of the verb to which they are joined.
↓
rogātus erō = I will have been asked

	FUTURE PERFECT PASSIVE INDICATIVE		
1st Sing.	rogātus **erō**	I shall (will) have been asked	[rogātus/rogāta/rogātum erō]
2nd Sing.	rogātus **eris**	You will have been asked	[rogātus/rogāta/rogātum eris]
3rd Sing.	rogātus **erit**	He/She/It will have been asked	[rogātus/rogāta/rogātum erit]
1st Pl.	rogātī **erimus**	We shall (will) have been asked	[rogātī/rogātae/rogāta erimus]
2nd Pl.	rogātī **eritis**	You (pl.) will have been asked	[rogātī/rogātae/rogāta eritis]
3rd Pl.	rogātī **erunt**	They will have been asked	[rogātī/rogātae/rogāta erunt]

SYSTEMS OF TENSES: FORMS

PRESENT SYSTEM

2nd
Principal
Part

PRESENT SYSTEM
OF TENSES

Present **Stem**

+

Connector **Vowel**

+

Endings

PRESENT STEM

ROG~~ĀRE~~
↓
rog-

CONNECTOR VOWELS

PRESENT		IMPERFECT		FUTURE	
a	e	a	e	ābō	ēbō
1	2	1	2	1	2
3	4	3	4	3	4
i	i	(i)e	ie	(i)am	iam

PRESENT SYSTEM OF TENSES (ACTIVE/PASSIVE) (3rd person singular form for each conjugation)					
	Present		Imperfect		Future	
1st	rogat	rogātur	rogābat	rogābātur	rogābit	rogābitur
2nd	docet	docētur	docēbat	docēbātur	docēbit	docēbitur
3rd	mittit	mittitur	mittēbat	mittēbātur	mittet	mittētur
3rd -IO	capit	capitur	capiēbat	capiēbātur	capiet	capiētur
4th	audit	audītur	audiēbat	audiēbātur	audiet	audiētur

PRESENT (All Verbs)		IMPERFECT (All Verbs)		FUTURE (1st & 2nd Conj.)		FUTURE (3rd & 4th Conj.)	
Active	Passive	Active	Passive	Active	Passive	Active	Passive
-ō	-r	-bam	-bar	-bō	-bor	-am	-ar
-s	-ris	-bās	-bāris	-bis	-beris	-ēs	-ēris
-t	-tur	-bat	-bātur	-bit	-bitur	-et	-ētur
-mus	-mur	-bāmus	-bāmur	-bimus	-bimur	-ēmus	-ēmur
-tis	-minī	-bātis	-bāminī	-bitis	-biminī	-ētis	-ēminī
-nt	-ntur	-bant	-bantur	-bunt	-buntur	-ent	-entur

SYSTEMS OF TENSES: FORMS

PERFECT SYSTEM

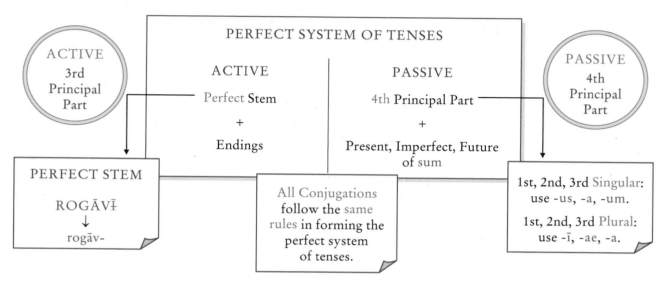

PERFECT SYSTEM OF TENSES

ACTIVE
3rd Principal Part

ACTIVE
Perfect Stem
+
Endings

PASSIVE
4th Principal Part
+
Present, Imperfect, Future of sum

PASSIVE
4th Principal Part

PERFECT STEM

ROGĀVĪ
↓
rogāv-

All Conjugations follow the same rules in forming the perfect system of tenses.

1st, 2nd, 3rd Singular: use -us, -a, -um.

1st, 2nd, 3rd Plural: use -ī, -ae, -a.

PERFECT SYSTEM OF TENSES (ACTIVE/PASSIVE)					
Perfect		Pluperfect		Future Perfect	
rogāvī	rogātus sum	rogāveram	rogātus eram	rogāverō	rogātus erō
rogāvistī	rogātus es	rogāverās	rogātus erās	rogāveris	rogātus eris
rogāvit	rogātus est	rogāverat	rogātus erat	rogāverit	rogātus erit
rogāvimus	rogātī sumus	rogāverāmus	rogātī erāmus	rogāverimus	rogātī erimus
rogāvistis	rogātī estis	rogāverātis	rogātī erātis	rogāveritis	rogātī eritis
rogāvērunt	rogātī sunt	rogāverant	rogātī erant	rogāverint	rogātī erunt

PERFECT (All Verbs)

Active	Passive
-ī	... sum
-istī	... es
-it	... est
-imus	... sumus
-istis	... estis
-ērunt	... sunt

PLUPERFECT (All Verbs)

Active	Passive
-eram	... eram
-erās	... erās
-erat	... erat
-erāmus	... erāmus
-erātis	... erātis
-erant	... erant

FUTURE PERFECT (All Verbs)

Active	Passive
-erō	... erō
-eris	... eris
-erit	... erit
-erimus	... erimus
-eritis	... eritis
-erint	... erunt

First Conjugation

-Ō
-ĀRE
-ĀVĪ
-ĀTUS

FIRST CONJUGATION

Typical Principal Parts:
rogō, rogāre, rogāvī, rogātus (to ask)

Some important unusual verbs exist:
dō, dare, dedī, datus (to give)
stō, stāre, stetī, status (to stand)

Present System:
Present Stem + Connector Vowel + Endings

Perfect System:
Active: Perfect Stem + Endings
Passive: 4th Principal Part + Endings

Dōnum **dabis**.
✦You will give✦ a gift.

PRESENT STEM
2nd Principal Part,
cut off -ĀRE.

PERFECT STEM
3rd Principal Part,
cut off -Ī.

PRESENT ACTIVE SYSTEM OF TENSES

PRESENT ↓ -A-	IMPERFECT ↓ -A- + BA	FUTURE ↓ -A- + BI	
rogō	rogābam	rogābō	INFINITIVE
rogās	rogābās	rogābis	rogāre
rogat	rogābat	rogābit	IMPERATIVE
rogāmus	rogābāmus	rogābimus	rogā
rogātis	rogābātis	rogābitis	rogāte
rogant	rogābant	rogābunt	

Dominant Vowel: **A**

PRESENT PASSIVE SYSTEM OF TENSES

PRESENT ↓ -A-	IMPERFECT ↓ -A- + BA	FUTURE ↓ -A- + BI	
rogor	rogābar	rogābor	INFINITIVE
rogāris	rogābāris	rogāberis	rogārī
rogātur	rogābātur	rogābitur	IMPERATIVE
rogāmur	rogābāmur	rogābimur	rogāre
rogāminī	rogābāminī	rogābiminī	rogāminī
rogantur	rogābantur	rogābuntur	

SECOND CONJUGATION

-ĒRE

-EŌ
-ĒRE
-UĪ
-TUS/-ITUS

SECOND CONJUGATION

Typical Principal Parts:
doceō, docēre, docuī, doctus (to teach)
habeō, habēre, habuī, habitus (to have)

Some important unusual verbs exist:
maneō, manēre, mānsī, mānsus (to stay)
videō, vidēre, vīdī, vīsus (to see)

Present System:
Present Stem + Connector Vowel + Endings

Perfect System:
Active: Perfect Stem + Endings
Passive: 4th Principal Part + Endings

Multās artēs **habēs**.
⋄You have⋄ many skills.

PRESENT STEM

2nd Principal Part, cut off -ĒRE.

PERFECT STEM

3rd Principal Part, cut off -Ī.

PRESENT ACTIVE SYSTEM OF TENSES

PRESENT ↓ -E-	IMPERFECT ↓ -E- + BA	FUTURE ↓ -E- + BI	
doceō	docēbam	docēbō	INFINITIVE
docēs	docēbās	docēbis	docēre
docet	docēbat	docēbit	IMPERATIVE
docēmus	docēbāmus	docēbimus	docē
docētis	docēbātis	docēbitis	docēte
docent	docēbant	docēbunt	

Dominant Vowel:
E

PRESENT PASSIVE SYSTEM OF TENSES

PRESENT ↓ -E-	IMPERFECT ↓ -E- + BA	FUTURE ↓ -E- + BI	
doceor	docēbar	docēbor	INFINITIVE
docēris	docēbāris	docēberis	docērī
docētur	docēbātur	docēbitur	IMPERATIVE
docēmur	docēbāmur	docēbimur	docēre
docēminī	docēbāminī	docēbiminī	docēminī
docentur	docēbantur	docēbuntur	

THIRD CONJUGATION

-Ō
-ERE

THIRD CONJUGATION

No "Typical" Verbs!
Memorize all principal parts carefully.
dūcō, dūcere, dūxī, ductus (to lead)
mittō, mittere, mīsī, missus (to send)
crēdō, crēdere, crēdidī, crēditus (to believe)

Present System:
Present Stem + Connector Vowel + Endings

Perfect System:
Active: Perfect Stem + Endings
Passive: 4th Principal Part + Endings

Fulmen **mittis**.
⬦You send⬦ a thunderbolt.

PRESENT STEM
2nd Principal Part,
cut off -ERE.

PERFECT STEM
3rd Principal Part,
cut off -Ī.

PRESENT ACTIVE SYSTEM OF TENSES

PRESENT ↓ -I-	IMPERFECT ↓ -E- + BA	FUTURE ↓ AM, ĒS, ET	
mittō	mittēbam	mittam	**INFINITIVE**
mittis	mittēbās	mittēs	mittere
mittit	mittēbat	mittet	
mittimus	mittēbāmus	mittēmus	**IMPERATIVE**
mittitis	mittēbātis	mittētis	mitte
mittunt	mittēbant	mittent	mittite

Dominant Vowel: **I/E**

~~BO BIS BIT~~

~~INT~~ ↓ UNT

PRESENT PASSIVE SYSTEM OF TENSES

PRESENT ↓ -I-	IMPERFECT ↓ -E- + BA	FUTURE ↓ AR, ĒRIS, ĒTUR	
mittor	mittēbar	mittar	**INFINITIVE**
mitteris	mittēbāris	mittēris	mittī
mittiturs	mittēbātur	mittētur	
mittimur	mittēbāmur	mittēmur	**IMPERATIVE**
mittiminī	mittēbāminī	mittēminī	mittere
mittuntur	mittēbantur	mittentur	mittiminī

~~IRIS~~ ↓ ERIS

~~INT~~ ↓ UNT

THIRD CONJUGATION

-ERE

SIMILAR-LOOKING THIRD CONJUGATION FORMS

PRESENT VS. FUTURE

Present: I + endings

Future: E + endings

mittit
He/She/It sends

mittet
He/She/It will send

Fīliam in pōmārium **mittit**.
◆She sends◆ her daughter into the orchard.

Fīliam in pōmārium **mittet**.
◆She will send◆ her daughter into the orchard.

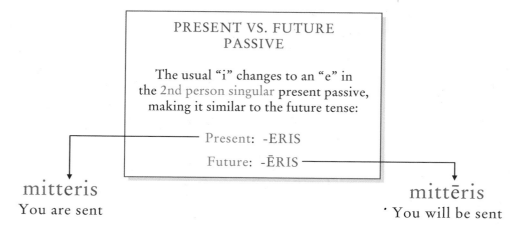

In pōmārium **mitteris**.
◆You are sent◆ into the orchard.

In pōmārium **mittēris**.
◆You will be sent◆ into the orchard.

PRESENT VS. FUTURE
PASSIVE

The usual "i" changes to an "e" in
the 2nd person singular present passive,
making it similar to the future tense:

Present: -ERIS

Future: -ĒRIS

mitteris
You are sent

mittēris
· You will be sent

THIRD CONJUGATION

-ERE

SECOND CONJUGATION VS. THIRD CONJUGATION

INFINITIVES

The 2nd and 3rd conjugations have very similar infinitives:

2nd Conjugation	3rd Conjugation
docēre	mittere
long mark	no long mark

TENSE FORMS WITH "E"

Both 2nd and 3rd conjugation have tenses that use e + ending:

2nd Conjugation	3rd Conjugation
docēs	mittēs
"you teach"	"you will send"
-e-	-e-
↓	↓
PRESENT tense	FUTURE tense
(Future is docēbit.)	(Present is mittit.)

WHAT TENSE IS INDICATED BY -ĒS, -ET, -ĒMUS, etc.?

↓

What conjugation is the verb?

2nd Principal Part: -ēre → 2nd Conjugation → E indicates Present Tense.

2nd Principal Part: -ere → 3rd Conjugation → E indicates Future Tense.

Flōrēs in manibus **tenēs**.
✦You hold✦ flowers in your hands.
(teneō, **tenēre**, tenuī, tentus)

Flōrēs ex terrā **crēscent**.
Flowers ✦will grow✦ out of the ground.
(crēscō, **crēscere**, crēvī, crētus)

Flōrēs in crīnibus **geris**.
✦You wear✦ flowers in your hair.
(gerō, **gerere**, gessī, gestus)

Third -IO Conjugation

-IŌ, -ERE

-IŌ, -ERE

THIRD -IO CONJUGATION

No "Typical" Verbs!
Memorize all principal parts carefully.
cap**iō**, cap**ere**, cēp**ī**, captus (to take, seize)
fug**iō**, fug**ere**, fūg**ī**, fugitus (to flee, flee from)

Present System:
Present Stem + Connector Vowel + Endings

Perfect System:
Active: Perfect Stem + Endings
Passive: 4th Principal Part + Endings

3rd -IO endings have some extra i's that
do not appear in the 3rd Conjugation.

Ab Sextō **fugiēmus**.
⬦We will flee⬦ from Sextus.

PRESENT STEM

2nd Principal Part,
cut off -ERE.

PERFECT STEM

3rd Principal Part,
cut off -Ī.

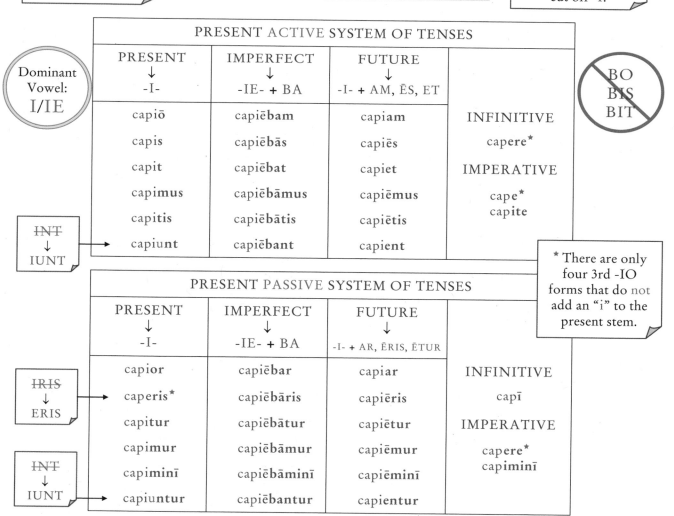

Dominant
Vowel:
I/IE

PRESENT ACTIVE SYSTEM OF TENSES			
PRESENT ↓ -I-	IMPERFECT ↓ -IE- + BA	FUTURE ↓ -I- + AM, ĒS, ET	
capiō	capiēbam	capiam	INFINITIVE
capis	capiēbās	capiēs	capere*
capit	capiēbat	capiet	IMPERATIVE
capimus	capiēbāmus	capiēmus	cape*
capitis	capiēbātis	capiētis	capite
capiunt	capiēbant	capient	

BO BIS BIT

INT ↓ IUNT

* There are only
four 3rd -IO
forms that do not
add an "i" to the
present stem.

PRESENT PASSIVE SYSTEM OF TENSES			
PRESENT ↓ -I-	IMPERFECT ↓ -IE- + BA	FUTURE ↓ -I- + AR, ĒRIS, ĒTUR	
capior	capiēbar	capiar	INFINITIVE
caperis*	capiēbāris	capiēris	capī
capitur	capiēbātur	capiētur	IMPERATIVE
capimur	capiēbāmur	capiēmur	capere*
capiminī	capiēbāminī	capiēminī	capiminī
capiuntur	capiēbantur	capientur	

IRIS ↓ ERIS

INT ↓ IUNT

FOURTH CONJUGATION

-ĪRE

-IŌ
-ĪRE
-ĪVĪ
-ĪTUS

FOURTH CONJUGATION

Typical Principal Parts:
audiō, audīre, audīvī, audītus (to hear)

Some important unusual verbs exist:
veniō, venīre, vēnī, ventus (to come)

Present System:
Present Stem + Connector Vowel + Endings

Perfect System:
Active: Perfect Stem + Endings
Passive: 4th Principal Part + Endings

Audīte, omnēs.
◇Listen,◇ everyone!

PRESENT STEM
2nd Principal Part,
cut off -ĪRE.

PERFECT STEM
3rd Principal Part,
cut off -Ī.

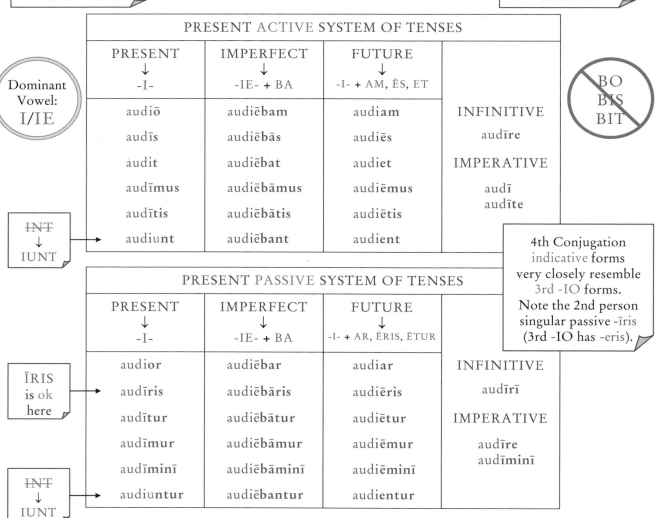

PRESENT ACTIVE SYSTEM OF TENSES

Dominant
Vowel:
I/IE

PRESENT ↓ -I-	IMPERFECT ↓ -IE- + BA	FUTURE ↓ -I- + AM, ĒS, ET	
audiō	audiēbam	audiam	**INFINITIVE**
audīs	audiēbās	audiēs	audīre
audit	audiēbat	audiet	**IMPERATIVE**
audīmus	audiēbāmus	audiēmus	audī
audītis	audiēbātis	audiētis	audīte
audiunt	audiēbant	audient	

~~INT~~ ↓ IUNT

~~BO BIS BIT~~

PRESENT PASSIVE SYSTEM OF TENSES

PRESENT ↓ -I-	IMPERFECT ↓ -IE- + BA	FUTURE ↓ -I- + AR, ĒRIS, ĒTUR	
audior	audiēbar	audiar	**INFINITIVE**
audīris	audiēbāris	audiēris	audīrī
audītur	audiēbātur	audiētur	**IMPERATIVE**
audīmur	audiēbāmur	audiēmur	audīre
audīminī	audiēbāminī	audiēminī	audīminī
audiuntur	audiēbantur	audientur	

ĪRIS
is ok
here

~~INT~~ ↓ IUNT

4th Conjugation
indicative forms
very closely resemble
3rd -IO forms.
Note the 2nd person
singular passive -īris
(3rd -IO has -eris).

INTRODUCTION TO IRREGULAR VERBS

PRESENT SYSTSEM OF TENSES

In the present, imperfect, and future tenses,
irregular verbs conjugate differently
from regular verbs.

Aqua perīculōsa **est.**
The water ⬦is⬦ dangerous.
(Present)

Hoc animal in aquā **erat.**
This animal ⬦was⬦ in the water.
(Imperfect)

Hoc animal **erit** magnum.
This animal ⬦will be⬦ big.
(Future)

Irregular verbs have unusual
principal parts which must be
memorized carefully!

e.g.
sum, esse, fuī, futūrus (to be)
volō, velle, voluī (to wish)

You can conjugate regular
verbs by manipulating
the 2nd principal part
(e.g. portāre → portābat),

but irregular verbs do not
function in the same way
(e.g. esse vs. erat).

PERFECT SYSTEM OF TENSES

The perfect, pluperfect, and future perfect
tenses are formed following the same rules
that apply to regular verbs.

ACTIVE

3rd Principal Part
+
Endings

FERŌ, FERRE, TULĪ, LĀTUS
(to bring, bear, endure)

Sometimes the principal parts
hardly resemble each other!

PASSIVE

4th Principal Part
+
Endings

Animālia multās hiemēs **tulerant.**
The animals ⬦had endured⬦ many winters.

(Pluperfect Active)

Ad hunc locum tempestāte **lātī erant.**
They ⬦had been carried⬦ to this place by a storm.

(Pluperfect Passive)

SUM, ESSE, FUĪ, FUTŪRUS
(TO BE)

SUM, ESSE, FUĪ, FUTURUS

↓

Present: "am," "is," "are"
Imperfect: "was," "were"
Future: "will be"

ACTIVE INFINITIVE

esse
(to be)

ACTIVE IMPERATIVE

es
este
(be!)

SUM, ESSE, FUĪ, FUTŪRUS PRESENT SYSTEM OF TENSES

Present	Imperfect	Future
sum	eram	erō
es	erās	eris
est	erat	eris
sumus	erāmus	erimus
estis	erātis	eritis
sunt	erant	erunt

SUM, ESSE, FUĪ, FUTŪRUS PERFECT SYSTEM OF TENSES

Perfect	Pluperfect	Future Perfect
fuī	fueram	fuerō
fuistī	fuerās	fueris
fuit	fuerat	fuerit
fuimus	fuerāmus	fuerimus
fuistis	fuerātis	fueritis
fuērunt	fuerant	fuerint

Sum cannot be conjugated simply by manipulating the 2nd principal part!

Imperfect & future endings are similar to -bam, -bās, -bat. . . & -bō, -bis, -bit. . .

These forms are regular. They use the perfect stem (fu-) and add endings.

Sentences with sum often contain predicate nominatives. (See p. 27)

Līberī sunt **laetī**.
The children are ⬦happy⬦.

3rd person forms can often be translated as "there is" or "there are," especially when the verb comes before the subject.

Erat rīsus in vultū tuō.
⬦There was⬦ a smile on your face.

SUM, ESSE, FUĪ, FUTŪRUS
(TO BE)

ALONE AND AS PART OF OTHER VERB FORMS

sum es est sumus estis sunt	Alone (**est**)	3rd Principal Part (not applicable)	4th Principal Part (amātus **est**)
	Present Active Indicative am, is, are	-----	Perfect Passive Indicative was/has been _verbed_

eram erās erat erāmus erātis erant	Alone (**erat**)	3rd Principal Part (amā**verat**)	4th Principal Part (amātus **erat**)
	Imperfect Active Indicative was, were	Pluperfect Active Indicative had _verbed_	Pluperfect Passive Indicative had been _verbed_

erō eris erit erimus eritis erunt	Alone (**erit**)	3rd Principal Part (amā**verit**)	4th Principal Part (amātus **erit**)
	Future Active Indicative will be	Future Perfect Active Indicative will have _verbed_ (-erint)	Future Perfect Passive Indicative will have been _verbed_

sim sīs sit sīmus sītis sint	Alone (**sit**)	3rd Principal Part (not applicable)	4th Principal Part (amātus **sit**)
	Present Active Subjunctive	-----	Perfect Passive Subjunctive

essem essēs esset essēmus essētis essent	Alone (**esset**)	3rd Principal Part (not applicable)	4th Principal Part (amātus **esset**)
	Imperfect Active Subjunctive	-----	Pluperfect Passive Subjunctive

POSSUM, POSSE, POTUĪ

(TO BE ABLE)

POSSUM, POSSE, POTUĪ

↓

Present: "am/is/are able"
Imperfect: "was/were able"
Future: "will be able"

ACTIVE
INFINITIVE

posse
(to be able)

ACTIVE
IMPERATIVE

-NONE-

POSSUM, POSSE, POTUĪ PRESENT SYSTEM OF TENSES		
Present	Imperfect	Future
possum	poteram	poterō
potes	poterās	poteris
potest	poterat	poterit
possumus	poterāmus	poterimus
potestis	poterātis	poteritis
possunt	poterant	poterunt

POSSUM, POSSE, POTUĪ PERFECT SYSTEM OF TENSES		
Perfect	Pluperfect	Future Perfect
potuī	potueram	potuerō
potuistī	potuerās	potueris
potuit	potuerat	potuerit
potuimus	potuerāmus	potuerimus
potuistis	potuerātis	potueritis
potuērunt	potuerant	potuerint

The forms of possum are based on the forms of sum:

Add pos when the form of sum starts with an "s."

Add pot when the form of sum starts with an "e."

sum
↓
possum

es
↓
potes

Note the difference between some very similar forms:

Imperfect	Pluperfect
poteram	potueram

Future	Fut. Perfect
poterō	potuerō

Sentences with possum usually include infinitives.

Saltāre possumus.
We are able ⬥to dance⬥.

Volō, Nōlō, Mālō
(to want, to not want, to prefer)

Volō, Velle, Voluī
(to wish, want)

Nōlō, Nōlle, Nōluī
(to not wish, not want, refuse)

[Combination of nōn & volō]

Mālō, Mālle, Māluī
(to prefer)

[Combination of magis & volō]

ACTIVE INFINITIVE

velle
nōlle
mālle

ACTIVE IMPERATIVE

nōlī
nōlīte
(none for volō & mālō)

Imperative of nōlō
+
Present Infinitive
↓
Do not *verb*!
(See p. 198)

Nōlī dēsistere.
✦Do not stop✦!

NOTE:
"You," "he/she/it," and "you (pl.)" forms are unusual for all three verbs.

Nōlō and mālō use modified versions of the unusual volō forms.

Volō, Nōlō, Mālō
Present Tense

volō	nōlō	mālō
vīs*	nōn vīs*	māvīs*
vult*	nōn vult*	māvult*
volumus	nōlumus	mālumus
vultis*	nōn vultis*	māvultis*
volunt	nōlunt	mālunt

Volō, Nōlō, Mālō
Present & Perfect Active System of Tenses

Present	Imperfect	Future	Perfect	Pluperfect	Future Perfect
volō	volēbam	volam	voluī	volueram	voluerō
vīs	volēbās	volēs	voluistī	voluerās	volueris
vult	volēbat	volet	voluit	voluerat	voluerit
volumus	volēbāmus	volēmus	voluimus	voluerāmus	voluerimus
vultis	volēbātis	volētis	voluistis	voluerātis	volueritis
volunt	volēbant	volent	voluērunt	voluerant	voluerint
nōlō	nōlēbam	nōlam	nōluī	nōlueram	nōluerō
mālō	mālēbam	mālam	māluī	mālueram	māluerō

Eō, Īre, Īvī or Iī, Itus

(to go)

Eō, Īre, Īvī or Iī, Itus

Present System of Tenses:
Note that all forms start with
an "i" except eō and eunt.

Perfect System of Tenses:
Either īvī or iī can be used
for the perfect stem.

ACTIVE
IMPERATIVE

ī
īte
(go!)

Eō, Īre, Īvī or Iī, Itus
PRESENT ACTIVE SYSTEM

Present	Imperfect	Future
eō	ībam	ībō
īs	ībās	ībis
it	ībat	ībit
īmus	ībāmus	ībimus
ītis	ībātis	ībitis
eunt	ībant	ībunt

Cochlea tertia celeriter ībat.
The third snail ⬩was going⬩ quickly.

Eō, Īre, Īvī or Iī, Itus
PERFECT ACTIVE SYSTEM

Perfect		Pluperfect		Future Perfect	
īvī	iī	īveram	ieram	īverō	ierō
īvistī	īstī*	īverās	ierās	īveris	ieris
īvit	iit	īverat	ierat	īverit	ierit
īvimus	iimus	īverāmus	ierāmus	īverimus	ierimus
īvistis	īstis*	īverātis	ierātis	īveritis	ieritis
īvērunt	iērunt	īverant	ierant	īverint	ierint

NOTE:

If iī is used for
the perfect stem,
forms that start with
iis- are condensed
to īs-.

iistī → īstī
iistis → īstis

EŌ, ĪRE, ĪVĪ OR IĪ, ITUS

(TO GO)

PASSIVE OF EŌ COMPOUNDS

PASSIVE INFINITIVE

īrī

COMPOUNDS OF EŌ

There are a number of compound verbs based on eō that use passive forms.

PASSIVE IMPERATIVE

īre
īminī

EŌ, ĪRE, ĪVĪ OR IĪ, ITUS PASSIVE VOICE*					
Present	Imperfect	Future	Perfect	Pluperfect	Future Perfect
eor	ībar	ībor	itus sum	itus eram	itus erō
īris	ībāris	īberis	itus es	itus erās	itus eris
ītur	ībātur	ībitur	itus est	itus erat	itus erit
īmur	ībāmur	ībimur	itī sumus	itī erāmus	itī erimus
īminī	ībāminī	ībiminī	itī estis	itī erātis	itī eritis
euntur	ībantur	ībuntur	itī sunt	itī erant	itī erunt

*Third person forms (such as ītur) may appear as impersonal passives (see. p. 265),

but passive forms of eō are generally restricted to compound verbs (e.g. adīmur).

SOME EŌ COMPOUNDS THAT MAY APPEAR IN THE PASSIVE VOICE

adeō - to approach

anteeō - to surpass

circumeō - to surround

ineō - to begin, start

praetereō - to leave out, neglect

Hic magus ā nūllō **anteībitur**.
This magician ⬧will be surpassed⬧ by no one.

FERŌ, FERRE, TULĪ, LĀTUS

(TO BRING, BEAR, ENDURE)

ACTIVE VOICE

ACTIVE INFINITIVE

ferre
(to bring)

ACTIVE VOICE

Ferō looks much like a
3rd conjugation verb.

Present
↓
*Some missing
connector vowels

Imperfect & Future
↓
Same as
3rd Conjugation

ACTIVE IMPERATIVE

fer
ferte
(bring!)

FERITE

FERŌ, FERRE, TULĪ, LĀTUS
PRESENT ACTIVE SYSTEM OF TENSES

Present	Imperfect	Future
ferō	ferēbam	feram
fers*	ferēbās	ferēs
fert*	ferēbat	feret
ferimus	ferēbāmus	ferēmus
fertis*	ferēbātis	ferētis
ferunt	ferēbant	ferent

Orbem in umerīs tuīs **fers**.
◇You bear◇ the world on your shoulders.

Capsulam ad lūdum **tulerās**.
◇You had brought◇ your bag to school.

FERŌ, FERRE, TULĪ, LĀTUS
PERFECT ACTIVE SYSTEM OF TENSES

Perfect	Pluperfect	Future Perfect
tulī	tuleram	tulerō
tulistī	tulerās	tuleris
tulit	tulerat	tulerit
tulimus	tulerāmus	tulerimus
tulistis	tulerātis	tuleritis
tulērunt	tulerant	tulerint

FERŌ, FERRE, TULĪ, LĀTUS
(TO BRING, BEAR, ENDURE)

PASSIVE VOICE

PASSIVE VOICE

Ferō looks much like
a 3rd conjugation verb.

Present	Imperfect & Future
↓	↓
*Some missing connector vowels	Same as 3rd Conjugation

PASSIVE INFINITIVE

ferrī
(to be brought)

PASSIVE IMPERATIVE

ferre
feriminī
(be brought!)

FERŌ, FERRE, TULĪ, LĀTUS PRESENT PASSIVE SYSTEM OF TENSES		
Present	Imperfect	Future
feror	ferēbar	ferar
ferris*	ferēbāris	ferēris
fertur*	ferēbātur	ferētur
ferimur	ferēbāmur	ferēmur
feriminī	ferēbāminī	ferēminī
feruntur	ferēbantur	ferentur

NOTE:

Active	Passive
fer-s	fer-ris
fer-t	fer-tur
fer-tis	fer-i-minī

Rānā ā puerō ad lūdum **ferētur**.
A frog ⬥will be brought⬥ to school by the boy.

Impetus ā tē **lātus est**.
The attack ⬥was endured⬥ by you.

FERŌ, FERRE, TULĪ, LĀTUS PERFECT PASSIVE SYSTEM OF TENSES		
Perfect	Pluperfect	Future Perfect
lātus **sum**	lātus **eram**	lātus **erō**
lātus **es**	lātus **erās**	lātus **eris**
lātus **est**	lātus **erat**	lātus **erit**
lātī **sumus**	lātī **erāmus**	lātī **erimus**
lātī **estis**	lātī **erātis**	lātī **eritis**
lātī **sunt**	lātī **erant**	·lātī **erunt**

Fīō, Fierī, Factus Sum
(to become, be made, happen)

INFINITIVE

fierī
(to become)

FĪŌ, FIERĪ, FACTUS SUM

Fīō is used as the passive of faciō.

This verb has active forms
in the present system of tenses,
but its meaning always expresses
the passive of faciō.

Forms resemble a 3rd -IO verb.

IMPERATIVE

fī
fīte
(become!)

Imperative forms of fīō
are very rare.

FĪŌ, FIERĪ, FACTUS SUM PRESENT SYSTEM OF TENSES		
Present	Imperfect	Future
fīō	fīēbam	fīam
fīs	fīēbās	fīēs
fit	fīēbat	fīet
fīmus	fīēbāmus	fīēmus
fītis	fīēbātis	fīētis
fīunt	fīēbant	fīent

FĪŌ, FIERĪ, FACTUS SUM PERFECT SYSTEM OF TENSES		
Perfect	Pluperfect	Future Perfect
factus sum	factus eram	factus erō
factus es	factus erās	factus eris
factus est	factus erat	factus erit
factī sumus	factī erāmus	factī erimus
factī estis	factī erātis	factī eritis
factī sunt	factī erant	factī erunt

PRESENT SYSTEM

Looks completely
unlike faciō.

PERFECT SYSTEM

Is the logical
passive of faciō.

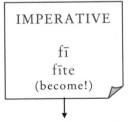

Fīetne aliquid malī?
⁺Will⁺ something bad ⁺happen⁺?

Dux nostra **fit**.
⁺She is made⁺ our leader.

NOTE:
Fīō can act as a
linking verb and
trigger a predicate
nominative

Soror mea **pernōta** facta est.
My sister became ⁺famous⁺.

DEPONENT VERBS

Fratrem meum **hortābar.**
◇I was encouraging◇ my brother.
↓
Imperfect Passive Indicative
translated actively

DEPONENT VERBS
↓

Forms:	Meaning:
Passive	Active

Mē **sequēminī.**
You (pl.) ◇will follow◇ me.
↓
Future Passive Indicative
translated actively

PRINCIPAL PARTS OF DEPONENT VERBS

hortor, hortārī, hortātus sum (to urge)

vereor, verērī, veritus sum (to fear)

sequor, sequī, secūtus sum (to follow)

patior, patī, passus sum (to allow)

orior, orīrī, ortus sum (to rise)

2ND PRINCIPAL PART

Note that the 2nd principal part is simply the passive infinitive.
(See p. 200)

PRESENT PASSIVE INFINITIVE

ārī			ērī
	1	2	
	3	4	
ī			īrī

PRINCIPAL PARTS

REGULAR VERB	amō 1st person singular present active indicative	amāre present active infinitive	amāvī 1st person singular perfect active indicative	amātus Perfect Passive Participle
DEPONENT VERB	hortor 1st person singular present passive indicative	hortārī present passive infinitive	✕	hortātus sum Perfect Passive Participle + sum

IMPERATIVES
(p. 197)

orīre
rise!

orīminī
rise (pl.)!

INFINITIVES
(pp. 200–203)

orīrī
to rise

ortus esse
to have risen

ortūrus esse*
to be about to rise

PARTICIPLES
(p. 216)

oriēns, orientis*
rising

ortus, -a, -um
having risen

ortūrus, -a, -um*
about to rise

SOME ACTIVE FORMS

Deponent verbs do use some active forms:

Present Participle:	-ns, -ntis	(p. 216)
Future Participle:	-ūrus	(p. 216)
Future Infinitive:	-ūrus esse	(p. 202)

SEMIDEPONENT VERBS

SEMIDEPONENT VERBS
↓
PRESENT SYSTEM OF TENSES:

Forms:	Meaning:
Active	Active

PERFECT SYSTEM OF TENSES:	
Forms:	Meaning:
Passive	Active

Contrā pāpiliōnēs saevissimōs pugnāre **ausus es**.
✧You dared✧ to fight against the very ferocious butterflies.

(Perfect Passive Indicative translated actively)

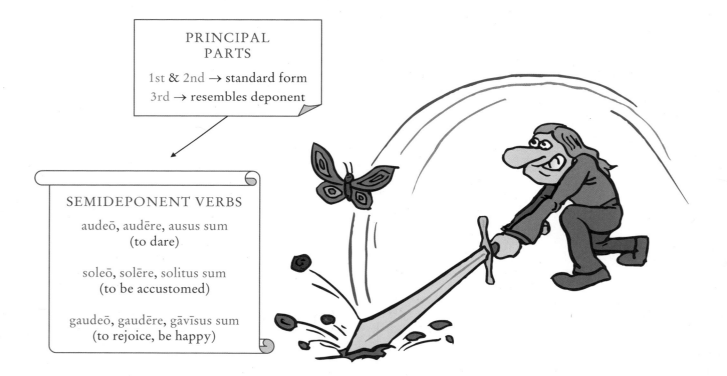

PRINCIPAL
PARTS

1st & 2nd → standard form
3rd → resembles deponent

SEMIDEPONENT VERBS

audeō, audēre, ausus sum
(to dare)

soleō, solēre, solitus sum
(to be accustomed)

gaudeō, gaudēre, gāvīsus sum
(to rejoice, be happy)

Effugere **ausus**, pāpiliō gladium tuum rīsit.
✧Having dared✧ to flee, the butterfly laughed at your sword.

(Perfect Passive Participle translated actively)

(See p. 216)

INDICATIVE SUMMARY

INDICATIVE MOOD

Indicates that someone
(I, you, he/she/it, we, you [pl.], they)
is doing some action.

PRESENT SYSTEM OF TENSES
(ACTIVE & PASSIVE: 2ND PRINCIPAL PART)

Present		Imperfect		Future			
ō	or	bam	bar	bō	bor	am	ar
s	ris	bās	bāris	bis	beris	ēs	ēris
t	tur	bat	bātur	bit	bitur	et	ētur
mus	mur	bāmus	bāmur	bimus	bimur	ēmus	ēmur
tis	minī	bātis	bāminī	bitis	biminī	ētis	ēminī
nt	ntur	bant	bantur	bunt	buntur	ent	entur

labōrat
he works

labōrās
you work

PERFECT SYSTEM OF TENSES
(ACTIVE: 3RD PRINCIPAL PART - PASSIVE: 4TH PRINCIPAL PART)

Perfect		Pluperfect		Future Perfect	
ī	. . . sum	eram	. . . eram	erō	. . . erō
istī	. . . es	erās	. . . erās	eris	. . . eris
it	. . . est	erat	. . . erat	erit	. . . erit
imus	. . . sumus	erāmus	. . . erāmus	erimus	. . . erimus
istis	. . . estis	erātis	. . . erātis	eritis	. . . eritis
ērunt	. . . sunt	erant	. . . erant	erint	. . . erunt

IMPERATIVE FORMS

VERB!

Present imperatives are 2nd person verb forms.

IMPERATIVE MOOD

Expresses commands.

Commands can be directed toward one **noun** or more than one noun.

↓

Present **Stem**

+

Endings

↓

"<u>VERB</u>!"

PRESENT STEM

Use 2nd principal part.

↓

Cut off -◇RE.

ACTIVE IMPERATIVE ENDINGS

ā	ē
āte	ēte
1	**2**
3	**4**
e	ī
ite	īte

PRESENT ACTIVE IMPERATIVE						
	1st Conj.	2nd Conj.	3rd Conj.	3rd -IO Conj.	4th Conj.	Translation
Sing.	rog**ā**	doc**ē**	mitt**e**	cap**e**	aud**ī**	<u>VERB</u>!
Pl.	rog**āte**	doc**ēte**	mitt**ite**	cap**ite**	aud**īte**	

Respondē, discipule!
✧Answer✧, student!

Respondēte, discipulī!
✧Answer✧, students!

IRREGULAR IMPERATIVES
(faciō, ferō, dūcō, dīcō)

dīc - say!
dūc - lead!
fac - do/make!
fer - bring!

PLURALS

facite, **ferte**, dūcite, dīcite

↓

HELPFUL RHYME

Dīc, dūc, fac, fer:
they should have an e,
but it isn't there!

IMPERATIVE FORMS

BE
VERBED!

Present
imperatives
are 2nd person
verb forms.

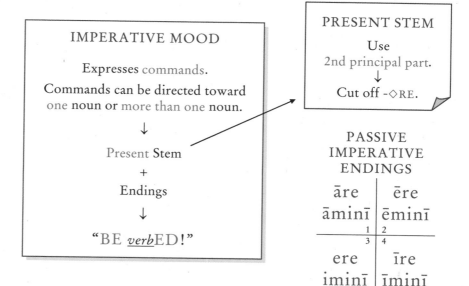

IMPERATIVE MOOD

Expresses commands.

Commands can be directed toward
one noun or more than one noun.

↓

Present Stem

+

Endings

↓

"BE *verb*ED!"

PRESENT STEM

Use
2nd principal part.

↓

Cut off -◇RE.

PASSIVE IMPERATIVE ENDINGS

āre	ēre
āminī	ēminī
1	**2**
3	**4**
ere	īre
iminī	īminī

PRESENT PASSIVE IMPERATIVE					
	1st Conj.	2nd Conj.	3rd Conj.	3rd -IO Conj.	4th Conj.	Translation
Sing.	rog**āre**	doc**ēre**	mitt**ere**	cap**ere**	aud**īre**	BE *VERB*ED!
Pl.	rog**āminī**	doc**ēminī**	mitt**iminī**	cap**iminī**	aud**īminī**	

Cibō **cōnfirmāre**, Brūte!
◊Be strengthened◊ by food, Brutus!

Cibō **cōnfirmāminī**, Brūte et Marce!
◊Be strengthened◊ by food, Brutus and Marcus!

IMPERATIVE FORMS

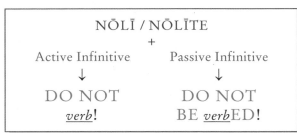

NŌLĪ / NŌLĪTE
+

Active Infinitive	Passive Infinitive
↓	↓
DO NOT *verb*!	DO NOT BE *verb*ED!

NŌLĪ
↓
Singular

Nōlī effugere, puer!
◊Do not flee◊, boy! (sing.)

Nōlī ab hostibus **superārī**, puer!
◊Do not be surpassed◊ by the enemy, boy! (sing.)

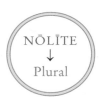

NŌLĪTE
↓
Plural

Nōlīte timēre, puerī!
◊Do not fear◊, boys! (pl.)

Nōlīte superārī, puerī!
◊Do not be surpassed◊, boys! (pl.)

IMPERATIVE FORMS

FUTURE ACTIVE AND PASSIVE

FUTURE IMPERATIVES

Rare forms - 2nd *and* 3rd person: translated just like the present imperative or the hortatory subjunctive.

(See p. 226)

↓

"<u>VERB</u>!", "LET. . .*verb*"

FUTURE IMPERATIVE CONNECTOR VOWELS

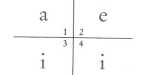

FUTURE IMPERATIVE FORMS				
	2ND PERSON		3RD PERSON	
	<u>Active</u>	<u>Passive</u>	<u>Active</u>	<u>Passive</u>
Sing.	rogā**tō**	rogā**tor**	rogā**tō**	rogā**tor**
Pl.	rogā**tōte**	---	roga**ntō**	roga**ntor**
	ask!	be asked!	let him/them ask!	let him/them be asked!

Tū pācem semper **petitō!**
Always ◇seek◇ peace!

Iūlia pācem semper **petitō!**
Let Julia always ◇seek◇ peace!

INFINITIVE FORMS

TO *verb* TO BE *verb*ED	ACTIVE	PASSIVE
1st Conjugation	**-ĀRE** rogāre (to ask)	**-ĀRĪ** rogārī (to be asked)
2nd Conjugation	**-ĒRE** docēre (to teach)	**-ĒRĪ** docērī (to be taught)
3rd Conjugation	**-ERE** mittere (to send)	**-Ī** mittī (to be sent)
3rd -IO Conjugation	**-ERE** capere (to seize)	**-Ī** capī (to be seized)
4th Conjugation	**-ĪRE** audīre (to hear)	**-ĪRĪ** audīrī (to be heard)

PRESENT
↓
-ĀRE
-ĀRĪ

Based on present stem.

fugārē
to chase

fugārī
to be chased

THIRD & THIRD -IO CONJUGATION

Passive infinitive may look very similar to the 3rd principal part, since both end in -ī. Pay close attention to the stem!

ī

Based on 2nd principal part (present stem).
↓
passive infinitive

Based on 3rd principal part (perfect stem).
↓
perfect indicative

dūcō, dūcere, dūxī, ductus (to lead)
↓
dūcī - passive infinitive
dūxī - perfect indicative

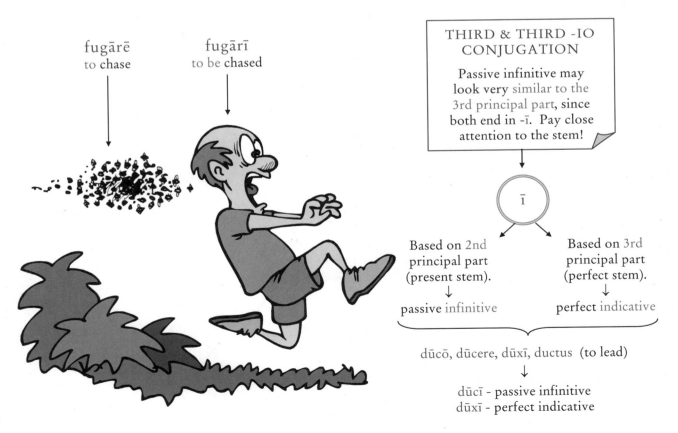

INFINITIVE FORMS

PERFECT ACTIVE AND PASSIVE

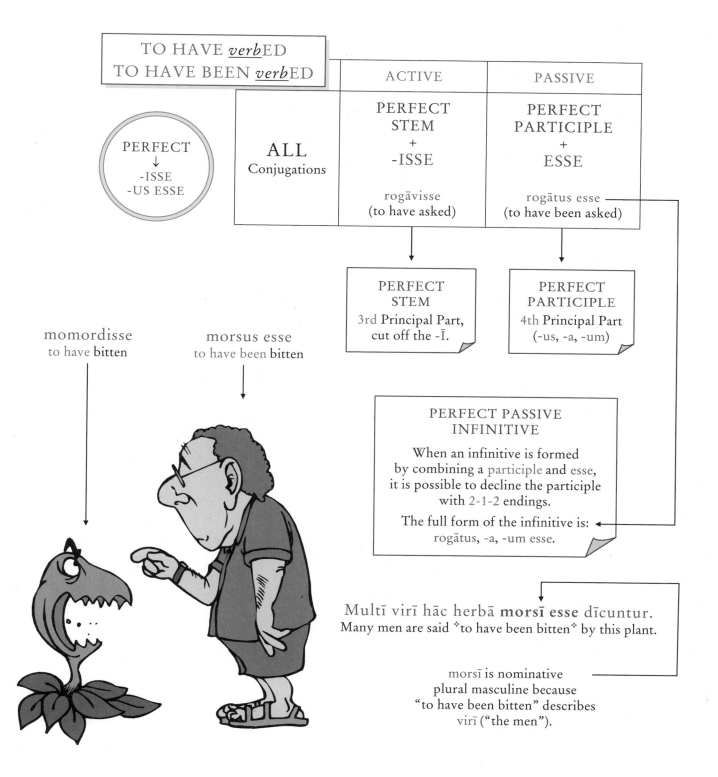

TO HAVE *verb*ED TO HAVE BEEN *verb*ED		ACTIVE	PASSIVE
PERFECT ↓ -ISSE -US ESSE	ALL Conjugations	PERFECT STEM + -ISSE rogāvisse (to have asked)	PERFECT PARTICIPLE + ESSE rogātus esse (to have been asked)

PERFECT
STEM
3rd Principal Part,
cut off the -ī.

PERFECT
PARTICIPLE
4th Principal Part
(-us, -a, -um)

momordisse
to have **bitten**

morsus esse
to have been **bitten**

PERFECT PASSIVE INFINITIVE

When an infinitive is formed
by combining a participle and esse,
it is possible to decline the participle
with 2-1-2 endings.

The full form of the infinitive is:
rogātus, -a, -um esse.

Multī virī hāc herbā **morsī esse** dīcuntur.
Many men are said ⁑to have been bitten⁑ by this plant.

morsī is nominative
plural masculine because
"to have been bitten" describes
virī ("the men").

INFINITIVE FORMS

TO BE ABOUT TO *verb*
TO BE ABOUT TO BE *verb*ED

	ACTIVE	PASSIVE
ALL Conjugations	FUTURE PARTICIPLE + ESSE	ACCUSATIVE SUPINE + ĪRĪ
	rogātūrus esse (to be about to ask)	rogātum īrī (to be about to be asked)

FUTURE
↓
-ŪRUS ESSE
-UM ĪRĪ

cultūrus esse
to be about to
cultivate

cultum īrī
to be about to
be cultivated

FUTURE
PARTICIPLE
4th Principal
Part
↓
-ūrus, -a, -um

ACCUSATIVE
SUPINE
4th Principal
Part
↓
-um
(See p. 263)

FUTURE ACTIVE INFINITIVE

When an infinitive is formed
by combining a participle and esse,
it is possible to decline the participle
with 2-1-2 endings.

The full form of the infinitive is:
rogātūrus, -a, -um esse.

Note that rogātum īrī
cannot be declined.

Pluvia **casūra esse** dicta est.
Rain was said ⬦to be about to fall⬦.

casūra is nominative
singular feminine because
"to be about to fall" describes
pluvia ("rain").

INFINITIVE FORMS

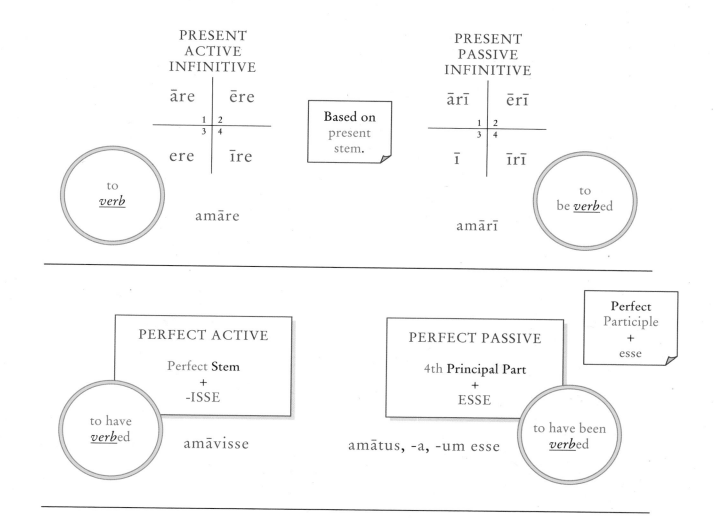

PRESENT ACTIVE INFINITIVE

āre	ēre
1	2
3	4
ere	īre

to *verb*

amāre

Based on present stem.

PRESENT PASSIVE INFINITIVE

ārī	ērī
1	2
3	4
ī	īrī

to be *verb*ed

amārī

PERFECT ACTIVE

Perfect **Stem**
+
-ISSE

to have *verb*ed

amāvisse

PERFECT PASSIVE

4th Principal Part
+
ESSE

to have been *verb*ed

amātus, -a, -um esse

Perfect Participle + esse

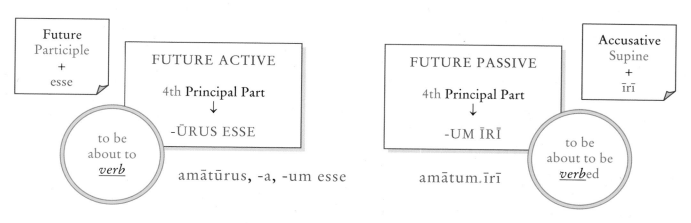

Future Participle + esse

FUTURE ACTIVE

4th **Principal Part**
↓
-ŪRUS ESSE

to be about to *verb*

amātūrus, -a, -um esse

FUTURE PASSIVE

4th **Principal Part**
↓
-UM ĪRĪ

to be about to be *verb*ed

amātum.īrī

Accusative Supine + īrī

INFINITIVE CONSTRUCTIONS

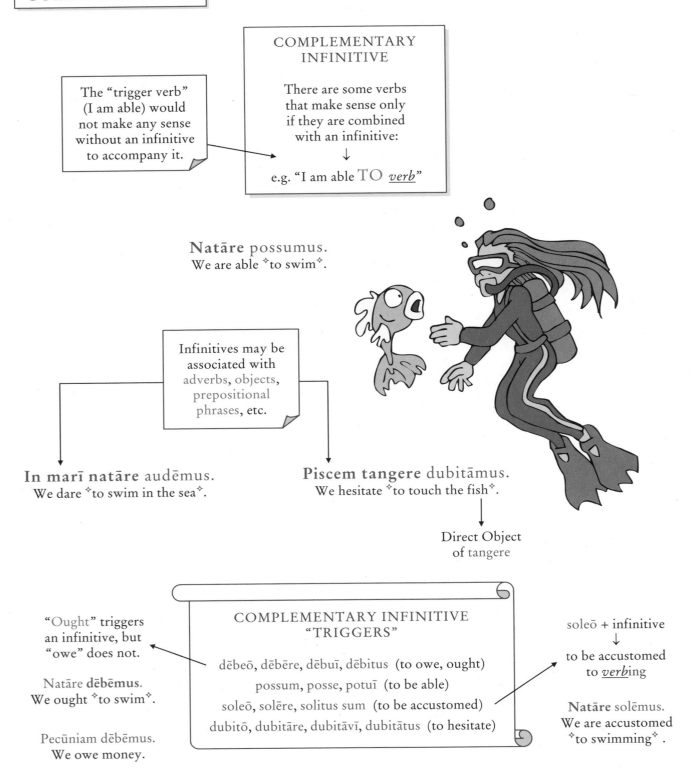

COMPLEMENTARY
INFINITIVE

There are some verbs
that make sense only
if they are combined
with an infinitive:
↓
e.g. "I am able TO *verb*"

The "trigger verb"
(I am able) would
not make any sense
without an infinitive
to accompany it.

Natāre possumus.
We are able ⋄to swim⋄.

Infinitives may be
associated with
adverbs, objects,
prepositional
phrases, etc.

In marī natāre audēmus.
We dare ⋄to swim in the sea⋄.

Piscem tangere dubitāmus.
We hesitate ⋄to touch the fish⋄.

Direct Object
of tangere

"Ought" triggers
an infinitive, but
"owe" does not.

Natāre **dēbēmus.**
We ought ⋄to swim⋄.

Pecūniam dēbēmus.
We owe money.

COMPLEMENTARY INFINITIVE
"TRIGGERS"

dēbeō, dēbēre, dēbuī, dēbitus (to owe, ought)
possum, posse, potuī (to be able)
soleō, solēre, solitus sum (to be accustomed)
dubitō, dubitāre, dubitāvī, dubitātus (to hesitate)

soleō + infinitive
↓
to be accustomed
to *verb*ing

Natāre solēmus.
We are accustomed
⋄to swimming⋄ .

INFINITIVE CONSTRUCTIONS

OBJECTIVE INFINITIVE

Infinitive can act as the
direct object of a verb.

↓

"TO _verb_," "_verb_ING"

Rēx pugnāre amāt.
The king loves ⬧to fight⬧.
The king loves ⬧fighting⬧.

Infinitive may be
associated with
adverbs, objects,
prepositional
phrases, etc.

Rēx equitem vincere cupit.
The king wants ⬧to beat the knight⬧.

Direct Object   Direct Object
of cupit   of vincere

Rēx cum equite pugnāre parat.
The king prepares ⬧to fight with the knight⬧.

Volāre possum.
I am able ⬧to fly⬧.

↓

Complementary:
"I am able" makes sense only
when followed by an infinitive.

OBJECTIVE VS. COMPLEMENTARY INFINITIVES

Both are examples of a situation
where a verb triggers an infinitive,
but a "complementary infinitive"
is a special situation when the
trigger verb can be satisfied only
by the presence of an infinitive.

Volāre cupiō.
I want ⬧to fly⬧.

↓

Objective:
"I want" makes sense when
followed by an infinitive, but it
could also be followed simply by a
noun ("I want bread.").

INFINITIVE CONSTRUCTIONS

SUBJECTIVE

To run
delights me.

It delights me
to run.

Running
delights me.

SUBJECTIVE INFINITIVE

Infinitive can act as a
nominative singular noun.

↓

Subject of
3rd person singular verb (-t):

↓

"TO *verb*," "*verb*ING"

Currere Marcum dēfatīgat.
⬦To run⬦ tires Marcus.
It tires Marcus ⬦to run⬦.
⬦Running⬦ tires Marcus.

Infinitive may be
associated with
adverbs, objects,
prepositional
phrases, etc.

Celeriter currere Marcum dēfatīgat.
⬦Running quickly⬦ tires Marcus.

Marcum vidēre mē dēfatīgat.
⬦Seeing Marcus⬦ tires me.

Direct Object
of vidēre

It is possible to join
a subject infinitive with
a predicate adjective. For
the purposes of adjective
agreement, the infinitive
is considered neuter.

Modifies "to run"
↓
Nominative Singular Neuter
↓

Bonum est cum amīcīs **currere.**
⬦To run⬦ with friends is good.
It is good ⬦to run⬦ with friends.
⬦Running⬦ with friends is good.

Modifies "to run"
↓
Nominative Singular Neuter
↓

Sub sōle **currere difficile** est.
⬦To run⬦ under the sun is difficult.
It is difficult ⬦to run⬦ under the sun.
⬦Running⬦ under the sun is difficult.

INFINITIVE CONSTRUCTIONS

WITH IMPERSONAL VERBS

INFINITIVE WITH
IMPERSONAL VERBS

Many impersonal verbs
can trigger an infinitive.

↓

"It is _____ TO _verb_."

COMMON IMPERSONAL VERBS

libet, libēre, libuit (it is pleasing)

licet, licēre, licuit (it is allowed)

necesse est, esse, fuit (it is necessary)

oportet, oportēre, oportuit (it is necessary)

decet, decēre, decuit (it is fitting)

Necesse erat **lūdere**.
It was necessary ⬧to have fun⬧.

Infinitive may be
associated with
adverbs, objects,
prepositional
phrases, etc.

Impersonal verbs
can be conjugated
in various tenses
just like any
other verb:

libēbat
↓
it was pleasing

Libet **vēritātem effugere**.
It is pleasing ⬧to escape reality⬧.

↓

Direct object
of effugere

INFINITIVE CONSTRUCTIONS

**INFINITIVE WITH
SUBJECT ACCUSATIVE**

There are several verbs that trigger an
Accusative + Infinitive phrase.

You will see that the accusative noun is
doing the action expressed by the infinitive;
therefore the construction is called:

"Infinitive with Subject Accusative"

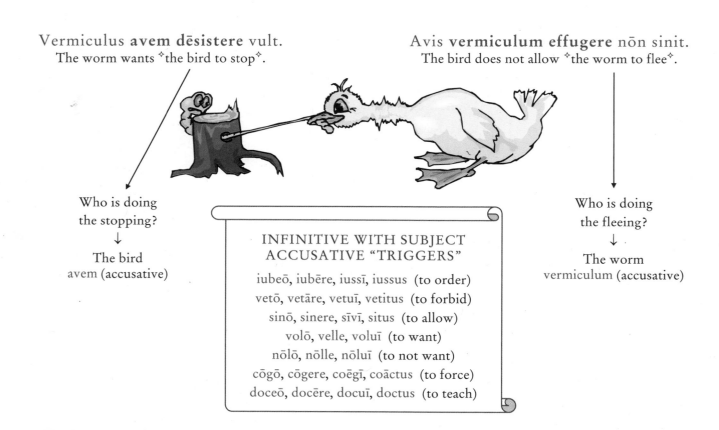

Vermiculus **avem dēsistere** vult.
The worm wants ⋄the bird to stop⋄.

Avis **vermiculum effugere** nōn sinit.
The bird does not allow ⋄the worm to flee⋄.

Who is doing
the stopping?
↓
The bird
avem (accusative)

Who is doing
the fleeing?
↓
The worm
vermiculum (accusative)

INFINITIVE WITH SUBJECT
ACCUSATIVE "TRIGGERS"

iubeō, iubēre, iussī, iussus (to order)
vetō, vetāre, vetuī, vetitus (to forbid)
sinō, sinere, sīvī, situs (to allow)
volō, velle, voluī (to want)
nōlō, nōlle, nōluī (to not want)
cōgō, cōgere, coēgī, coāctus (to force)
doceō, docēre, docuī, doctus (to teach)

Tē vincere cupimus.

Accusatives may function as the
subject or the direct object of an
infinitive. Use context to decide
on the correct interpretation.

We want ⋄you to conquer⋄.
(Tē is the subject
of vincere.)

We want ⋄to conquer you⋄.
(Tē is the object
of vincere.)

INFINITIVE CONSTRUCTIONS

WITH SUBJECT ACCUSATIVE – TRANSLATING WITH "THAT"

THAT

INFINITIVE WITH SUBJECT ACCUSATIVE

Sometimes it is impossible to translate an accusative + infinitive phrase with the traditional infinitive translation "to verb."

An alternative is:

Accusative + Infinitive

↓

"THAT *accusative verb*"

Tē tacēre opus est.
It is necessary ✧that you be quiet✧.

Tē clāmāre mē terret.
✧That you are shouting✧ scares me.
It scares me ✧that you are shouting✧.

Tē tam magnum **esse** malum est.
It is bad ✧that you are✧ so big.

Livia   Brutus

TWO ACCUSATIVES

When a sentence contains two accusatives and an infinitive, the first accusative is usually the subject of the infinitive, and the second is usually the direct object.

Subject of   Direct Object of   Perfect
terruisse   terruisse   Infinitive

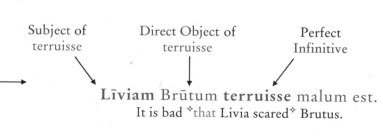

Līviam Brūtum **terruisse** malum est.
It is bad ✧that Livia scared✧ Brutus.

INFINITIVE IN AN INDIRECT STATEMENT

OVERVIEW

INDIRECT STATEMENT

Verbs of
thinking, perceiving, knowing, saying,
etc. can trigger indirect statements.

"THAT"

SUBJECT
↓
Accusative

VERB
↓
Infinitive

In Latin, it is often
unnecessary to state the
subject of an indicative
verb, but you must
always state the subject
of an indirect statement.

DIRECT STATEMENT
The sun is setting.
↓
INDIRECT STATEMENT
You say that the sun is setting.

Although your English
translation contains the
word "that," no extra
word appears in Latin
to express this.

You say ⋄that the sun is setting⋄.
Dīcis **sōlem occidere**.

Subject of Indirect Statement:
Accusative

Verb in Indirect Statement:
Infinitive

INDIRECT STATEMENT "TRIGGERS"

arbitror, arbitrārī, arbitrātus sum (to think)
exīstimō, exīstimāre, exīstimāvī, exīstimātus (to think)
putō, putāre, putāvī, putātus (to think)

audiō, audīre, audīvī, audītus (to hear)
sentiō, sentīre, sēnsī, sēnsus (to feel, realize)
videō, vidēre, vīdī, vīsus (to see)

cognōscō, cognōscere, cognōvī, cognitus (to find out, learn)
intellegō, intellegere, intellēxī, intellectus (to understand)
nesciō, nescīre, nescīvī, nescītus (to not know)
sciō, scīre, scīvī, scītus (to know)

dīcō, dīcere, dīxī, dictus (to say)
fateor, fatērī, fassus sum (to confess)
negō, negāre, negāvī, negātus (to deny, say. . .not)
referō, referre, rettulī, relātus (to report)

crēdō, crēdere, crēdidī, crēditus (to believe)
spērō, spērāre, spērāvī, spērātus (to hope)

INFINITIVE IN AN INDIRECT STATEMENT

TENSE OF THE INFINITIVE
↓
Indicates that the action in the indirect statement
takes place before, at the same time as, or after
the verb that triggers the indirect statement.

In indirect statements, the infinitive is translated
with an indicative phrasing rather than with "to."

PRESENT
↓
SAME
TIME

Dīcis sōlem occidere.
You say ⋄that the sun is setting.⋄

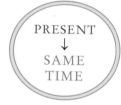

PERFECT
↓
BEFORE

FUTURE
↓
AFTER

Dīcis sōlem iam occidisse.
You say ⋄that the sun set⋄ already.

Dīcis sōlem occāsūrum esse.
You say ⋄that the sun will set⋄.

Putābam vōs vocātōs esse.
I thought that you (pl.) ⋄had been called⋄.

Sciēbam mātrem ventūram esse.
I knew that mother ⋄would come⋄.

Accusative: accusative is required
in indirect statement.

Plural: "you (pl.)" is plural.

Masculine: this "you (pl.)"
happens to be a group of men.

PERFECT PASSIVE
Infinitive
(amātus esse)
&
FUTURE ACTIVE
Infinitive
(amātūrus esse)
↓
Must agree with the
accusative subject
of the indirect statement.

Accusative: accusative is required
in indirect statement.

Singular: mātrem is singular.

Feminine: mātrem is feminine.

INFINITIVE IN AN INDIRECT STATEMENT

TRANSLATING THE INFINITIVE

ACTIVE INFINITIVES			
Sequence	PRESENT Infinitive	PERFECT Infinitive	FUTURE Infinitive
1°	"*verb*s"	"*verb*ed"	"will *verb*"
2°	"was *verb*ing"	"had *verb*ed"	"would *verb*"

1° (PRIMARY) SEQUENCE

Main verb is present, future, or future perfect. (See p. 231)

2° (SECONDARY) SEQUENCE

Main verb is imperfect, perfect, or pluperfect. (See p. 231)

PASSIVE INFINITIVES			
Sequence	PRESENT Infinitive	PERFECT Infinitive	FUTURE Infinitive
1°	"is *verb*ed"	"was *verb*ed"	"will be *verb*ed"
2°	"was being *verb*ed"	"had been *verb*ed"	"would be *verb*ed"

NOTE:

The future passive infinitive rarely appears.

FUTURE

1°: "will"

2°: "would"

MISSING "ESSE"

The future active and perfect passive infinitives sometimes appear without esse.

Spērō tē tūtum in itinere **futūrum**.
I hope that you ⋄will be⋄ safe on your journey.
(Spērō tē tūtum in itinere **futūrum esse**.)

REVIEW OF INFINITIVE FORMS			
	Present	Perfect	Future
Active	amāre	amāvisse	amātūrus esse
Passive	amārī	amātus esse	amātum īrī

INFINITIVE IN AN INDIRECT STATEMENT

ACTIVE INFINITIVES			
SEQUENCE	TENSE OF INFINITIVE	TRANSLATION OF INFINITIVE	EXAMPLE
1°	present	_verb_s, is _verb_ing, does _verb_	crēdō tē **audīre** I believe that you ⁺are hearing⁺.
1°	perfect	_verb_ed, was _verb_ing, did _verb_, has _verb_ed	crēdō tē **audīvisse** I believe that you ⁺heard⁺.
1°	future	will _verb_	crēdō tē **auditūrum esse** I believe that you ⁺will hear⁺.
2°	present	was _verb_ing	crēdidī tē **audīre** I believed that you ⁺were hearing⁺.
2°	perfect	had _verb_ed	crēdidī tē **audīvisse** I believed that you ⁺had heard⁺.
2°	future	would _verb_	crēdidī tē **auditūrum esse** I believed that you ⁺would hear⁺.

PASSIVE INFINITIVES			
SEQUENCE	TENSE OF INFINITIVE	TRANSLATION OF INFINITIVE	EXAMPLE
1°	present	is _verb_ed, is being _verb_ed	crēdō tē **audīrī** I believe that you ⁺are being heard⁺.
1°	perfect	was _verb_ed, was being _verb_ed, has been _verb_ed	crēdō tē **audītum esse** I believe that you ⁺were heard⁺.
1°	future	will be _verb_ed	crēdō tē **audītum īrī** I believe that you ⁺will be heard⁺.
2°	present	was being _verb_ed	crēdidī tē **audīrī** I believed that you ⁺were being heard⁺.
2°	perfect	had been _verb_ed	crēdidī tē **audītum esse** I believed that you ⁺had been heard⁺.
2°	future	would be _verb_ed	crēdidī tē **audītum īrī** I believed that you ⁺would be heard⁺.

INFINITIVE IN AN INDIRECT STATEMENT

HE/SHE/IT/THEY SUBJECTS

REFLEXIVE VS. DEMONSTRATIVE

If the subject of the indirect statement
is "he," "she," "it," or "they" and
refers back to the subject of the trigger verb,
use the reflexive sē as the subject accusative.

Otherwise, use is, ea, id in the accusative
with the appropriate number and gender.

Claudia negat **sē** mūrem timēre.
Claudia denies that ⧫she⧫ fears the mouse.

Subject of Trigger Verb $=$ Subject of Indirect Statement

Mūs scit **eam** magnopere timēre.
The mouse knows that ⧫she⧫ (Claudia) is very afraid.

Subject of Trigger Verb $\neq$ Subject of Indirect Statement

PARTICIPLES

PARTICIPLE

↓

VERBAL ADJECTIVE

(a verb acting as an adjective)

Brendan calls Sara about the canceled meeting.

Comes from the verb "to cancel," but acts as an adjective modifying "meeting."

Miriam hears Sara talking.

Comes from the verb "to talk," but acts as an adjective modifying "Sara."

NOTE:

Experiment with English word order. The participle can be placed before or after the noun it modifies.

We see the ⋄smiling woman⋄.   We see the ⋄woman smiling⋄.

PARTICIPLES

audiēns
"listening"

1 Termination
Third Declension
Adjective with
I-Stem Endings

-NS, -NTIS
↓
*verb*ing

ABLATIVE
SINGULAR

May end in
-ī or -e.
(See p. 82)

*verb*ING

PRESENT ACTIVE
PARTICIPLE
↓
(1st) rogāns, rogantis
(2nd) docēns, docentis
(3rd) mittēns, mittentis
(3rd -IO) capiēns, capientis
(4th) audiēns, audientis

institūta
"[having been] trained"

4ᵀᴴ
Principal Part
↓
[having been]
*verb*ed

2-1-2
Adjective

[HAVING BEEN] *verb*ED

PERFECT PASSIVE
PARTICIPLE
↓
4th Principal Part
(rogātus, -a, -um)

spectātūrus
"about/intending/going to look"

-ŪRUS
↓
about to/
intending to/
going to
verb

2-1-2
Adjective

ABOUT TO *verb*
INTENDING TO *verb*
GOING TO *verb*

FUTURE ACTIVE
PARTICIPLE
↓
4th Principal Part with -ūrus
(rogātūrus, -a, -um)

PARTICIPLES

VERBAL ADJECTIVES

Participles are adjectives, so they must agree with the noun they modify in case, number, and gender.

Since participles are formed from verbs, they can be combined with objects, prepositional phrases, adverbs, etc.

Umbra **fēlem persequēns** gaudet.
The ghost ✧pursuing the cat✧ rejoices.

Direct Object
of persequēns

Nominative Singular
Feminine in agreement
with umbra

TRANSLATING PARTICIPLES AS CLAUSES

PARTICIPLES AS CLAUSES

You can often translate participles by converting them into clauses by adding the words below:

who/which/that (Relative Clause)
when/once/while (Temporal Clause)
since (Causal Clause)
although (Concessive Clause)

Umbra fēlem **persequēns** gaudet.
The ghost ✧[who is] pursuing✧ the cat rejoices.

Fēlēs **dormiēns** petīta est. ——————
The cat was attacked ✧[while she was] sleeping✧.

→ PRESENT PARTICIPLE
Same time as the main action.

Fēlem **petītam** iuvābimus. ——————
We will help the cat ✧[since she has been] attacked✧.

→ PERFECT PARTICIPLE
Before the main action.

Fēlēs **effugitūra** tamen timēbat. ——————
✧[Although she was] about to escape✧, the cat was still afraid.

→ FUTURE PARTICIPLE
About to happen
after the main action.

PARTICIPLES

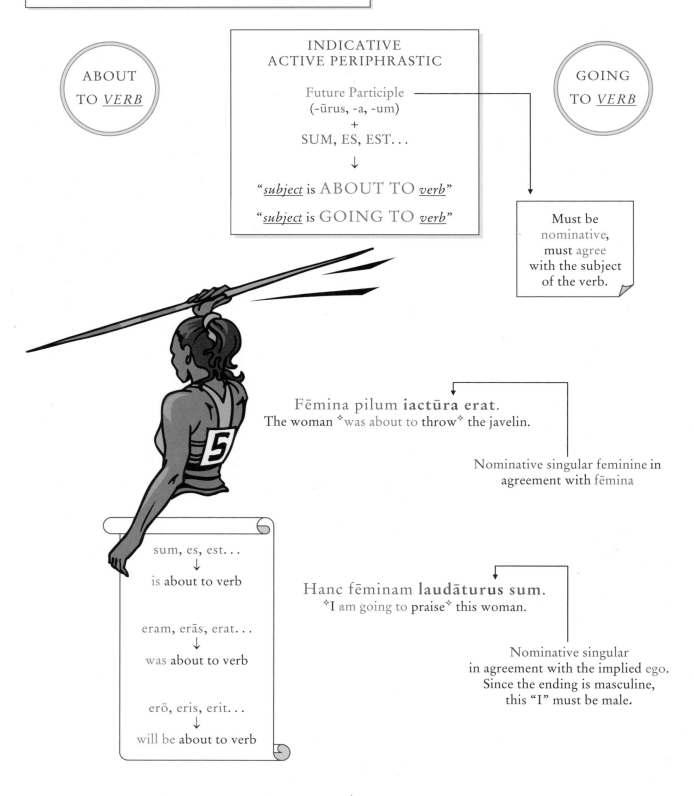

ABOUT
TO *VERB*

INDICATIVE
ACTIVE PERIPHRASTIC

Future Participle
(-ūrus, -a, -um)
+
SUM, ES, EST . . .

↓

"*subject* is ABOUT TO *verb*"

"*subject* is GOING TO *verb*"

GOING
TO *VERB*

Must be
nominative,
must agree
with the subject
of the verb.

Fēmina pilum **iactūra erat**.
The woman ⋄was about to throw⋄ the javelin.

Nominative singular feminine in
agreement with fēmina

sum, es, est . . .
↓
is about to verb

eram, erās, erat . . .
↓
was about to verb

erō, eris, erit . . .
↓
will be about to verb

Hanc fēminam **laudāturus sum**.
⋄I am going to praise⋄ this woman.

Nominative singular
in agreement with the implied ego.
Since the ending is masculine,
this "I" must be male.

PARTICIPLES

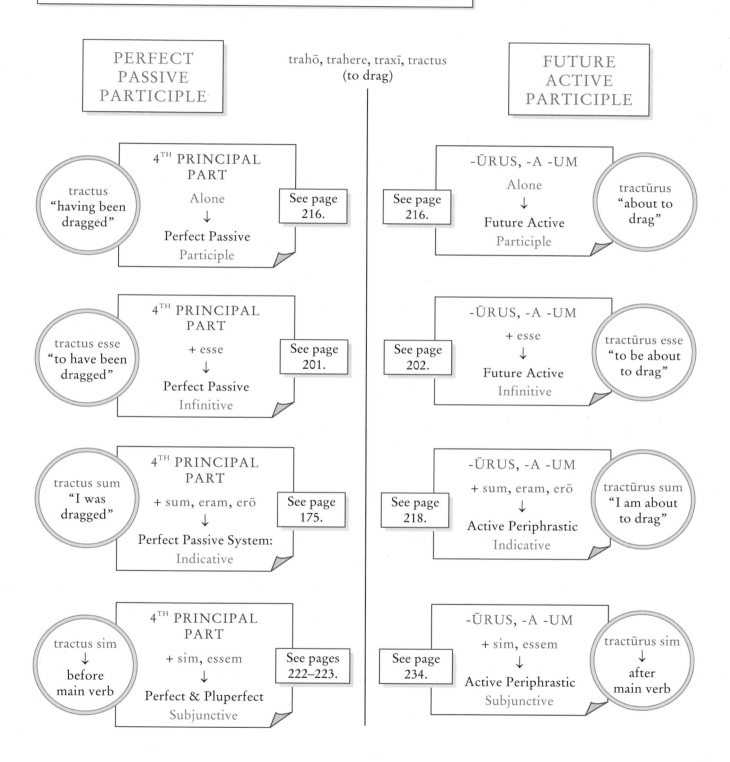

PERFECT PASSIVE PARTICIPLE

trahō, trahere, traxī, tractus
(to drag)

FUTURE ACTIVE PARTICIPLE

tractus
"having been dragged"

4TH PRINCIPAL PART

Alone
↓
Perfect Passive
Participle

See page 216.

-ŪRUS, -A -UM

Alone
↓
Future Active
Participle

See page 216.

tractūrus
"about to drag"

tractus esse
"to have been dragged"

4TH PRINCIPAL PART

+ esse
↓
Perfect Passive
Infinitive

See page 201.

-ŪRUS, -A -UM

+ esse
↓
Future Active
Infinitive

See page 202.

tractūrus esse
"to be about to drag"

tractus sum
"I was dragged"

4TH PRINCIPAL PART

+ sum, eram, erō
↓
Perfect Passive System:
Indicative

See page 175.

-ŪRUS, -A -UM

+ sum, eram, erō
↓
Active Periphrastic
Indicative

See page 218.

tractūrus sum
"I am about to drag"

tractus sim
↓
before
main verb

4TH PRINCIPAL PART

+ sim, essem
↓
Perfect & Pluperfect
Subjunctive

See pages 222–223.

-ŪRUS, -A -UM

+ sim, essem
↓
Active Periphrastic
Subjunctive

See page 234.

tractūrus sim
↓
after
main verb

SUBJUNCTIVE FORMS

Indicative	Subjunctive
rogāmus	rogēmus
docēmus	doceāmus
mittimus	mittāmus
capimus	capiāmus
audīmus	audiāmus

PRESENT SUBJUNCTIVE

Present Stem
+
wE EAt cAvIAr vowel
+
Endings

(-m, -s, -t, -mus, -tis, -nt)
(-r, -ris, -tur, -mur, -minī, -ntur)

ROGĀRE
↓
ROGE-
↓
ROGEM

wE EAt cAvIAr

| 1st | 2nd | 3rd | 3rd -IO & |
| conj. | conj. | conj. | 4th conj. |

DOCĒRE
↓
DOCEA-
↓
DOCEAM

PRESENT ACTIVE SUBJUNCTIVE

1st Conj.	2nd Conj.	3rd Conj.	3rd -IO Conj.	4th Conj.
rogem	doceam	mittam	capiam	audiam
rogēs	doceās	mittās	capiās	audiās
roget	doceat	mittat	capiat	audiat
rogēmus	doceāmus	mittāmus	capiāmus	audiāmus
rogētis	doceātis	mittātis	capiātis	audiātis
rogent	doceant	mittant	capiant	audiant

PRESENT PASSIVE SUBJUNCTIVE

1st Conj.	2nd Conj.	3rd Conj.	3rd -IO Conj.	4th Conj.
roger	docear	mittar	capiar	audiar
rogēris	doceāris	mittāris	capiāris	audiāris
rogētur	doceātur	mittātur	capiātur	audiātur
rogēmur	doceāmur	mittāmur	capiāmur	audiāmur
rogēminī	doceāminī	mittāminī	capiāminī	audiāminī
rogentur	doceantur	mittantur	capiantur	audiantur

SUBJUNCTIVE FORMS

IMPERFECT ACTIVE AND PASSIVE

IMPERFECT SUBJUNCTIVE

Present Active Infinitive
(2nd principal part)

+

Endings
(-m, -s, -t, -mus, -tis, -nt)
(-r, -ris, -tur, -mur, -minī, -ntur)

ROGĀRE
↓
ROGĀREM

DOCĒRE
↓
DOCĒREM

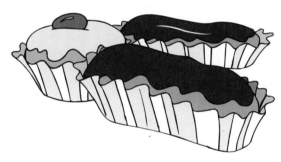

Rogāvī quid **ederēs.**
I asked what ⋄you were eating⋄.

IMPERFECT ACTIVE SUBJUNCTIVE

1st Conj.	2nd Conj.	3rd Conj.	3rd -IO Conj.	4th Conj.
rogārem	docērem	mitterem	caperem	audīrem
rogārēs	docērēs	mitterēs	caperēs	audīrēs
rogāret	docēret	mitteret	caperet	audīret
rogārēmus	docērēmus	mitterēmus	caperēmus	audīrēmus
rogārētis	docērētis	mitterētis	caperētis	audīrētis
rogārent	docērent	mitterent	caperent	audīrent

IMPERFECT PASSIVE SUBJUNCTIVE

1st Conj.	2nd Conj.	3rd Conj.	3rd -IO Conj.	4th Conj.
rogārer	docērer	mitterer	caperer	audīrer
rogārēris	docērēris	mitterēris	caperēris	audīrēris
rogārētur	docērētur	mitterētur	caperētur	audīrētur
rogārēmur	docērēmur	mitterēmur	caperēmur	audīrēmur
rogārēminī	docērēminī	mitterēminī	caperēminī	audīrēminī
rogārentur	docērentur	mitterentur	caperentur	audīrentur

SUBJUNCTIVE FORMS

PERFECT ACTIVE AND PASSIVE

<table>
<tr><td>

**PERFECT ACTIVE
SUBJUNCTIVE**

Perfect Stem
(3rd principal part, cut off -ī)

+

Endings

↓

-erim	-erīmus
-erīs	-erītis
-erit	-erint

</td><td>

**PERFECT PASSIVE
SUBJUNCTIVE**

Perfect Passive Participle
(4th principal part)

+

Present Subjunctive
of sum, esse

↓

sim	sīmus
sīs	sītis
sit	sint

</td></tr>
</table>

Endings resemble
the Future Perfect
Indicative except for
the 1st person singular.

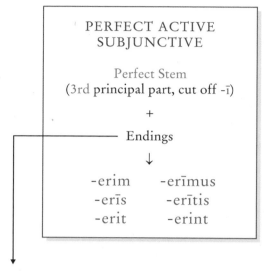

ROGĀVĪ
↓
ROGĀVERIM

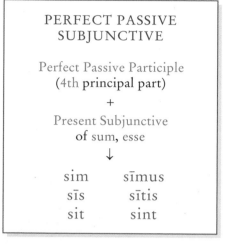

ROGĀTUS
↓
ROGĀTUS
SIM

PERFECT ACTIVE SUBJUNCTIVE	PERFECT PASSIVE SUBJUNCTIVE
All conjugations follow the same formula	
rogāverim	rogātus sim
rogāverīs	rogātus sīs
rogāverit	rogātus sit
rogāverīmus	rogātī sīmus
rogāverītis	rogātī sītis
rogāverint	rogātī sint

Nominative Plural
Feminine in agreement
with corōnae

↓

The 4th principal part must
take on masculine, feminine,
or neuter characteristics
to match the subject!

rogātus, -a, -um
sim, sīs, sit

&

rogātī, -ae, -a
sīmus, sītis, sint

Quaeris cūr corōnae illīs **dātae sint.**
You ask why garlands ⁺were given⁺ to those people.

SUBJUNCTIVE FORMS

PLUPERFECT ACTIVE AND PASSIVE

PLUPERFECT ACTIVE SUBJUNCTIVE

Perfect Stem
(3rd principal part, cut off -ī)
+
ISSE
+
-m, -s, -t, -mus, -tis, -nt
↓

-issem	-issēmus
-issēs	-issētis
-isset	-issent

PLUPERFECT PASSIVE SUBJUNCTIVE

Perfect Passive Participle
(4th principal part)
+
Imperfect Subjunctive
of sum, esse
↓

essem	essēmus
essēs	essētis
esset	essent

Note that the 3rd principal part + isse is simply the perfect active infinitive.

Note that the imperfect subjunctive of sum is formed according to the rules on p. 221 (present active infinitive + endings).

PLUPERFECT ACTIVE SUBJUNCTIVE	PLUPERFECT PASSIVE SUBJUNCTIVE
All conjugations follow the same formula	
rogāvissem	rogātus essem
rogāvissēs	rogātus essēs
rogāvisset	rogātus esset
rogāvissēmus	rogātī essēmus
rogāvissētis	rogātī essētis
rogāvissent	rogātī essent

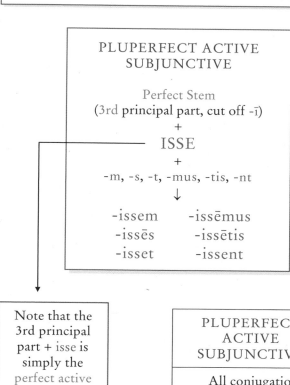

ROGĀVĪ
↓
ROGĀVISSE
↓
ROGĀVISSEM

ROGĀTUS
↓
ROGĀTUS
ESSEM

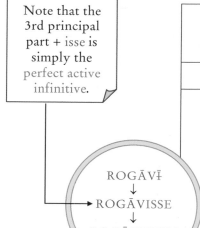

The 4th principal part must take on masculine, feminine, or neuter characteristics to match the subject!

rogātus, -a, -um
essem, essēs, esset
&
rogātī, -ae, -a
essēmus, essētis, essent

Nominative Singular
Neuter in agreement
with oppidum
↓

Quaesīvī quandō oppidum **conditum esset**.
I asked when the town ⋄had been founded⋄.

SUBJUNCTIVE FORMS

SUMMARY OF FORMS

PRESENT SUBJUNCTIVE	Present Stem + wE EAt cAvIAr +	-m, -s, -t, -mus, -tis, -nt -r, -ris, -tur, -mur, -minī, -ntur

IMPERFECT SUBJUNCTIVE	Present Active Infinitive +	-m, -s, -t, -mus, -tis, -nt -r, -ris, -tur, -mur, -minī, -ntur

PERFECT SUBJUNCTIVE	Active: Perfect Stem +	-erim, -erīs, -erit, -erīmus, -erītis, -erint
	Passive: 4th Principal Part +	sim, sīs, sit, sīmus, sītis, sint

PLUPERFECT SUBJUNCTIVE	Active: Perfect Stem +	-issem, -issēs, -isset, -issēmus, -issētis, -issent
	Passive: 4th Principal Part +	essem, essēs, esset, essēmus, essētis, essent

SUBJUNCTIVE FORMS OF PORTŌ, PORTĀRE, PORTĀVĪ, PORTĀTUS (TO CARRY)

	PRESENT	IMPERFECT	PERFECT	PLUPERFECT
Active:	portet	portāret*	portāverit	portāvisset*
Passive:	portētur	portārētur	portātus sit	portātus esset

NOTE:

Imperfect Subjunctive =
Present Infinitive + Endings

Pluperfect Subjunctive =
Perfect Infinitive + Endings

FUTURE
Subjunctive

FUTURE
PERFECT
Subjunctive

SUBJUNCTIVE FORMS

IRREGULAR VERBS

	SUM	POSSUM	VOLŌ	NŌLŌ	MĀLŌ	EŌ	FERŌ	FĪŌ
PRESENT	sim	possim	velim	nōlim	mālim	eam	feram	fīam
	sīs	possīs	velis	nōlis	mālis	eās	ferās	fīās
	sit	possit	velit	nōlit	mālit	eat	ferat	fīat
	sīmus	possīmus	velimus	nōlimus	mālimus	eāmus	ferāmus	fīāmus
	sītis	possītis	velitis	nōlitis	mālitis	eātis	ferātis	fīātis
	sint	possint	velint	nōlint	mālint	eant	ferant	fīant
IMPERFECT	essem	possem	vellem	nōllem	māllem	īrem	ferrem	fierem
	essēs	possēs	vellēs	nōllēs	māllēs	īrēs	ferrēs	fierēs
	esset	posset	vellet	nōllet	māllet	īret	ferret	fieret
	essēmus	possēmus	vellēmus	nōllēmus	māllēmus	īrēmus	ferrēmus	fierēmus
	essētis	possētis	vellētis	nōllētis	māllētis	īrētis	ferrētis	fierētis
	essent	possent	vellent	nōllent	māllent	īrent	ferrent	fierent
PERFECT	fuerim	potuerim	voluerim	nōluerim	māluerim	īverim / ierim	tulerim	factus sim
	fuerīs	potuerīs	voluerīs	nōluerīs	māluerīs	īverīs / ierīs	tulerīs	factus sīs
	fuerit	potuerit	voluerit	nōluerit	māluerit	īverit / ierit	tulerit	factus sit
	fuerīmus	potuerīmus	voluerīmus	nōluerīmus	māluerīmus	etc.	etc.	factī sīmus
	fuerītis	potuerītis	voluerītis	nōluerītis	māluerītis	itus sim / itus sīs / itus sit / etc.	lātus sim / lātus sīs / lātus sit / etc.	factī sītis
	fuerint	potuerint	voluerint	nōluerint	māluerint			factī sint
PLUPERFECT	fuissem	potuissem	voluissem	nōluissem	māluissem	īvissem / īssem	tulissem	factus essem
	fuissēs	potuissēs	voluissēs	nōluissēs	māluissēs	īvissēs / īssēs	tulissēs	factus essēs
	fuisset	potuisset	voluisset	nōluisset	māluisset	īvisset / īsset	tulisset	factus esset
	fuissēmus	potuissēmus	voluissēmus	nōluissēmus	māluissēmus	etc.	etc.	factī essēmus
	fuissētis	potuissētis	voluissētis	nōluissētis	māluissētis	itus essem / itus essēs / itus esset / etc.	lātus essem / lātus essēs / lātus esset / etc.	factī essētis
	fuissent	potuissent	voluissent	nōluissent	māluissent			factī essent

> Present Subjunctive forms are irregular, but the imperfect, perfect, and pluperfect are formed just as for any other verb.

INDEPENDENT SUBJUNCTIVE USES

Present

Independent

HORTATORY/JUSSIVE/VOLITIVE

HORTATORY SUBJUNCTIVE
(Also called "jussive" or
"volitive" subjunctive)

Conveys an exhortation/command.
↓
Present Subjunctive

(LET)

(*VERB*!)

TRANSLATION

1ST AND 3RD PERSON:
"LET *subject verb*"

2ND PERSON:
"*VERB*!"

Ad urbem **ambulēmus.**
⬩Let us walk⬩ to the city!

Marcus ā nōbis **servētur.**
⬩Let Marcus be saved⬩ by us!

Patriam tuam **dēfendās.**
⬩Defend⬩ your fatherland!

Cīvēs bonī **sītis.**
⬩Be⬩ good citizens!

(LET...
NOT)

(DO
NOT
VERB!)

NEGATIVE
HORTATORY SUBJUNCTIVE

nē
+
Present Subjunctive

PERFECT
SUBJUNCTIVE

Often, the perfect
subjunctive appears in
negative hortatory
expressions.

Nē Marcus in aquam **pellātur.**
⬩Let⬩ Marcus ⬩not be pushed⬩ into the water!

Nē volāre **temptēs,** phoenīcoptere.
⬩Do not try⬩ to fly, flamingo.

Nē dīcere **temptāverint.**
⬩Let them not try⬩ to speak!

Nē mē **timuerīs.**
⬩Do not fear⬩ me!

INDEPENDENT SUBJUNCTIVE USES

Present
Imperfect
Pluperfect

Independent

OPTATIVE

> ## OPTATIVE SUBJUNCTIVE
>
> ### UTINAM
> +
> Present, Imperfect, Pluperfect
> Subjunctive
> ↓
> ## "IF ONLY," "WOULD THAT"

> ### UTINAM NĒ
> ↓
> "would that. . .not"

MAY

PRESENT SUBJUNCTIVE

"would that I may *verb*"

(Possible wish for the present/future)

Utinam brevis **sit** hic labor.
Would that this task ⬧may be⬧ brief.

Brevis **sit** hic labor.
⬧May⬧ this task ⬧be⬧ brief.

→

> Utinam may be omitted with the present subjunctive, but not with other tenses.
>
> Take care to avoid confusing optative (wish) and hortatory (command).
>
> (See pp. 226, 228)

WERE

IMPERFECT SUBJUNCTIVE

"would that I were *verb*ing"
"would that I *verb*ed"

(Unfulfilled longing pertaining to the present)

Utinam nunc **volārem**.
If only I ⬧were flying⬧ now.

Utinam hunc labōrem **amārem**.
If only I ⬧liked⬧ this task.

HAD

PLUPERFECT SUBJUNCTIVE

"would that I had *verb*ed"

(Unfulfilled longing pertaining to the past)

Utinam nē tantam illuviem **fēcissem**.
Would that I ⬧had not made⬧ such a great mess.

INDEPENDENT SUBJUNCTIVE USES

OPTATIVE VS. HORTATORY SUBJUNCTIVE

If utinam is omitted before a present tense optative subjunctive, the optative may easily be mistaken for a hortatory construction.

Take careful note of the difference between the two, and use context to decide which is intended:

↓

Hortatory: command, exhortation
Optative: wish, hope

Epistulam ad tē **mittāmus.**
◇Let us send◇ a letter to you.

Epistulam hodiē **accipiāmus.**
◇May we receive◇ a letter today!

We command ourselves to send a letter.

We wish that we will receive a letter.

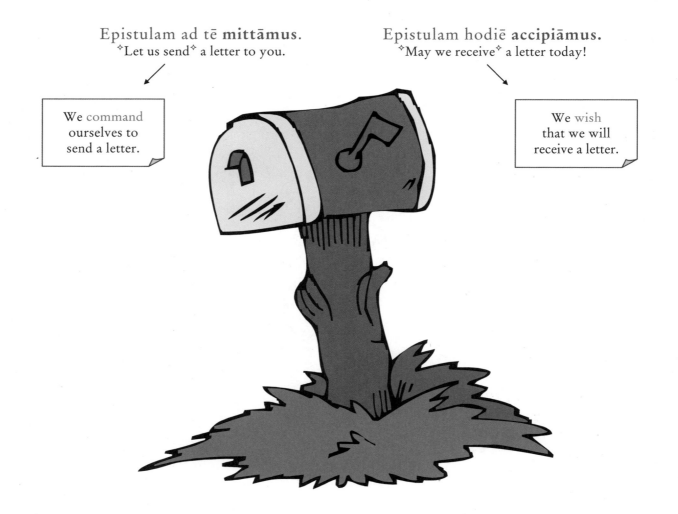

INDEPENDENT SUBJUNCTIVE USES

DELIBERATIVE

DELIBERATIVE SUBJUNCTIVE

Appears in questions.

"SHOULD I *verb*? / AM I TO *verb*?"
(Present Subjunctive)

"SHOULD I HAVE *verb*ed? / WAS I TO *verb*?"
(Imperfect Subjunctive)

Brūtus sōlus **temptet** hunc labōrem ferre?
⬥Should⬥ Brutus ⬥try⬥ to bear this task alone?

Quem amīcum **vocet** Brūtus?
What friend ⬥is⬥ Brutus ⬥to call⬥?

Quid **faceret** Brūtus?
What ⬥was⬥ Brutus ⬥to do⬥?

Quōmodō Brūtus perīculum **vitāret**?
How ⬥should⬥ Brutus ⬥have avoided⬥ danger?

INDEPENDENT SUBJUNCTIVE USES

Present
Imperfect
Pluperfect

Independent

POTENTIAL

POTENTIAL SUBJUNCTIVE

WOULD   MAY
COULD   MIGHT

(Present & Imperfect & Pluperfect
Subjunctive)

There are many different
ways of phrasing the
potential subjunctive in
English. Keep all of them
in mind and pick the one
that best seems to fit
the context.

WOULD/COULD/ETC. "HAVE"

If the verb is imperfect,
it is often appropriate
to add "have," and it is
always appropriate when
the verb is pluperfect.

PRESENT TENSE

Deals with
what is possible in
the present/future.

Quis familiam dēfendere **dubitet**?
Who ⁺would hesitate⁺ to defend his family?

IMPERFECT TENSE

Deals with what
was possible in
the past.

Quis eō tempore bellum **cuperet**?
Who ⁺could have desired⁺ war at that time?

COMMON POTENTIAL SUBJUNCTIVE PHRASE

aliquis **dīcat**. . .
Someone may say. . .

The apodoses
of subjunctive
conditions are
potential
subjunctives.

Sī perīculum veniat, **pugnem**.
If danger should come, ⁺I would fight⁺.

Sī in perīculō essēs, tē **iuvārem**.
If you were in danger, ⁺I would be helping⁺ you.

PLUPERFECT TENSE

The potential use
of the pluperfect
subjunctive appears
most frequently
in conditions.

Nisi nāvēs dēlētae essent, **effūgissētis**.
If the ships had not been destroyed, you (pl.) ⁺would have fled⁺.

SEQUENCE OF TENSES IN DEPENDENT CLAUSES

PRIMARY VS. SECONDARY SEQUENCE

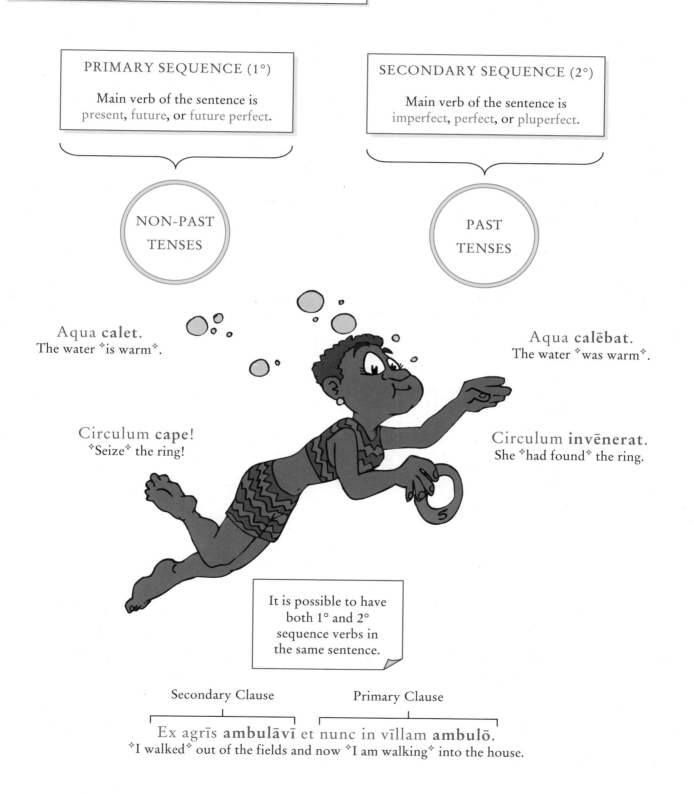

PRIMARY SEQUENCE (1°)

Main verb of the sentence is present, future, or future perfect.

SECONDARY SEQUENCE (2°)

Main verb of the sentence is imperfect, perfect, or pluperfect.

NON-PAST TENSES

PAST TENSES

Aqua **calet**.
The water ⬦is warm⬦.

Aqua **calēbat**.
The water ⬦was warm⬦.

Circulum **cape**!
⬦Seize⬦ the ring!

Circulum **invēnerat**.
She ⬦had found⬦ the ring.

It is possible to have both 1° and 2° sequence verbs in the same sentence.

Secondary Clause   Primary Clause

Ex agrīs **ambulāvī** et nunc in vīllam **ambulō**.
⬦I walked⬦ out of the fields and now ⬦I am walking⬦ into the house.

SEQUENCE OF TENSES IN DEPENDENT CLAUSES

INDICATIVE	SAME TIME	SUBJUNCTIVE
Action happens	AFTER	Action happens
NOW	BEFORE	SAME TIME AS MAIN VERB
or		or
AFTER NOW		AFTER MAIN VERB
or		or
BEFORE NOW		BEFORE MAIN VERB

These translations apply to subjunctive verbs in dependent clauses.

MAIN VERB	DEPENDENT SUBJUNCTIVE VERB	
	SAME TIME / AFTER (Incomplete at the time of the main verb)	BEFORE (Complete at the time of the main verb)
1° (Primary Sequence) Present Future Future Perfect	PRESENT SAME TIME - "*verb*s" AFTER - "will *verb*"	PERFECT BEFORE - "*verb*ed"
2° (Secondary Sequence) Imperfect Perfect Pluperfect	IMPERFECT SAME TIME - "was *verb*ing" AFTER - "would *verb*"	PLUPERFECT BEFORE - "had *verb*ed"

Present & Imperfect
↓
Action happens at the same time as or after the main verb.

Perfect & Pluperfect
↓
Action happened before the main verb.

Common sense and context clues will help you tell a "same time" situation from an "after" situation.

SEQUENCE OF TENSES IN DEPENDENT CLAUSES

> Given an English sentence,
> how do you translate the
> dependent verb into Latin?

PRIMARY SEQUENCE

I ask why you are leaving.	SAME TIME	present subjunctive	rogō cūr **abeās**
I fear that you will leave.	AFTER	present subjunctive	timeō nē **abeās**
I do not know when you left.	BEFORE	perfect subjunctive	nesciō quandō **abīverīs**

SECONDARY SEQUENCE

I asked why you were leaving.	SAME TIME	imperfect subjunctive	rogāvī cūr **abīrēs**
I feared that you would leave.	AFTER	imperfect subjunctive	timēbam ne **abīrēs**
I did not know when you had left.	BEFORE	pluperfect subjunctive	nesciēbam quandō **abīvissēs**

> Given a Latin sentence,
> how do you translate the
> dependent verb into English?

PRIMARY SEQUENCE

timeō nē **abeās**	present subjunctive	SAME TIME/ AFTER	I fear that you are leaving. I fear that you will leave.
nesciō quandō **abīverīs**	perfect subjunctive	BEFORE	I do not know when you left.

SECONDARY SEQUENCE

timēbam ne **abīrēs**	imperfect subjunctive	SAME TIME/ AFTER	I feared that you were leaving. I feared that you would leave.
nesciēbam quandō **abīvissēs**	pluperfect subjunctive	BEFORE	I did not know when you had left.

> **NOTE:**
>
> Some dependent clauses (such as
> purpose clauses and indirect commands)
> have special translation rules.
>
> When this book indicates
> that a dependent clause is translated
> "according to the sequence of tenses,"
> no special rules are in place and
> the guidelines on this page
> should be followed.

Cum animum fortem habeās, nihil tē terret.
Since ⬦you have⬦ a brave heart, nothing scares you.

SEQUENCE OF TENSES IN DEPENDENT CLAUSES

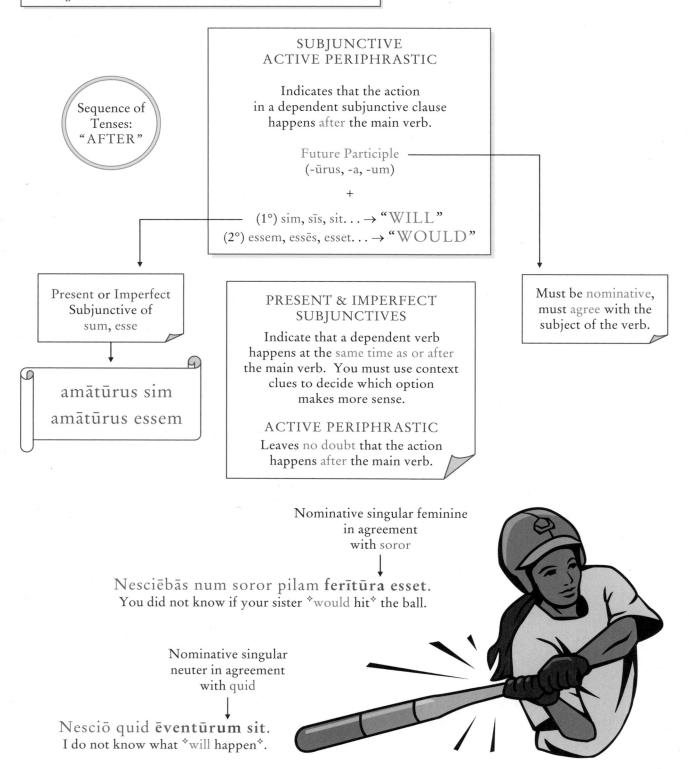

Sequence of
Tenses:
"AFTER"

SUBJUNCTIVE ACTIVE PERIPHRASTIC

Indicates that the action
in a dependent subjunctive clause
happens after the main verb.

Future Participle
(-ūrus, -a, -um)

+

(1°) sim, sīs, sit... → "WILL"
(2°) essem, essēs, esset... → "WOULD"

Present or Imperfect
Subjunctive of
sum, esse

amātūrus sim
amātūrus essem

PRESENT & IMPERFECT SUBJUNCTIVES

Indicate that a dependent verb
happens at the same time as or after
the main verb. You must use context
clues to decide which option
makes more sense.

ACTIVE PERIPHRASTIC

Leaves no doubt that the action
happens after the main verb.

Must be nominative,
must agree with the
subject of the verb.

Nominative singular feminine
in agreement
with soror

Nesciēbās num soror pilam **ferītūra esset**.
You did not know if your sister ⁺would hit⁺ the ball.

Nominative singular
neuter in agreement
with quid

Nesciō quid **ēventūrum sit**.
I do not know what ⁺will happen⁺.

DEPENDENT SUBJUNCTIVE USES

Present
&
Imperfect

Dependent

PURPOSE

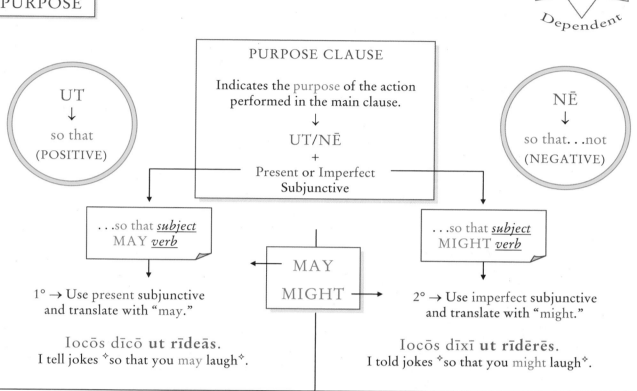

PURPOSE CLAUSE

Indicates the purpose of the action
performed in the main clause.
↓
UT/NĒ
+
Present or Imperfect
Subjunctive

UT
↓
so that
(POSITIVE)

NĒ
↓
so that. . .not
(NEGATIVE)

. . .so that *subject*
MAY *verb*

. . .so that *subject*
MIGHT *verb*

MAY
MIGHT

1° → Use present subjunctive
and translate with "may."

2° → Use imperfect subjunctive
and translate with "might."

Iocōs dīcō **ut rīdeās**.
I tell jokes ⋄so that you may laugh⋄.

Iocōs dīxī **ut rīdērēs**.
I told jokes ⋄so that you might laugh⋄.

It is often possible
to use an alternate
translation for nē.
↓
"LEST"

Iocōs dīcō **nē doleās**.
I tell jokes ⋄so that you may not be sad⋄.
I tell jokes ⋄lest you be sad⋄.

If the main verb and
the dependent verb
have the same subject:
↓
"[IN ORDER] TO"

Hūc venimus **ut requiēscāmus**.
We come here ⋄so that we may relax⋄.
We come here ⋄[in order] to relax⋄.

Hūc vēnimus **ut requiēscerēmus**.
We came here ⋄so that we might relax⋄.
We came here ⋄[in order] to relax⋄.

DEPENDENT SUBJUNCTIVE USES

RESULT

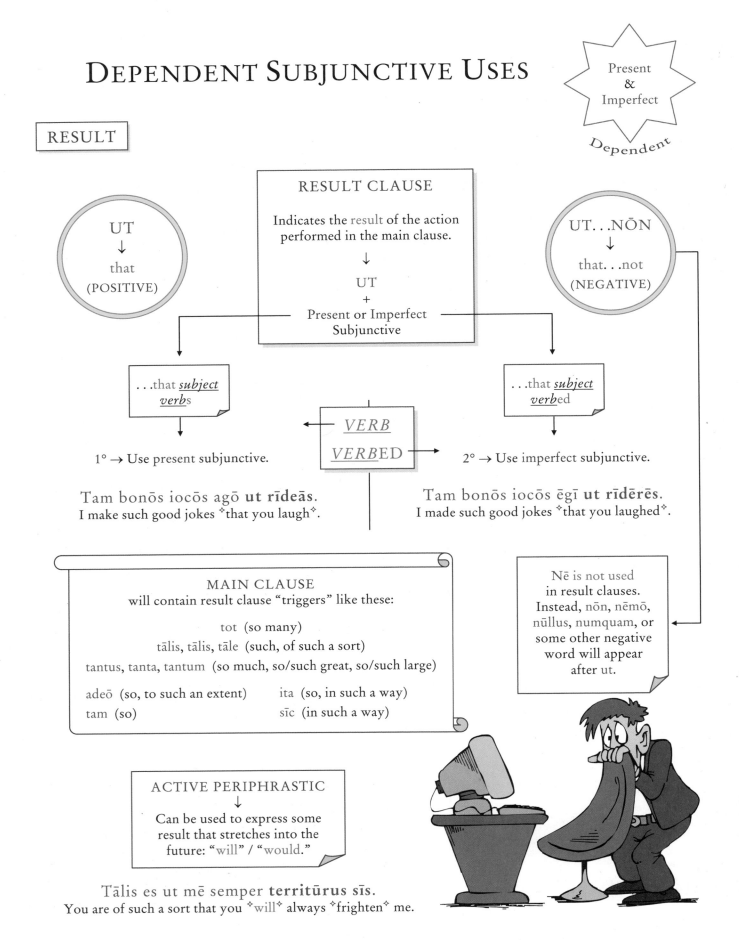

UT
↓
that
(POSITIVE)

RESULT CLAUSE

Indicates the result of the action performed in the main clause.

↓

UT
+
Present or Imperfect
Subjunctive

UT…NŌN
↓
that…not
(NEGATIVE)

…that *subject verbs*

VERB
VERBED

…that *subject verbed*

1° → Use present subjunctive.

2° → Use imperfect subjunctive.

Tam bonōs iocōs agō **ut rīdeās**.
I make such good jokes ◇that you laugh◇.

Tam bonōs iocōs ēgī **ut rīdērēs**.
I made such good jokes ◇that you laughed◇.

MAIN CLAUSE
will contain result clause "triggers" like these:

tot (so many)

tālis, tālis, tāle (such, of such a sort)

tantus, tanta, tantum (so much, so/such great, so/such large)

adeō (so, to such an extent)   ita (so, in such a way)

tam (so)   sīc (in such a way)

Nē is not used
in result clauses.
Instead, nōn, nēmō,
nūllus, numquam, or
some other negative
word will appear
after ut.

ACTIVE PERIPHRASTIC
↓
Can be used to express some
result that stretches into the
future: "will" / "would."

Tālis es ut mē semper **territūrus sīs**.
You are of such a sort that you ◇will◇ always ◇frighten◇ me.

DEPENDENT SUBJUNCTIVE USES

RESULT – SUBSTANTIVE

> efficiō ut + subjunctive → I bring it about that. . .
>
> accidit ut + subjunctive → It happens that. . .
>
> necesse est ut + subjunctive → It is necessary that. . .

Effēcistī **ut laudārēris.**
You brought it about ⁺that you were praised⁺.

Accidit **ut laudārēris.**
It happened ⁺that you were praised.⁺

Necesse est **ut laudēris.**
It is necessary ⁺that you be praised.⁺

> This construction can also be called a "Noun Clause of Fact."

> ACCIDIT is used *only* in the 3rd person singular.
>
> Be careful not to confuse the present and the perfect, which are identical.
>
> Look at the tense of the subjunctive to determine whether the sentence is in primary or secondary sequence.

Present Subjunctive
↓
Primary Sequence:
accidit must be present.

Imperfect Subjunctive
↓
Secondary Sequence:
accidit must be perfect.

Accidit ut cibō careāmus.
⁺It happens⁺ that we are without food.

Accidit ut cibō carērēmus.
⁺It happened⁺ that we were without food.

DEPENDENT SUBJUNCTIVE USES

INDIRECT COMMAND

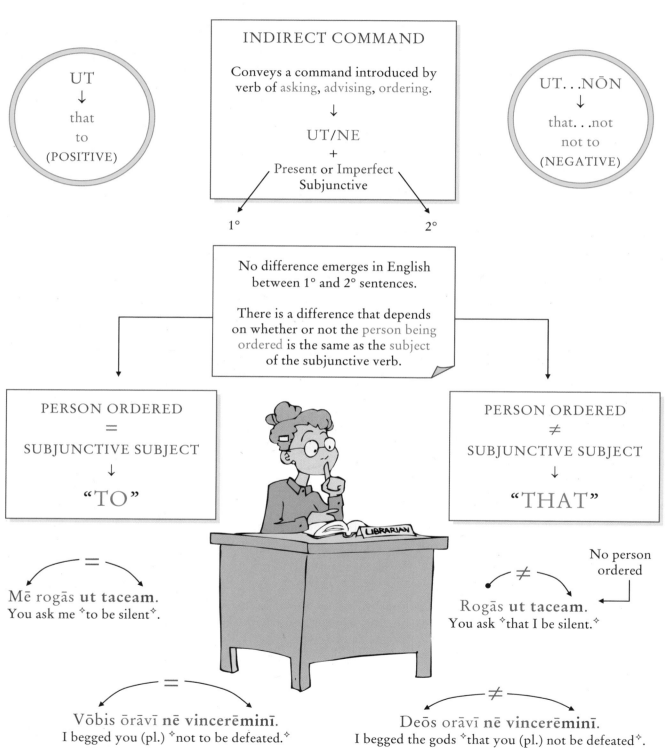

UT
↓
that
to
(POSITIVE)

INDIRECT COMMAND

Conveys a command introduced by
verb of asking, advising, ordering.
↓
UT/NE
+
Present or Imperfect
Subjunctive

1°   2°

UT...NŌN
↓
that...not
not to
(NEGATIVE)

No difference emerges in English
between 1° and 2° sentences.

There is a difference that depends
on whether or not the person being
ordered is the same as the subject
of the subjunctive verb.

PERSON ORDERED
=
SUBJUNCTIVE SUBJECT
↓
"TO"

PERSON ORDERED
≠
SUBJUNCTIVE SUBJECT
↓
"THAT"

=
Mē rogās **ut** taceam.
You ask me ⁀to be silent⁀.

≠   No person
ordered
Rogās **ut** taceam.
You ask ⁀that I be silent.⁀

=
Vōbis ōrāvī **nē** vincerēminī.
I begged you (pl.) ⁀not to be defeated.⁀

≠
Deōs ōrāvī **nē** vincerēminī.
I begged the gods ⁀that you (pl.) not be defeated⁀.

DEPENDENT SUBJUNCTIVE USES

Present
&
Imperfect

Dependent

INDIRECT COMMAND – INTRODUCTORY VERBS

VERBS THAT TRIGGER INDIRECT COMMANDS

Some verbs that trigger indirect commands take the "person ordered" in the dative, some take the accuastive, and others take ā/ab + ablative.

Canem rogāvī ut sedēret.
I asked ✦the dog✦ to sit.

Canī mandāvī ut sedēret.
I ordered ✦the dog✦ to sit.

Ā cane petīvī ut sedēret.
I asked ✦the dog✦ to sit.

VERBS THAT TRIGGER INDIRECT COMMANDS

ACCUSATIVE

moneō, monēre, monuī, monitus (to warn, advise)
ōrō, ōrāre, ōrāvī, ōrātus (to beg)
rogō, rogāre, rogāvī, rogātus (to ask, ask for)

DATIVE

persuādeō, persuādēre, persuāsī, persuāsus (to persuade)
imperō, imperāre, imperāvī, imperātus (to order)
mandō, mandāre, mandāvī, mandātus (to order)

ā/ab + ABLATIVE

petō, petere, petīvī, petītus (to seek, ask)
quaerō, quaerere, quaesīvī, quaesītus (to seek; ask)
postulō, postulāre, postulāvī, postulātus (to demand, ask)

nōs rogābunt
↓
they will ask ✦us✦

nōbis imperāvit
↓
he ordered ✦us✦

ā nōbis petis
↓
you ask ✦[of] us✦

DEPENDENT SUBJUNCTIVE USES

Present
Imperfect
Perfect
Pluperfect

Dependent

FEAR

UT
↓
that...◇NOT◇
(NEGATIVE)

FEARING CLAUSE

"I fear that ___dependent clause___"
↓
UT/NĒ
+
Present, Imperfect, Perfect, Pluperfect
Subjunctive

NĒ
↓
that
(POSITIVE)

Translate
subjunctives
according to
Sequence of
Tenses.

FEARING CLAUSE TRIGGERS

timeō, timēre, timuī (to fear)
metuō, metuere, metuī (to fear)
vereor, verērī, veritus sum (to fear)

timōrem habēre (to have fear)
metum habēre (to have fear)

Timeō nē capiāris.
I fear ◇that you are being captured◇.
I fear ◇that you will be captured◇.

Timuī ut effugerēs.
I feared ◇that you were not escaping◇.
I feared ◇that you would not escape◇.

Timeō nē captus sīs.
I fear ◇that you were captured◇.

UT/NĒ REVERSAL

Nē → "That"
Ut → "That...not"

Nē sounds positive and ut
sounds negative, but this is
merely a convenient way of
translating a Latin concept
into English.

Timuī ut effūgissēs.
I feared ◇that you had not escaped◇.

Timeō nē capiātur.

Latin Concept	English Translation
I am afraid... may he not be captured!	=	I am afraid that he will be captured.

Timeō ut capiātur.

Latin Concept	English Translation
I am afraid... may he be captured!	=	I am afraid that he will not be captured.

DEPENDENT SUBJUNCTIVE USES

SUMMARY OF SUBJUNCTIVES USING *UT* AND *NĒ*

HORTATORY
(Independent - Present)

Never uses ut

"Let *subject verb*"
"*Verb*!"

No triggers

Discēdāmus.
Let us depart.

Discēdās.
Depart!

Nē discēdāmus.
Let us not depart.

Nē discēdās.
Do not depart!

PURPOSE
(Dependent - Present & Imperfect)

"So that *subject* may/might *verb*"

No triggers

Veniō ut te videam.
I am coming so that I may see you.

Vēnī ut te vidērem.
I came so that I might see you.

RESULT
(Dependent - Present & Imperfect,
Active Periphrastic)

Never uses nē

"that *subject verbs*/*verb*ed"
"that *subject* will/would *verb*"

Triggers: tot, tantus, talis, sīc, ita, tam,
necesse est, accidit, efficiō

Tam fortis es ut tē laudēmus.
You are so brave that we praise you.
. . .ut tē laudātūrī sīmus. - . . .that we will priaise you.

Tam fortis erās ut tē laudārēm.
You were so brave that we praised you.
. . .ut tē laudātūrī essēmus. - . . .that we would praise you.

Effēcī ut caperēris.
I brought it about that you were captured.

INDIRECT COMMAND
(Dependent - Present & Imperfect)

"that *subject verb*"
"to *verb*"

Triggers: imperō, persuādeō, mandō,
moneō, ōrō, rogō, petō, postulō, quaerō

Imperō ut laborēs.
I order that you work.

Tibi imperō ut laborēs.
I order you to work.

Imperāvī ut laborārēs.
I ordered that you work.

Tibi imperāvī ut laborārēs.
I ordered you to work.

FEARING
(Dependent - All Tenses)

ut ↓ not

"I fear that ___dependent clause___"

Translate verb using Sequence of Tenses
Triggers: timeō, metuō, vereor,
timōrem habēre, metum habēre

Timēs nē vincar. - You fear that I am being conquered.
. . .that I will be conquered.
Timēs nē victus sim. - You fear that I was conquered.

Timēbās nē vincerer. - You feared that I was being conquered.
. . .that I would be conquered.
Timēbās nē victus essem. - You feared that I had been conquered.

DEPENDENT SUBJUNCTIVE USES

INDIRECT QUESTION

INDIRECT QUESTION

Direct: Where are you going?
Indirect: I ask where you are going.
↓
Begins with some interrogative word.
(cūr, ubi, num, quis, quid)
+
Present, Imperfect, Perfect, Pluperfect
Subjunctive

An indirect question *does not* have to have a question mark at the end!

Introduced by verbs of saying, asking, knowing, perceiving, etc.

Translate subjunctives according to Sequence of Tenses.

Rogāvī **num hīc mānsūrus essēs annōn.**
I asked ⋄whether you would stay here or not⋄.

Dīc **unde vēnerīs et quō itūrus sīs.**
Say ⋄where you came from and where you will go⋄.

IMPORTANT INTERROGATIVES

quis, quid (who?, what?)
quī, quae, quod (what _noun_ ?)
quālis, quālis, quāle (of what sort?)
quantus, quanta, quantum (how much/great?)
quot (how many?)

cūr (why?)
quandō (when?)
quomodō (how?)
quō (where? [destination])
ubi (where? [location])
unde (where from?)

num (whether, if)
sīve...sīve (whether...or)
utrum...an (whether...or)
utrum...annōn (whether...or not)
utrum...necne (whether...or not)

Nesciō **cūr subrīdeās.**
I do not know ⋄why you are smiling⋄.

DEPENDENT SUBJUNCTIVE USES

Present
Imperfect
Perfect
Pluperfect

Dependent

CUM CLAUSES

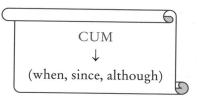

CUM
↓
(when, since, although)

CUM CLAUSES

Cum can introduce a dependent clause with an indicative or a subjunctive verb.

Cum has several different meanings, and context will help you pick the right one.

Translate subjunctives according to Sequence of Tenses.

"WHEN"
↓
Temporal Clause
(Indicative)

"WHEN"
↓
Temporal: when one thing occurs, something else happens to be going on. The events are otherwise unconnected.

Circumstantial: when one thing occurs, it triggers another thing.

"WHEN"
↓
Circumstantial
Clause
(Indicative or
Subjunctive)

Cum advēnistī, salīre parābam.
⬥When you arrived⬥, I was preparing to jump.

Cum ades, minus timeō.
⬥When you are near⬥, I am less afraid.

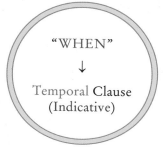

Cum clauses may have more than one valid interpretation.

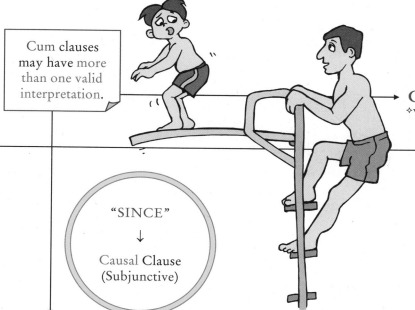

1° - Indicative is used
2° - Subjunctive is used

Cum adessēs, minus timēbam.
⬥When you were near⬥, I was less afraid

"SINCE"
↓
Causal Clause
(Subjunctive)

"ALTHOUGH"
↓
Concessive Clause
(Subjunctive)

Cum adessēs, minus timēbam.
⬥Since you were near⬥, I was less afraid.

Cum magnopere timērem, saluī!
⬥Although I was very afraid⬥, I jumped.

DEPENDENT SUBJUNCTIVE USES

Present
Imperfect
Perfect
Pluperfect

Dependent

> If the subject of the cum clause is the same as the subject of the independent clause, the sentence may be structured as follows:
>
> <u>subject</u>   <u>cum clause</u>   <u>independent clause</u>
>
> Marcus [cum dēfessus esset] [currere dēbēbat].
> Although Marcus was tired, he had to run.

Sextus cum bene sē cēlāvisset āb amīcīs tamen inventus est.
Athough Sextus had hidden himself well, he was nevertheless found by his friends.

cum (when, since, although)

tamen (nevertheless, yet, still)

tum (at that time)

Tamen often appears in the independent clause that accompanies a concessive ("although") cum clause.

Tum may appear in the independent clause that accompanies a temporal ("when") cum clause.

Cum timeāmus, ursum tamen spectāmus.
Although we are afraid, we ⬧still⬧ watch the bear.

Tum vigilābāmus cum ursus vēnit.
We were awake ⬧at that time⬧ when the bear came.

> COMMON PHRASE
>
> quae cum ita **sint/essent**
> ↓
> "since these things
> are/were so"

DEPENDENT SUBJUNCTIVE USES

Present
Imperfect
Perfect
Pluperfect

Dependent

RELATIVE CLAUSES OF CHARACTERISTIC – OVERVIEW

The sort of person who. . .

RELATIVE CLAUSE OF CHARACTERISTIC

Relative clause that intends to describe the antecedent. Tells you what kind of <u>*noun*</u> the antecedent is.

↓

quī, quae, quod
+
Present, Imperfect, Perfect, Pluperfect Subjunctive

Translate subjunctives according to Sequence of Tenses.

Often, no extra words are necessary, but sometimes it helps to add:

THE SORT OF
or
WOULD

Antōnia est fēmina **quae bēstiās amet.**
Antonia is a woman ⬦who likes animals⬦.
Antonia is ⬦the sort of⬦ woman ⬦who likes animals⬦.

Antōniam, **quae muscae numquam noceat,** laudāmus.
We praise Antonia, ⬦who would never hurt a fly⬦.

Antōnia erat fēmina **quae nūllī animālī nocuisset.**
Antonia was ⬦the sort of⬦ woman ⬦who had not hurt any creature⬦.

INDICATIVE RELATIVE CLAUSE
↓
Intends to relate factual information about the antecedent.

SUBJUNCTIVE CLAUSE OF CHARACTERISTIC
↓
Intends to describe what kind of person/thing the antecedent is.

Vir **quī pecūniam meam rapuit.**
the man ⬦who stole my money⬦

Vir **quī pecūniam rapiat.**
the sort of man ⬦who steals money⬦

DEPENDENT SUBJUNCTIVE USES

CLAUSES OF CHARACTERISTIC – IMAGINED ANTECEDENTS

Clauses of Characteristic are used
when the antecedent is an imagined noun
because the indicative is allowed only
in concrete, definite situations.

IMAGINED NOUN

A person, place, or thing which
may or may not actually exist,

OR

An unspecified / generalized
person, place, or thing.

Amīcum petis **cuī cōnfīdere possīs**.
You are looking for a friend ⬧whom you can trust⬧.

Hominēs melius vident **quī quattuor oculōs habeant**.
People ⬧who have four eyes⬧ see better.

DEPENDENT SUBJUNCTIVE USES

Present
Imperfect
Perfect
Pluperfect

Dependent

CLAUSES OF CHARACTERISTIC – COMMON PHRASES

---

est [is] quī

he is the sort of person who. . .
there is one who. . .
↓
(A form of is, ea, id
may or may not appear).

↓

Pīrāta est quī avēs amet.
The pirate ⬥is the sort of person who⬥ likes birds.

---

sunt [eī] quī

they are the sort of people who. . .
there are some who. . .
↓
(A form of is, ea, id
may or may not appear).

↓

Sunt eī quī avēs dēspiciant.
⬥There are those who⬥ despise birds.

---

quis est quī
sōlus est quī
ūnus est quī

who is there who. . .
he is the only one who. . .
there is one who. . .

↓

Quis erat quī avēs timēret?
⬥Who was there who⬥ feared birds?

NEGATIVE ANTECEDENTS

In addition to "imagined"
antecedents (see p. 246),
relative clauses of characteristic
are also used to describe
"negative" antecedents
(no one, nothing, etc.).

↓

nēmō est quī
nihil est quod
nūllus est quī

there is no one who. . .
there is nothing which. . .
there is no _____ who/which. . .

↓

Nēmō erat quī avibus nocēre vellet.
⬥There was no one who⬥ wanted to harm the birds.

DEPENDENT SUBJUNCTIVE USES

Present
&
Imperfect

Dependent

RELATIVE CLAUSES OF PURPOSE

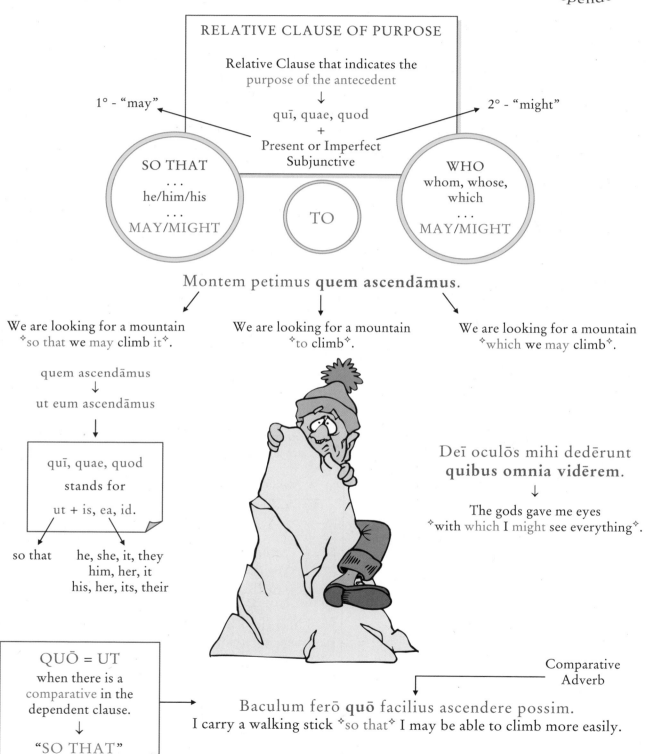

RELATIVE CLAUSE OF PURPOSE

Relative Clause that indicates the
purpose of the antecedent
↓
quī, quae, quod
+
Present or Imperfect
Subjunctive

1° - "may"

2° - "might"

SO THAT
. . .
he/him/his
. . .
MAY/MIGHT

TO

WHO
whom, whose,
which
. . .
MAY/MIGHT

Montem petimus **quem ascendāmus**.

We are looking for a mountain
⋄so that we may climb it⋄.

We are looking for a mountain
⋄to climb⋄.

We are looking for a mountain
⋄which we may climb⋄.

quem ascendāmus
↓
ut eum ascendāmus
↓

quī, quae, quod
stands for
ut + is, ea, id.

so that

he, she, it, they
him, her, it
his, her, its, their

Deī oculōs mihi dedērunt
quibus omnia vidērem.
↓
The gods gave me eyes
⋄with which I might see everything⋄.

Comparative
Adverb

QUŌ = UT
when there is a
comparative in the
dependent clause.
↓
"SO THAT"

Baculum ferō **quō** facilius ascendere possim.
I carry a walking stick ⋄so that⋄ I may be able to climb more easily.

DEPENDENT SUBJUNCTIVE USES

Present
Imperfect
Perfect
Pluperfect

Dependent

DEPENDENT CLAUSES IN INDIRECT DISCOURSE

DEPENDENT CLAUSES IN INDIRECT DISCOURSE

If a dependent clause appears as part of an indirect statement, command, or question:

↓

Verb is subjunctive.

↓

Translate according to the sequence of tenses.

COMMON DEPENDENT CLAUSES

Clauses that start with "who/whom/whose/which," "because," "when," "where," etc.

The subjunctive verb indicates when the action happens relative to the main (independent) verb.

Rogō {num fēmina illa virō [**quī cum eā sedeat**] nūpserit}.
I ask if that woman married the man ⋄who is sitting with her⋄.

(Relative clause within an Indirect Question)

RELATIVE CLAUSES

Be careful to determine whether a subjunctive verb appears in a relative clause simply because the clause is in indirect discourse or because the subjunctive is needed to indicate characteristic or purpose.

(See pp. 245-248)

Tē ōrāvī {ut fēminam invenīrēs [**quae idōnea mihi esset**]}.
I begged you to find a woman ⋄who would be suitable for me⋄.

(Relative clause of Characteristic within an Indirect Command)

DEPENDENT SUBJUNCTIVE USES

Present
&
Imperfect

Dependent

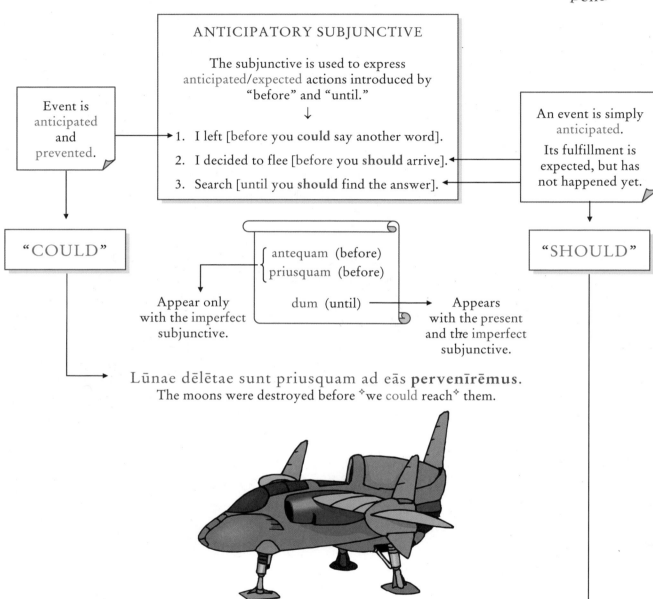

ANTICIPATORY SUBJUNCTIVE

The subjunctive is used to express
anticipated/expected actions introduced by
"before" and "until."

↓

1. I left [before you **could** say another word].

2. I decided to flee [before you **should** arrive].

3. Search [until you **should** find the answer].

Event is
anticipated
and
prevented.

An event is simply
anticipated.

Its fulfillment is
expected, but has
not happened yet.

"COULD"

"SHOULD"

{ antequam (before)
priusquam (before)

dum (until)

Appear only
with the imperfect
subjunctive.

Appears
with the present
and the imperfect
subjunctive.

Lūnae dēlētae sunt priusquam ad eās **pervenīrēmus**.
The moons were destroyed before ⬧we could reach⬧ them.

Per stēllās errābimus dum domum novam **inveniāmus**.
We will wander through the stars until ⬧we should find⬧ a new home.

NOTE:
priusquam & antequam
may be written as
prius. . .quam and ante. . .quam.

Prius effūgī **quam** mē caperēs.
I fled ⬧before⬧ you could catch me.

NOTE:
dum + indicative → while
dum + subjunctive → until

CONDITIONS

Indicative

Independent
+
Dependent

THE PARTS OF A CONDITION

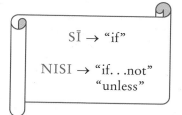

SĪ → "if"

NISI → "if. . .not"
"unless"

IF you are Julius Caesar,   THEN I am Mickey Mouse!

PROTASIS
(Dependent
Clause)

APODOSIS
(Independent
Clause)

INDICATIVE CONDITIONS

Present
Indicatives

SIMPLE PRESENT CONDITION

Sī gaudēs, gaudeō.
If you rejoice, I rejoice.

Imperfect
or
Perfect
Indicatives

SIMPLE PAST CONDITION

Sī dīcēbātis, audiēbāmus.
If you were speaking, we were listening.

Sī pugnāvistī, vīcistī.
If you fought, you won.

Sī dīcēs, audiam.
If you speak, I will listen.

Future
or
Future Perfect
Indicatives

SIMPLE FUTURE CONDITION
(FUTURE MORE VIVID)

Sī veniēs, gaudēbimus.
If you ⬦come⬦, we will rejoice.

Sī capta eris, omnia āmīserimus.
If you ⬦are captured⬦, we will have lost everything.

In English,
Future & Future Perfect
verbs in the protasis
are translated as if
they were present.

(No will/will have
after "if.")

CONDITIONS

Present
Imperfect
Pluperfect
Subjunctive

Independent
+
Dependent

SUBJUNCTIVE CONDITIONS

FUTURE LESS VIVID CONDITION
(Protasis may or may not end up happening.)

PRESENT   +   PRESENT
Subjunctive   Subjunctive
↓   ↓
"if I SHOULD *verb*"   "then I WOULD *verb*"

PRESENT
Subjunctives
should/would

Sī ventus **flet, cadat** arbor.
If the wind ⋄should blow⋄, the tree ⋄would fall⋄.

PRESENT CONTRARY TO FACT CONDITION
(Implies that the protasis is not being fulfilled right now.)

IMPERFECT   +   IMPERFECT
Subjunctive   Subjunctive
↓   ↓
"if I WERE *verb*ING"   "then I WOULD *verb*"
"if I *verb*ED"   "then I WOULD BE *verb*ING"

IMPERFECT
Subjunctives
were/would

Sī meliōrem secūrem **habērem**,   Sī plūrēs virī **labōrārent**,
auxilium nōn **dēsīderārem**.   arbor nōn iam **stāret**.
If I ⋄owned⋄ a better axe,   If more men ⋄were working⋄,
I ⋄would⋄ not ⋄need⋄ help.   the tree no longer ⋄would be standing⋄.

PAST CONTRARY TO FACT CONDITION
(Implies that the protasis was not fulfilled in the past.)

PLUPERFECT   +   PLUPERFECT
Subjunctive   Subjunctive
↓   ↓
"if I HAD *verb*ed"   "then I WOULD HAVE *verb*ed"

PLUPERFECT
Subjunctives
had/would have

Nisi secūrem **tūlissem**, arbor nōn **cecidisset**.
If I ⋄had not brought⋄ my axe, the tree ⋄would not have fallen⋄.

CONDITIONS

Indicative
Subjunctive
&
Substitutions

Independent
+
Dependent

FUTURE CONDITIONS

FUTURE MORE VIVID	FUTURE LESS VIVID
↓	↓
Used when it is likely that the protasis will come true.	Used when it is uncertain whether the protasis will come true.

Panicking besieged citizens might say. . .

Vincēmur sī ille exercitus inrumpet.
We will be conquered if that army breaks through.

People might say in peacetime. . .

Quid faciāmus sī bellum hūc veniat?
What would we do if war should come here?

MIXED CONDITIONS & SUBSTITUTIONS

MIXED CONDITIONS

Combination of one type of protasis and a different type of apodosis.

Sī dēlicuissem, dolērēs!
If I ⬩had melted⬩, you ⬩would be sad⬩!

(Past Contrary to Fact Protasis
+
Present Contrary to Fact Apodosis)

SUBSTITUTIONS

Imperatives and ablative absolutes may take the place of one element of the condition.

Sī sōlem videās, fuge!
If you ⬩should see⬩ the sun, ⬩flee⬩!

(Future Less Vivid Protasis
+
Imperative Apodosis)

Sōle fulgente, dēlicuissem.
⬩With the sun shining⬩, I would have melted.
⬩If the sun had shone⬩, I would have melted.

(Ablative Absolute Protasis
+
Past Contrary to Fact Apodosis)

In addition to sī & nisi, ablative absolutes can express "if".

Sōle fulgente, dēliquēscam.
⬩With the sun shining⬩, I would melt.
⬩If the sun should shine⬩, I would melt.

(Ablative Absolute Protasis
+
Future Less Vivid Apodosis)

GERUNDS

GERUNDS
are
NOUNS.

GERUND

"Verbal Noun"
↓
A verb form
that acts as a noun:
↓
"*verb*ING"

Connor has no fear of falling.

Verb "to fall" acts ←
as a genitive noun.

Do not confuse the gerund
with the present participle!
↓
Participle = Adjective
Gerund = Noun

Peter hears Joe talking.
(Adjective modifying Joe)

He expresses himself by talking.
(Ablative noun)

Gerunds are
singular
2nd Declension
neuter nouns.

FORMING GERUNDS

Present **Stem** of Verb
+
Connector **Vowel**
+
-NDUM

-NDUM
↓
*VERB*ING

___

rogand**ī**

rogand**ō**

rogand**um**

rogand**ō**

*The nominative gerund
is never actually used.

GERUND FORMS			
1st Conj.	roga**ndum**	→	asking
2nd Conj.	doce**ndum**	→	teaching
3rd Conj.	mitte**ndum**	→	sending
3rd -IO	capie**ndum**	→	seizing
4th Conj.	audie**ndum**	→	hearing

Nōs **cantandō** dēlectās.
You delight us ⬦by singing⬦.

Gerunds sometimes take direct
objects, though a gerundive
construction is more common.
(See pp. 256-257)

GERUND
CONNECTOR
VOWELS

a	e
1	2
3	4
(i)e	ie

Amorem **carmina cantandī** habeō.
I have a love ⬦of singing songs⬦.

GERUNDIVES

GERUNDIVES
are
ADJECTIVES
and their job is to
modify nouns.

GERUNDIVES
(Future Passive Participle)

Present Stem of Verb
+
Connector Vowel
+
-NDUS, -A, -UM
↓
"TO BE _verb_ED"

GERUNDIVE
CONNECTOR
VOWELS

a	e
1	2
3	4
(i)e	ie

-NDUS
↓
TO BE
_VERB_ED

Be careful not
to confuse the
gerundive with
the passive
infinitive!
The gerundive
is an adjective!

GERUNDIVE FORMS

1st Conj.	rogandus, -a, -um	→	to be asked
2nd Conj.	docendus, -a, -um	→	to be taught
3rd Conj.	mittendus, -a, -um	→	to be sent
3rd -IO	capiendus, -a, -um	→	to be seized
4th Conj.	audiendus, -a, -um	→	to be heard

Ā puellā **timendā** dēfendēbāmur.
We were being defended by a girl ⋄to be feared⋄.
(Gerundive modifying puellā)

Timērī vult.
She wants ⋄to be feared⋄.
(Passive Infinitive)

_VERB_ING
THE
NOUN

"VERBING THE NOUN"

Gerundive + Noun
is more commonly translated:

"_VERB_ING THE _NOUN_"

The noun that
the gerundive
modifies receives
the action of the
gerundive.

"VERBING THE NOUN"
↓
Verbal phrase which acts as a
noun in Latin

tabulārum frangendārum
of breaking the boards

(Genitive Plural)

tabulīs frangendīs
by breaking the boards

(Ablative Plural)

Tabulā frangendā artem ostendis.
You show your skill ⋄by breaking the board⋄.

GERUNDS AND GERUNDIVES

GERUND VS. GERUNDIVE

Both the gerund and the gerundive
can be used to express
"verbing the noun."

The gerund must be used for
special object verbs.

Gerund + Noun

Form of Noun
↓
Accusative or
special object case.

Gerundive + Noun

Form of Noun
↓
Same form
as gerundive.

mātrem honōrandō
by honoring mother

↓

Ablative Gerund
+
Accusative Direct Object

mātre honōrandā
by honoring mother

↘

Ablative Gerundive
+
Ablative Noun

mātrī placendō
by pleasing mother

↓

Ablative Gerund
+
Special Object Noun
(Placeō takes a dative object.)

The gerundive is the most
common way to express
"verbing the noun."

In general, a gerund may
take an accusative object
only if it appears in the
genitive or in the ablative
without a preposition.

GERUND
is a
Noun

↓

2nd declension
neuter noun
endings only

You can remember
that the gerundive
modifies a noun and
that the gerund
does not by
recalling that the
gerundive is an
adjective.

GERUNDIVE
is an
Adjective

↓

2-1-2 adjective
endings
(all genders)

GERUNDS AND GERUNDIVES

Gerund without object → _verb_ing
Gerund with object → _verb_ing the _noun_
Gerundive + Noun → _verb_ing the _noun_

CAUSĀ/GRĀTIĀ
+
GENITIVE
↓
For the sake of

AD
+
ACCUSATIVE
↓
For the
purpose of

NOTE:
Causā and grātiā
mean "for the
sake of" only if
they are in the
ablative case.

ACCUSATIVE NOTE:
When "_verb_ing"
acts as a direct object
(She loves sailing),
the infinitive is used
instead of an accusative
gerund or gerundive.

GENITIVE
↓
"OF _verb_ing [the _noun_]"

Timōrem **mōnstrī videndī** habēs. (Gerundive)
You have a fear ⁺of seeing the monster⁺.

Inimīcōs vincendī causā surgis. (Gerund)
You get up ⁺for the sake of conquering enemies⁺.

CAUSĀ/GRĀTIĀ + Genitive:
FOR THE SAKE OF

ACCUSATIVE
↓
Object of Preposition

Ad omnēs servandōs vigilā. (Gerundive)
Stay awake ⁺for the purpose of saving everyone⁺.

Ad vincendum vēnistī! (Gerund)
You came ⁺for the purpose of conquering⁺.

AD + Accusative:
FOR THE PURPOSE OF

DATIVE
↓
"TO/FOR _verb_ing [the _noun_]"

Mōnstrō vincendō operam das. (Gerundive)
You devote effort ⁺to conquering the monster⁺.

Arma mea **vincendō** idōnea sunt. (Gerund)
My weapons are suitable ⁺for conquering⁺.

ABLATIVE
↓
"BY/WITH _verb_ing [the _noun_]"
Object of Preposition

Dē **mōnstrō vincendō** somniās. (Gerundive)
You dream ⁺about conquering the monster⁺.

Vincendō fāmam augēbis. (Gerund)
You will increase your fame ⁺by conquering⁺.

PASSIVE PERIPHRASTIC

MUST BE
VERBED

NOMINATIVE NOUN
+
GERUNDIVE
(agreeing with nominative noun)
+
SUM, ES, EST...
↓
"*Noun* MUST BE *verbed*."

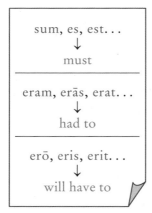

sum, es, est...
↓
must

eram, erās, erat...
↓
had to

erō, eris, erit...
↓
will have to

Nominative
plural
neuter

Gerundive:
nominative
plural neuter
agreeing with
signa

3rd Plural:
because the
subject signa
is a "they"

Signa **legenda sunt**.
Signs ⬦must be read⬦.

Gerundive:
nominative singular
agreeing with "you."
-us indicates that the
"you" is masculine.

2nd Singular:
indicates that the
subject is "you".
↓
No Nominative is
necessary.

Dūcendus erās.
⬦You had to be led⬦.

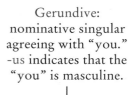

INDIRECT STATEMENT
According to the rules
of indirect statement. . .

nominative   sum/eram/erō
↓   ↓
accusative   esse/fuisse/futūrum esse

Dīcō **discipulās docendās esse**.
I say that ⬦the students must be taught⬦.

LITERAL MEANING
Note that the passive
periphrastic treats the
gerundive as an adjective
meaning "to be *verb*ed."
(See p. 255)

Signa legenda sunt.
The signs are to be read.
↓
The signs must be read.

PASSIVE PERIPHRASTIC

STANDARD – WITH DATIVE OF AGENT

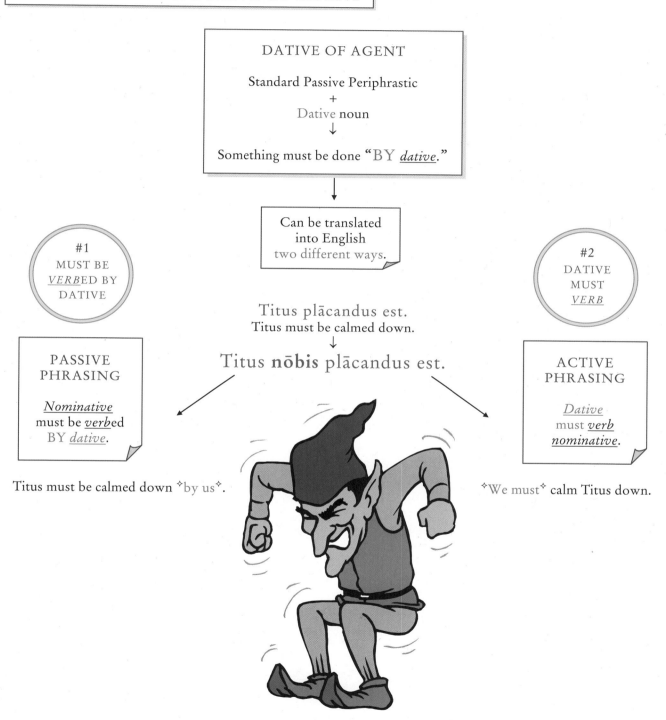

DATIVE OF AGENT

Standard Passive Periphrastic
+
Dative noun
↓
Something must be done "BY *dative*."

Can be translated
into English
two different ways.

#1
MUST BE
*VERB*ED BY
DATIVE

#2
DATIVE
MUST
VERB

Titus plācandus est.
Titus must be calmed down.
↓
Titus **nōbis** plācandus est.

PASSIVE
PHRASING

Nominative
must be *verb*ed
BY *dative*.

ACTIVE
PHRASING

Dative
must *verb*
nominative.

Titus must be calmed down ⟡by us⟡.

⟡We must⟡ calm Titus down.

Rogāvī cūr Titus **tibi** adligandus esset.
I asked why Titus had to be tied up ⟡by you⟡.
I asked why ⟡you had to⟡ tie up Titus.

Passive Periphrastic

IMPERSONAL

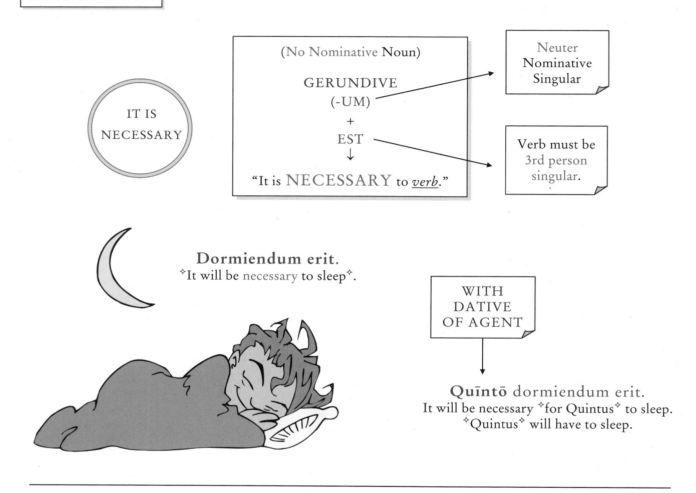

IT IS
NECESSARY

(No Nominative Noun)

GERUNDIVE
(-UM)
+
EST
↓
"It is NECESSARY to *verb*."

Neuter
Nominative
Singular

Verb must be
3rd person
singular.

Dormiendum erit.
◇It will be necessary to sleep◇.

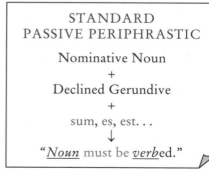

WITH
DATIVE
OF AGENT

Quīntō dormiendum erit.
It will be necessary ◇for Quintus◇ to sleep.
◇Quintus◇ will have to sleep.

STANDARD
PASSIVE PERIPHRASTIC

Nominative Noun
+
Declined Gerundive
+
sum, es, est. . .
↓
"*Noun* must be *verb*ed."

Pizza edenda est.
Pizza must be eaten.

IMPERSONAL
PASSIVE PERIPHRASTIC

Gerundive (-um)
+
est
↓
"It is necessary to *verb*."

Edendum est.
It is necessary to eat.

PASSIVE PERIPHRASTIC

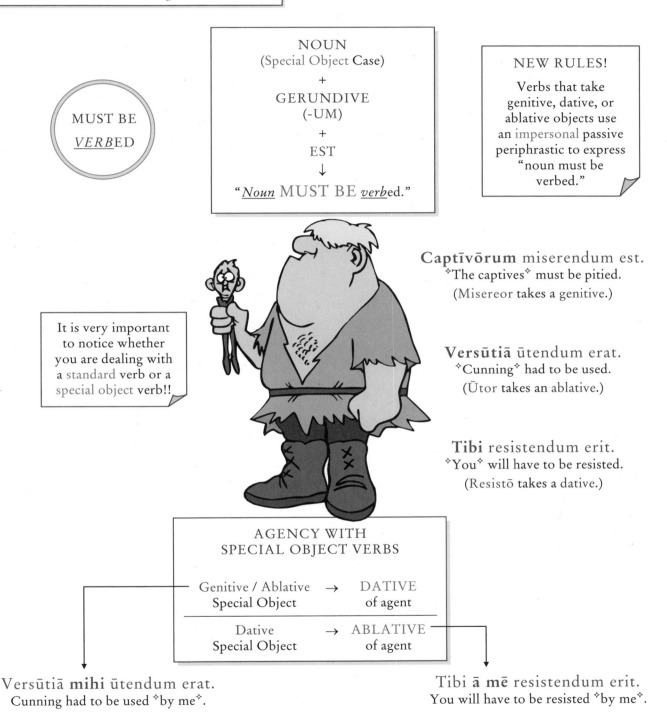

MUST BE
***VERB*ED**

NOUN
(Special Object **Case**)
+
GERUNDIVE
(-UM)
+
EST
↓
"*Noun* MUST BE *verb*ed."

NEW RULES!

Verbs that take genitive, dative, or ablative objects use an impersonal passive periphrastic to express "noun must be verbed."

It is very important to notice whether you are dealing with a standard verb or a special object verb!!

Captīvōrum miserendum est.
⬧The captives⬧ must be pitied.
(Misereor takes a genitive.)

Versūtiā ūtendum erat.
⬧Cunning⬧ had to be used.
(Ūtor takes an ablative.)

Tibi resistendum erit.
⬧You⬧ will have to be resisted.
(Resistō takes a dative.)

AGENCY WITH SPECIAL OBJECT VERBS

| Genitive / Ablative Special Object | → | DATIVE of agent |
| Dative Special Object | → | ABLATIVE of agent |

Versūtiā **mihi** ūtendum erat.
Cunning had to be used ⬧by me⬧.

Tibi **ā mē** resistendum erit.
You will have to be resisted ⬧by me⬧.

Captīvōrum **tibi** miserendum est.
The captives must be pitied ⬧by you⬧.

PASSIVE PERIPHRASTIC

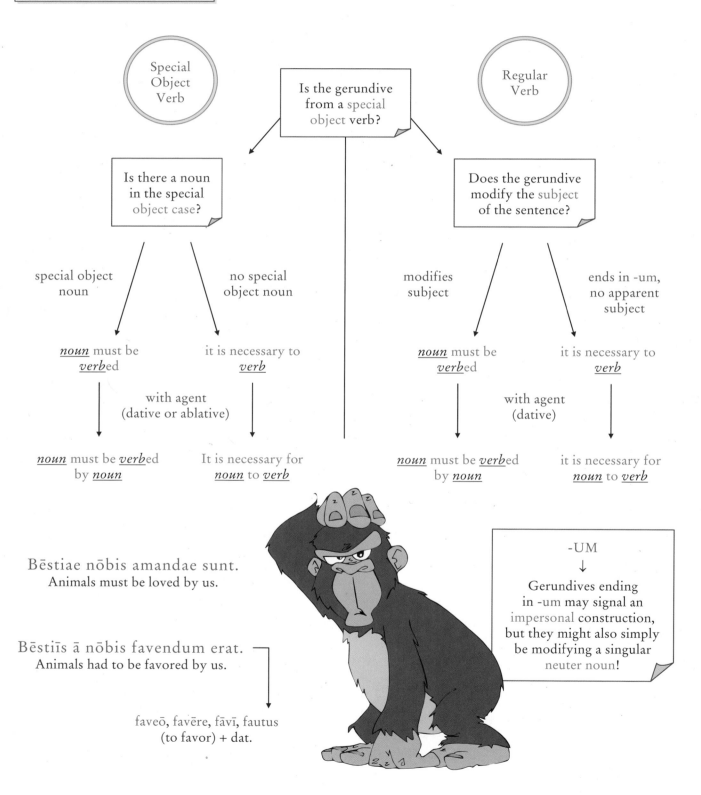

Special
Object
Verb

Is the gerundive
from a special
object verb?

Regular
Verb

Is there a noun
in the special
object case?

Does the gerundive
modify the subject
of the sentence?

special object
noun

no special
object noun

modifies
subject

ends in -um,
no apparent
subject

noun must be
_verb_ed

it is necessary to
verb

noun must be
_verb_ed

it is necessary to
verb

with agent
(dative or ablative)

with agent
(dative)

noun must be _verb_ed
by _noun_

It is necessary for
noun to _verb_

noun must be _verb_ed
by _noun_

it is necessary for
noun to _verb_

Bēstiae nōbis amandae sunt.
Animals must be loved by us.

Bēstiīs ā nōbis favendum erat.
Animals had to be favored by us.

faveō, favēre, fāvī, fautus
(to favor) + dat.

-UM
↓
Gerundives ending
in -um may signal an
impersonal construction,
but they might also simply
be modifying a singular
neuter noun!

SUPINE FORMS AND SYNTAX

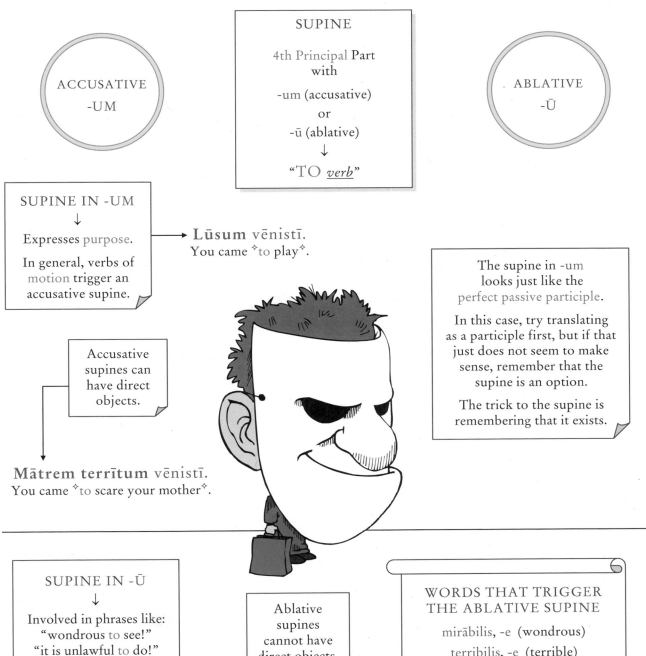

ACCUSATIVE -UM

ABLATIVE -Ū

SUPINE

4th Principal Part
with
-um (accusative)
or
-ū (ablative)
↓
"TO *verb*"

SUPINE IN -UM
↓
Expresses purpose.

In general, verbs of motion trigger an accusative supine.

Lūsum vēnistī.
You came ⬧to play⬧.

The supine in -um looks just like the perfect passive participle.

In this case, try translating as a participle first, but if that just does not seem to make sense, remember that the supine is an option.

The trick to the supine is remembering that it exists.

Accusative supines can have direct objects.

Mātrem terrītum vēnistī.
You came ⬧to scare your mother⬧.

SUPINE IN -Ū
↓
Involved in phrases like:
"wondrous to see!"
"it is unlawful to do!"

Ablative supines cannot have direct objects.

WORDS THAT TRIGGER THE ABLATIVE SUPINE

mirābilis, -e (wondrous)
terribilis, -e (terrible)
facilis, -e (easy)
difficilis, -e (difficult)
nefās est (it is unlawful)
fās est (it is lawful)
opus est (it is necessary)

Persōnam terribilem vīsū in ludō gerēbās.
At school you were wearing a mask terrible ⬧to see⬧.

Hoc nefās est factū!
This is unlawful ⬧to do⬧!

Translating "To"

Errāre est hūmānum.
⬧To err⬧ is human.

WHAT ROLE
does "to *verb*"
play in the sentence?

Omnia **scīre** volō.
I want ⬧to know⬧ everything.

Tē Rōmam **venīre** iubeō.
I order you ⬧to come⬧ to Rome.

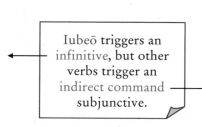

Iubeō triggers an infinitive, but other verbs trigger an indirect command subjunctive.

Tibi ōrō ut Rōmam **veniās**.
I beg you ⬧to come⬧ to Rome.

Vēnī ut tē **vidērem**.
I came ⬧to see⬧ you.

Ad tē **videndum** vēnī.
I came ⬧to see⬧ you.

Tē **vīsum** vēnī.
I came ⬧to see⬧ you.

Subjunctive	Gerund(ive)	Supine
Purpose Clause	ad + Accusative	Accusative

IMPERSONAL PASSIVE

IMPERSONAL PASSIVE

The passive voice can be used to indicate that *verb*ing occurs without specifying any particular subject.

There are a number of possible phrasings:

"*verb*ING OCCURS/TAKES PLACE"
"THERE IS *verb*ING"

Difficile est vāsa pulchra fōrmāre, sed dīligenter cotīdiē **labōrātur**.
It is difficult to fashion beautiful vessels, but ⁺working⁺ carefully ⁺takes place⁺ every day.

PERFECT SYSTEM

In the perfect system of tenses, the neuter ending -um is used on the 4th principal part.

In lūdō dē multīs rēbus **doctum est**.
⁺There was teaching⁺ about many things in school.

ACTIVE PHRASING

Often, impersonal passives can be phrased in the active.

You must rely on context to help you determine the most likely subject.

Difficile discipulīs est, sed dīligenter **labōrātur**.
It is difficult for the students, but ⁺they work⁺ carefully.

ALTERNATE FORMS

2ND PERSON SINGULAR PASSIVE PERSONAL ENDING

-r, **-ris**, -tur, -mur, -minī, -ntur

-ris   =   -re

(rogābe**ris**)   (rogābe**re**)

↓

⬧You will be asked⬧

3RD PERSON PLURAL PERFECT ACTIVE INDICATIVE

-ī, -istī, -it, -imus, -istis, **-erunt**

-ērunt   =   -ēre

(rogāvē**runt**)   (rogāvē**re**)

↓

⬧They asked⬧

Frāgīsne **dēlectāre**, soror?
Are you delighted by strawberries, sister?

(dēlectāre = dēlectāris)

Omnia frāga **devōrāvēre**.
⬧They devoured⬧ all the strawberries.

(devōrāvēre = devōrāvērunt)

↓

The -re form is tricky:
in the present tense it often
looks the same as the present
active infinitive.

SUM, ESSE, FUĪ, FUTŪRUS FUTURE ACTIVE INFINITIVE

futūrus esse = fore

Sciō Rōmānōs potentissimōs **fore**.
I know that the Romans ⬧will be⬧ very powerful.

(fore = futūrōs esse)

SUM, ESSE, FUĪ, FUTŪRUS IMPERFECT SUBJUNCTIVE

essem,
etc.   =   forem,
         etc.

essem, essēs, esset,   forem, forēs, foret,
essēmus, essētis, essent   forēmus, forētis, forent

Rogāvī num potentissimī **forētis**.
I asked if you (pl.) ⬧would be⬧ very powerful.

(forētis = essētis)

Noun, Adjective, and Pronoun Forms

FIRST Declension		SECOND Declension Masculine			SECOND Declension Neuter		THIRD Declension Masc./Fem.		THIRD Declension Neuter		THIRD I-STEM Masc./Fem.		THIRD I-STEM Neuter	
-a	-ae	-us/-ius, -r		-ī	-um	-a	-------	-ēs	-------	-a	-------	-ēs	-------	-ia
-ae	-ārum	-ī		-ōrum	-ī	-ōrum	-is	-um	-is	-um	-is	-ium	-is	-ium
-ae	-īs	-ō		-īs	-ō	-īs	-ī	-ibus	-ī	-ibus	-ī	-ibus	-ī	-ibus
-am	-ās	-um		-ōs	-um	-a	-em	-ēs	-------	-a	-em	-īs / -ēs	-------	-ia
-ā	-īs	-ō		-īs	-ō	-īs	-e	-ibus	-e	-ibus	-e	-ibus	-ī	-ibus
-a	-ae	-e/-ī, -r		-ī	-um	-a	-------	-ēs	-------	-a	-------	-ēs	-------	-ia

FOURTH Declension Masculine		FOURTH Declension Neuter		FIFTH Declension	
-us	-ūs	-ū	-ua	-ēs	-ēs
-ūs	-uum	-ūs	-uum	-eī	-ērum
-uī	-ibus	-ū	-ibus	-eī	-ēbus
-um	-ūs	-ū	-ua	-em	-ēs
-ū	-ibus	-ū	-ibus	-ē	-ēbus
-us	-ūs	-ū	-ua	-ēs	-ēs

2-1-2
ADJECTIVES
use the same forms
as 1st and 2nd
declension
nouns.

THIRD Declension ADJECTIVE			
-------	-ēs	-------	-ia
-is	-ium	-is	-ium
-ī	-ibus	-ī	-ibus
-em	-īs / -ēs	-------	-ia
-ī	-ibus	-ī	-ibus
-------	-ēs	-------	-ia

PERSONAL PRONOUNS (1st and 2nd Person)				REFLEXIVE PRONOUNS (1st, 2nd, 3rd Person)					
I	You	We	You (pl.)	Myself	Yourself	Ourselves	Yourselves	Himself	Themselves
ego	tū	nōs	vōs	----	----	----	----	----	----
meī	tuī	nostrum/-ī	vestrum/-ī	meī	tuī	nostrum/-ī	vestrum/-ī	suī	suī
mihi	tibi	nōbis	vōbis	mihi	tibi	nōbis	vōbis	sibi	sibi
mē	tē	nōs	vōs	mē	tē	nōs	vōs	sē	sē
mē	tē	nōbis	vōbis	mē	tē	nōbis	vōbis	sē	sē

HIC, HAEC, HOC (THIS/THESE)						ILLE, ILLA, ILLUD (THAT/THOSE)						IS, EA, ID (THIS/THESE, THAT/THOSE)					
hic	haec	hoc	hī	hae	haec	ille	illa	illud	illī	illae	illa	is	ea	id	eī	eae	ea
huius	huius	huius	hōrum	hārum	hōrum	illīus	illīus	illīus	illōrum	illārum	illōrum	eius	eius	eius	eōrum	eārum	eōrum
huic	huic	huic	hīs	hīs	hīs	illī	illī	illī	illīs	illīs	illīs	eī	eī	eī	eīs	eīs	eīs
hunc	hanc	hoc	hōs	hās	haec	illum	illam	illud	illōs	illās	illa	eum	eam	id	eōs	eās	ea
hōc	hāc	hōc	hīs	hīs	hīs	illō	illā	illō	illīs	illīs	illīs	eō	eā	eō	eīs	eīs	eīs

QUĪ, QUAE, QUOD (Relative Pronoun/Interrogative Adjective)						QUIS, QUID (Interrogative Pronoun)					
quī	quae	quod	quī	quae	quae	quis	quid	quī	quae	quae
cuius	cuius	cuius	quōrum	quārum	quōrum	cuius	cuius	quōrum	quārum	quōrum
cui	cui	cui	quibus	quibus	quibus	cui	cui	quibus	quibus	quibus
quem	quam	quod	quōs	quās	quae	quem	quid	quōs	quās	quae
quō	quā	quō	quibus	quibus	quibus	quō	quō	quibus	quibus	quibus

VERB FORMS

CHARACTERISTICS OF VERBS:
- **Person:** first, second, third
- **Number:** singular, plural
- **Voice:** active, passive
- **Mood:** indicative, imperative, infinitive, subjunctive, participle
- **Tense:** see chart below. . .

VERB TENSES						
	Present	Imperfect	Future	Perfect	Pluperfect	Future Perfect
Indicative	✓	✓	✓	✓	✓	✓
Imperative	✓		✓			
Infinitive	✓		✓	✓		
Subjunctive	✓	✓		✓	✓	
Participle	✓		✓	✓		

PRESENT STEM (from 2nd principal part)	PERFECT STEM (from 3rd principal part)	PARTICIPIAL STEM (from 4th principal part)
Indicative: Present Active & Passive Imperfect Active & Passive Future Active & Passive	**Indicative:** Perfect Active Pluperfect Active Future Perfect Active	**Indicative:** Perfect Passive Pluperfect Passive Future Perfect Passive
Infinitive: Present Active & Passive	**Infinitive** (active): Perfect Active	**Infinitive:** Perfect Passive Future Active & Passive
Imperative: Present Active & Passive Future Active & Passive	**Imperative:** ------	**Imperative:** ------
Subjunctive: Present Active & Passive Imperfect Active & Passive	**Subjunctive:** Perfect Active Pluperfect Active	**Subjunctive:** Perfect Passive Pluperfect Passive
Participle: Present Active Gerundive	**Participle:** ------	**Participle:** Perfect Passive Future Active

rogātus/a/um sum, es, est
rogātī/ae/a sumus, estis, sunt

Remember: many forms that are based on the 4th principal part can be declined with 2-1-2 endings.

rogātus/a/um sim, sīs, sit
rogātī/ae/a sīmus, sītis, sint

INDICATIVE

Forms such as rogātus est and rogātī sunt are listed in the charts that follow, but feminine and neuter forms are also possible.

SUBJUNCTIVE

Forms such as rogātus sit and rogātī sint are listed in the charts that follow, but feminine and neuter forms are also possible.

FIRST CONJUGATION

rogō, rogāre, rogāvī, rogātus (to ask)

-ĀRE

INDICATIVE

ACTIVE

Present	_Imperfect_	_Future_		_Perfect_	_Pluperfect_	_Future Perfect_
rogō	rogābam	rogābō		rogāvī	rogāveram	rogāverō
rogās	rogābās	rogābis		rogāvistī	rogāverās	rogāveris
rogat	rogābat	rogābit		rogāvit	rogāverat	rogāverit
rogāmus	rogābāmus	rogābimus		rogāvimus	rogāverāmus	rogāverimus
rogātis	rogābātis	rogābitis		rogāvistis	rogāverātis	rogāveritis
rogant	rogābant	rogābunt		rogāvērunt	rogāverant	rogāverint

PASSIVE

Present	_Imperfect_	_Future_		_Perfect_	_Pluperfect_	_Future Perfect_
rogor	rogābar	rogābor		rogātus sum	rogātus eram	rogātus erō
rogāris	rogābāris	rogāberis		rogātus es	rogātus erās	rogātus eris
rogātur	rogābātur	rogābitur		rogātus est	rogātus erat	rogātus erit
rogāmur	rogābāmur	rogābimur	-us, -a, -um	rogātī sumus	rogātī erāmus	rogātī erimus
rogāminī	rogābāminī	rogābiminī	-ī, -ae, -a	rogātae estis	rogātī erātis	rogātī eritis
rogantur	rogābantur	rogābuntur		rogāta sunt	rogātī erant	rogātī erunt

IMPERATIVE

PRESENT ACTIVE			PRESENT PASSIVE	
2nd Person	_3rd Person_		_2nd Person_	_3rd Person_
rogā / rogāte	------		rogāre / rogāminī	------

FUTURE ACTIVE			FUTURE PASSIVE	
2nd Person	_3rd Person_		_2nd Person_	_3rd Person_
rogātō / rogātōte	rogātō / rogantō		rogātor / -----	rogātor / rogantor

INFINITIVE

	ACTIVE				PASSIVE	
Present	_Perfect_	_Future_		_Present_	_Perfect_	_Future_
rogāre	rogāvisse	rogātūrus, -a, -um esse		rogārī	rogātus, -a, -um esse	rogātum īrī

PARTICIPLE

Present Active	_Perfect Passive_	_Future Active_	_Gerundive_
rogāns, rogantis	rogātus, -a, -um	rogātūrus, -a, -um	rogandus, -a, -um

GERUND	SUPINE
amandī, -ō, -um, -ō	amātum / amātū

SUBJUNCTIVE

ACTIVE

Present	_Imperfect_		_Perfect_	_Pluperfect_
rogem	rogārem		rogāverim	rogāvissem
rogēs	rogārēs		rogāverīs	rogāvissēs
roget	rogāret		rogāverit	rogāvisset
rogēmus	rogārēmus		rogāverīmus	rogāvissēmus
rogētis	rogārētis		rogāverītis	rogāvissētis
rogent	rogārent		rogāverint	rogāvissent

PASSIVE

Present	_Imperfect_		_Perfect_	_Pluperfect_
roger	rogārer		rogātus sim	rogātus essem
rogēris	rogārēris		rogātus sīs	rogātus essēs
rogetur	rogārētur		rogātus sit	rogātus esset
rogēmur	rogārēmur	-us, -a, -um	rogātī sīmus	rogātī essēmus
rogēminī	rogārēminī	-ī, -ae, -a	rogātī sītis	rogātī essētis
rogentur	rogārentur		rogātī sint	rogātī essent

SECOND CONJUGATION

doceō, docēre, docuī, doctus (to teach)

-ĒRE

INDICATIVE

ACTIVE

Present	Imperfect	Future		Perfect	Pluperfect	Future Perfect
doceō	docēbam	docēbō		docuī	docueram	docuerō
docēs	docēbās	docēbis		docuistī	docuerās	docueris
docet	docēbat	docēbit		docuit	docuerat	docuerit
docēmus	docēbāmus	docēbimus		docuimus	docuerāmus	docuerimus
docētis	docēbātis	docēbitis		docuistis	docuerātis	docueritis
docent	docēbant	docēbunt		docuērunt	docuerant	docuerint

PASSIVE

Present	Imperfect	Future		Perfect	Pluperfect	Future Perfect
doceor	docēbar	docēbor		doctus sum	doctus eram	doctus erō
docēris	docēbāris	docēberis		doctus es	doctus erās	doctus eris
docētur	docēbātur	docēbitur	-us, -a, -um	doctus est	doctus erat	doctus erit
docēmur	docēbāmur	docēbimur	-ī, -ae, -a	doctī sumus	doctī erāmus	doctī erimus
docēminī	docēbāminī	docēbiminī		doctī estis	doctī erātis	doctī eritis
docentur	docēbantur	docēbuntur		doctī sunt	doctī erant	doctī erunt

IMPERATIVE

PRESENT ACTIVE
2nd Person: docē / docēte 3rd Person: -----

PRESENT PASSIVE
2nd Person: docēre / docēminī 3rd Person: -----

FUTURE ACTIVE
2nd Person: docētō / docētōte 3rd Person: docētō / docentō

FUTURE PASSIVE
2nd Person: docētor / ----- 3rd Person: docētor / docentor

INFINITIVE

ACTIVE
Present: docēre Perfect: docuisse Future: doctūrus, -a, -um esse

PASSIVE
Present: docērī Perfect: doctus, -a, -um esse Future: doctum īrī

PARTICIPLE

Present Active: docēns, docentis Perfect Passive: doctus, -a, -um Future Active: doctūrus, -a, -um Gerundive: docendus, -a, -um

GERUND
docendī, -ō, -um, -ō

SUPINE
doctum / doctū

SUBJUNCTIVE

ACTIVE

Present	Imperfect		Perfect	Pluperfect
doceam	docērem		docuerim	docuissem
doceās	docērēs		docuerīs	docuissēs
doceat	docēret		docuerit	docuisset
doceāmus	docērēmus		docuerīmus	docuissēmus
doceātis	docērētis		docuerītis	docuissētis
doceant	docērent		docuerint	docuissent

PASSIVE

Present	Imperfect		Perfect	Pluperfect
docear	docērer		doctus sim	doctus essem
doceāris	docērēris		doctus sīs	doctus essēs
doceātur	docērētur	-us, -a, -um	doctus sit	doctus esset
doceāmur	docērēmur	-ī, -ae, -a	doctī sīmus	doctī essēmus
doceāminī	docērēminī		doctī sītis	doctī essētis
doceantur	docērentur		doctī sint	doctī essent

THIRD CONJUGATION

mittō, mittere, mīsī, missus (to send)

-ERE

INDICATIVE

ACTIVE

Present	_Imperfect_	_Future_		_Perfect_	_Pluperfect_	_Future Perfect_
mittō	mittēbam	mittam		mīsī	mīseram	mīserō
mittis	mittēbās	mittēs		mīsistī	mīserās	mīseris
mittit	mittēbat	mittet		mīsit	mīserat	mīserit
mittimus	mittēbāmus	mittēmus		mīsimus	mīserāmus	mīserimus
mittitis	mittēbātis	mittētis		mīsistis	mīserātis	mīseritis
mittunt	mittēbant	mittent		mīsērunt	mīserant	mīserint

PASSIVE

Present	_Imperfect_	_Future_		_Perfect_	_Pluperfect_	_Future Perfect_
mittor	mittēbar	mittar		missus sum	missus eram	missus erō
mitteris	mittēbāris	mittēris	-us, -a, -um	missus es	missus erās	missus eris
mittitur	mittēbātur	mittētur	-ī, -ae, -a	missus est	missus erat	missus erit
mittimur	mittēbāmur	mittēmur		missī sumus	missī erāmus	missī erimus
mittiminī	mittēbāminī	mittēminī		missī estis	missī erātis	missī eritis
mittuntur	mittēbantur	mittentur		missī sunt	missī erant	missī erunt

IMPERATIVE

PRESENT ACTIVE		PRESENT PASSIVE	
2nd Person	_3rd Person_	_2nd Person_	_3rd Person_
mitte / mittite	-----	mittere / mittiminī	-----

FUTURE ACTIVE		FUTURE PASSIVE	
2nd Person	_3rd Person_	_2nd Person_	_3rd Person_
mittitō / mittitōte	mittitō / mittuntō	mittitor / -----	mittitor / mittuntor

INFINITIVE

	ACTIVE				PASSIVE	
Present	_Perfect_	_Future_		_Present_	_Perfect_	_Future_
mittere	mīsisse	missūrus, -a, -um esse		mittī	missus, -a, -um esse	missum īrī

PARTICIPLE

Present Active	_Perfect Passive_	_Future Active_	_Gerundive_
mittēns, mittentis	missus, -a, -um	missūrus, -a, -um	mittendus, -a, -um

GERUND	**SUPINE**
mittendī, -ō, -um, -ō	missum / missū

SUBJUNCTIVE

ACTIVE

Present	_Imperfect_		_Perfect_	_Pluperfect_
mittam	mitterem		mīserim	mīsissem
mittās	mitterēs		mīserīs	mīsissēs
mittat	mitteret		mīserit	mīsisset
mittāmus	mitterēmus		mīserīmus	mīsissēmus
mittātis	mitterētis		mīserītis	mīsissētis
mittant	mitterent		mīserint	mīsissent

PASSIVE

Present	_Imperfect_		_Perfect_	_Pluperfect_
mittar	mitterer		missus sim	missus essem
mittāris	mitterēris		missus sīs	missus essēs
mittātur	mitterētur	-us, -a, -um	missus sit	missus esset
mittāmur	mitterēmur	-ī, -ae, -a	missī sīmus	missī essēmus
mittāminī	mitterēminī		missī sītis	missī essētis
mittantur	mitterentur		missī sint	missī essent

THIRD -IO CONJUGATION

capiō, capere, cēpī, captus (to take, seize)

-IŌ, -ERE

INDICATIVE

ACTIVE

Present	*Imperfect*	*Future*		*Perfect*	*Pluperfect*	*Future Perfect*
capiō	capiēbam	capiam		cēpī	cēperam	cēperō
capis	capiēbās	capiēs		cēpistī	cēperās	cēperis
capit	capiēbat	capiet		cēpit	cēperat	cēperit
capimus	capiēbāmus	capiēmus		cēpimus	cēperāmus	cēperimus
capitis	capiēbātis	capiētis		cēpistis	cēperātis	cēperitis
capiunt	capiēbant	capient		cēpērunt	cēperant	cēperint

PASSIVE

Present	*Imperfect*	*Future*		*Perfect*	*Pluperfect*	*Future Perfect*
capior	capiēbar	capiar		captus sum	captus eram	captus erō
caperis	capiēbāris	capiēris		captus es	captus erās	captus eris
capitur	capiēbātur	capiētur	-us, -a, -um	captus est	captus erat	captus erit
capimur	capiēbāmur	capiēmur	-ī, -ae, -a	captī sumus	captī erāmus	captī erimus
capiminī	capiēbāminī	capiēminī		captī estis	captī erātis	captī eritis
capiuntur	capiēbantur	capientur		captī sunt	captī erant	captī erunt

IMPERATIVE

PRESENT ACTIVE		PRESENT PASSIVE	
2nd Person	*3rd Person*	*2nd Person*	*3rd Person*
cape / capite	-----	capere / capiminī	-----
FUTURE ACTIVE		FUTURE PASSIVE	
2nd Person	*3rd Person*	*2nd Person*	*3rd Person*
capitō / capitōte	capitō / capiuntō	capitor / -----	capitor / capiuntor

INFINITIVE

	ACTIVE			PASSIVE	
Present	*Perfect*	*Future*	*Present*	*Perfect*	*Future*
capere	cēpisse	captūrus, -a, -um esse	capī	captus, -a, -um esse	captum īrī

PARTICIPLE

Present Active	*Perfect Passive*	*Future Active*	*Gerundive*
capiēns, capientis	captus, -a, -um	captūrus, -a, -um	capiendus, -a, -um

GERUND	**SUPINE**
capiendī, -ō, -um, -ō	captum / captū

SUBJUNCTIVE

ACTIVE

Present	*Imperfect*		*Perfect*	*Pluperfect*
capiam	caperem		cēperim	cēpissem
capiās	caperēs		cēperīs	cēpissēs
capiat	caperet		cēperit	cēpisset
capiāmus	caperēmus		cēperīmus	cēpissēmus
capiātis	caperētis		cēperītis	cēpissētis
capiant	caperent		cēperint	cēpissent

PASSIVE

Present	*Imperfect*		*Perfect*	*Pluperfect*
capiar	caperer		captus sim	captus essem
capiāris	caperēris		captus sīs	captus essēs
capiātur	caperētur	-us, -a, -um	captus sit	captus esset
capiāmur	caperēmur	-ī, -ae, -a	captī sīmus	captī essēmus
capiāminī	caperēminī		captī sītis	captī essētis
capiantur	caperentur		captī sint	captī essent

FOURTH CONJUGATION

audiō, audīre, audīvī, audītus (to hear, listen)

-IRE

INDICATIVE

ACTIVE

Present	*Imperfect*	*Future*		*Perfect*	*Pluperfect*	*Future Perfect*
audiō	audiēbam	audiam		audīvī	audīveram	audīverō
audīs	audiēbās	audiēs		audīvistī	audīverās	audīveris
audit	audiēbat	audiet		audīvit	audīverat	audīverit
audīmus	audiēbāmus	audiēmus		audīvimus	audīverāmus	audīverimus
audītis	audiēbātis	audiētis		audīvistis	audīverātis	audīveritis
audiunt	audiēbant	audient		audīvērunt	audīverant	audīverint

PASSIVE

Present	*Imperfect*	*Future*		*Perfect*	*Pluperfect*	*Future Perfect*
audior	audiēbar	audiar		audītus sum	audītus eram	audītus erō
audīris	audiēbāris	audiēris		audītus es	audītus erās	audītus eris
audītur	audiēbātur	audiētur		audītus est	audītus erat	audītus erit
audīmur	audiēbāmur	audiēmur		audītī sumus	audītī erāmus	audītī erimus
audīminī	audiēbāminī	audiēminī		audītī estis	audītī erātis	audītī eritis
audiuntur	audiēbantur	audientur		audītī sunt	audītī erant	audītī erunt

-us, -a, -um
-ī, -ae, -a

IMPERATIVE

PRESENT ACTIVE

2nd Person	*3rd Person*
audī / audīte	-----

FUTURE ACTIVE

2nd Person	*3rd Person*
audītō / audītōte	audītō / audiuntō

PRESENT PASSIVE

2nd Person	*3rd Person*
audīre / audīminī	-----

FUTURE PASSIVE

2nd Person	*3rd Person*
audītor / -----	audītor / audiuntor

INFINITIVE

ACTIVE

Present	*Perfect*	*Future*
audīre	audīvisse	audītūrus, -a, -um esse

PASSIVE

Present	*Perfect*	*Future*
audīrī	audītus, -a, -um esse	audītum īrī

PARTICIPLE

Present Active	*Perfect Passive*	*Future Active*	*Gerundive*
audiēns, audientis	audītus, -a, -um	audītūrus, -a, -um	audiendus, -a, -um

GERUND

audiendī, -ō, -um, -ō

SUPINE

audītum / audītū

SUBJUNCTIVE

ACTIVE

Present	*Imperfect*		*Perfect*	*Pluperfect*
audiam	audīrem		audīverim	audīvissem
audiās	audīrēs		audīverīs	audīvissēs
audiat	audīret		audīverit	audīvisset
audiāmus	audīrēmus		audīverīmus	audīvissēmus
audiātis	audīrētis		audīverītis	audīvissētis
audiant	audīrent		audīverint	audīvissent

PASSIVE

Present	*Imperfect*		*Perfect*	*Pluperfect*
audiar	audīrer		auditus sim	auditus essem
audiāris	audīrēris		auditus sīs	auditus essēs
audiātur	audīrētur		auditus sit	auditus esset
audiāmur	audīrēmur		audītī sīmus	audītī essēmus
audiāminī	audīrēminī		audītī sītis	audītī essētis
audiantur	audīrentur		audītī sint	audītī essent

-us, -a, -um
-ī, -ae, -a

SUM, ESSE, FUĪ, FUTŪRUS

(to be)

INDICATIVE

ACTIVE

Present	_Imperfect_	_Future_	_Perfect_	_Pluperfect_	_Future Perfect_
sum	eram	erō	fuī	fueram	fuerō
es	erās	eris	fuistī	fuerās	fueris
est	erat	erit	fuit	fuerat	fuerit
sumus	erāmus	erimus	fuimus	fuerāmus	fuerimus
estis	erātis	eritis	fuistis	fuerātis	fueritis
sunt	erant	erunt	fuērunt	fuerant	fuerint

IMPERATIVE

PRESENT ACTIVE

2nd Person	_3rd Person_
es / este	-----

FUTURE ACTIVE

2nd Person	_3rd Person_
estō / estōte	estō / suntō

INFINITIVE

ACTIVE

Present	_Perfect_	_Future_
esse	fuisse	futūrus, -a, -um esse
		*fore

PARTICIPLE

Present Active	_Perfect Passive_	_Future Active_	_Gerundive_
-----	-----	futūrus, -a, -um	-----

GERUND

SUPINE

SUBJUNCTIVE

ACTIVE

Present	_Imperfect_		_Perfect_	_Pluperfect_
sim	essem	*forem	fuerim	fuissem
sīs	essēs	*forēs	fueris	fuissēs
sit	esset	*foret	fuerit	fuisset
sīmus	essēmus	*forēmus	fuerimus	fuissēmus
sītis	essētis	*forētis	fueritis	fuissētis
sint	essent	*forent	fuerint	fuissent

*Note the alternate forms of the future active infinitive and the imperfect subjunctive.

Possum, Posse, Potuī

(to be able)

INDICATIVE
ACTIVE

Present	*Imperfect*	*Future*	*Perfect*	*Pluperfect*	*Future Perfect*
possum	poteram	poterō	potuī	potueram	potuerō
potes	poterās	poteris	potuistī	potuerās	potueris
potest	poterat	poterit	potuit	potuerat	potuerit
possumus	poterāmus	poterimus	potuimus	potuerāmus	potuerimus
potestis	poterātis	poteritis	potuistis	potuerātis	potueritis
possunt	poterant	poterunt	potuērunt	potuerant	potuerint

IMPERATIVE	INFINITIVE

INFINITIVE
ACTIVE

Present	*Perfect*	*Future*
posse	potuisse	-----

IMPERATIVE

PARTICIPLE

Present Active	*Perfect Passive*	*Future Active*	*Gerundive*
potēns, potentis	-----	-----	-----

GERUND	SUPINE
-----	-----

SUBJUNCTIVE
ACTIVE

Present	*Imperfect*	*Perfect*	*Pluperfect*
possim	possem	potuerim	potuissem
possīs	possēs	potuerīs	potuissēs
possit	posset	potuerit	potuisset
possīmus	possēmus	potuerīmus	potuissēmus
possītis	possētis	potuerītis	potuissētis
possint	possent	potuerint	potuissent

VOLŌ, VELLE, VOLUĪ

(to wish, want)

INDICATIVE
ACTIVE

Present	Imperfect	Future	Perfect	Pluperfect	Future Perfect
volō	volēbam	volam	voluī	volueram	voluerō
vīs	volēbās	volēs	voluistī	voluerās	volueris
vult	volēbat	volet	voluit	voluerat	voluerit
volumus	volēbāmus	volēmus	voluimus	voluerāmus	voluerimus
vultis	volēbātis	volētis	voluistis	voluerātis	volueritis
volunt	volēbant	volent	voluērunt	voluerant	voluerint

IMPERATIVE	**INFINITIVE**		
		ACTIVE	
	Present	Perfect	Future
-----	velle	voluisse	-----

PARTICIPLE

Present Active	Perfect Passive	Future Active	Gerundive
volēns, volentis	-----	-----	-----

GERUND	**SUPINE**
-----	-----

SUBJUNCTIVE
ACTIVE

Present	Imperfect	Perfect	Pluperfect
velim	vellem	voluerim	voluissem
velīs	vellēs	voluerīs	voluissēs
velit	vellet	voluerit	voluisset
velīmus	vellēmus	voluerīmus	voluissēmus
velītis	vellētis	voluerītis	voluissētis
velint	vellent	voluerint	voluissent

NŌLŌ, NŌLLE, NŌLUĪ

(to not wish, not want, refuse)

INDICATIVE

ACTIVE

Present	Imperfect	Future	Perfect	Pluperfect	Future Perfect
nōlō	nōlēbam	nōlam	nōluī	nōlueram	nōluerō
nōn vīs	nōlēbās	nōlēs	nōluistī	nōluerās	nōlueris
nōn vult	nōlēbat	nōlet	nōluit	nōluerat	nōluerit
nōlumus	nōlēbāmus	nōlēmus	nōluimus	nōluerāmus	nōluerimus
nōn vultis	nōlēbātis	nōlētis	nōluistis	nōluerātis	nōlueritis
nōlunt	nōlēbant	nōlent	nōluērunt	nōluerant	nōluerint

IMPERATIVE

PRESENT ACTIVE

2nd Person	3rd Person
nōlī / nōlīte	-----

FUTURE ACTIVE

2nd Person	3rd Person
nōlītō / nōlītōte	nōlītō / nōluntō

INFINITIVE

ACTIVE

Present	Perfect	Future
nōlle	nōluisse	-----

PARTICIPLE

Present Active	Perfect Passive	Future Active	Gerundive
nōlēns, nōlentis	-----	-----	-----

GERUND

SUPINE

SUBJUNCTIVE

ACTIVE

Present	Imperfect	Perfect	Pluperfect
nōlim	nōllem	nōluerim	nōluissem
nōlīs	nōllēs	nōluerīs	nōluissēs
nōlit	nōllet	nōluerit	nōluisset
nōlīmus	nōllēmus	nōluerīmus	nōluissēmus
nōlītis	nōllētis	nōluerītis	nōluissētis
nōlint	nōllent	nōluerint	nōluissent

Mālō, Mālle, Māluī

(to prefer)

INDICATIVE

Active

Present	Imperfect	Future	Perfect	Pluperfect	Future Perfect
mālō	mālēbam	mālam	māluī	mālueram	māluerō
māvīs	mālēbās	mālēs	māluistī	māluerās	mālueris
māvult	mālēbat	mālet	māluit	māluerat	māluerit
mālumus	mālēbāmus	mālēmus	māluimus	māluerāmus	māluerimus
māvultis	mālēbātis	mālētis	māluistis	māluerātis	mālueritis
mālunt	mālēbant	mālent	māluērunt	māluerant	māluerint

IMPERATIVE	INFINITIVE

IMPERATIVE

INFINITIVE

Active

Present	Perfect	Future
mālle	māluisse	-----

PARTICIPLE

Present Active	Perfect Passive	Future Active	Gerundive
-----	-----	-----	-----

GERUND

SUPINE

SUBJUNCTIVE

Active

Present	Imperfect	Perfect	Pluperfect
mālim	māllem	māluerim	māluissem
mālīs	māllēs	māluerīs	māluissēs
mālit	māllet	māluerit	māluisset
mālīmus	māllēmus	māluerīmus	māluissēmus
mālītis	māllētis	māluerītis	māluissētis
mālint	māllent	māluerint	māluissent

Eō, Īre, Īvī or Iī, Itus

(to go)

INDICATIVE

ACTIVE

Present	Imperfect	Future
eō	ībam	ībō
īs	ībās	ībis
it	ībat	ībit
īmus	ībāmus	ībimus
ītis	ībātis	ībitis
eunt	ībant	ībunt

Perfect		Pluperfect		Future Perfect	
īvī	iī	īveram	ieram	īverō	ierō
īvistī	īstī	īverās	ierās	īveris	ieris
īvit	iit	īverat	ierat	īverit	ierit
īvimus	iimus	īverāmus	ierāmus	īverimus	ierimus
īvistis	īstis	īverātis	ierātis	īveritis	ieritis
īvērunt	iērunt	īverant	ierant	īverint	ierint

PASSIVE

Present	Imperfect	Future
eor	ībar	ībor
īris	ībāris	īberis
ītur	ībātur	ībitur
īmur	ībāmur	ībimur
īminī	ībāminī	ībiminī
euntur	ībantur	ībuntur

-us, -a, -um
-ī, -ae, -a →

Perfect	Pluperfect	Future Perfect
itus sum	itus eram	itus erō
itus es	itus erās	itus eris
itus est	itus erat	itus erit
itī sumus	itī erāmus	itī erimus
itī estis	itī erātis	itī eritis
itī sunt	itī erant	itī erunt

IMPERATIVE

	PRESENT ACTIVE			PRESENT PASSIVE	
2nd Person		3rd Person	2nd Person		3rd Person
ī / īte		-----	īre / īminī		-----
	FUTURE ACTIVE			FUTURE PASSIVE	
2nd Person		3rd Person	2nd Person		3rd Person
ītō / ītōte		ītō / euntō	ītor / -----		ītor / euntor

INFINITIVE

	ACTIVE			PASSIVE	
Present	Perfect	Future	Present	Perfect	Future
īre	īvisse / īsse	itūrus, -a, -um esse	īrī	itus, -a, -um esse	itum īrī

PARTICIPLE

Present Active	Perfect Passive	Future Active	Gerundive
iēns, euntis	itus, -a, -um	itūrus, a, -um	eundus, -a -um

GERUND	SUPINE
eundī, -ō, -um, -ō	itum / itū

SUBJUNCTIVE

ACTIVE

Present	Imperfect
eam	īrem
eās	īrēs
eat	īret
eāmus	īrēmus
eātis	īrētis
eant	īrent

Perfect		Pluperfect	
īverim	ierim	īvissem	īssem
īverīs	ierīs	īvissēs	īssēs
īverit	ierit	īvisset	īsset
īverīmus	ierīmus	īvissēmus	īssēmus
īverītis	ierītis	īvissētis	īssētis
īverint	ierint	īvissent	īssent

PASSIVE

Present	Imperfect
ear	īrer
eāris	īrēris
eātur	īrētur
eāmur	īrēmur
eāminī	īrēminī
eantur	īrentur

-us, -a, -um
-ī, -ae, -a →

Perfect	Pluperfect
itus sim	itus essem
itus sīs	itus essēs
itus sit	itus esset
itī sīmus	itī essēmus
itī sītis	itī essētis
itī sint	itī essent

Ferō, Ferre, Tulī, Lātus

(to bring, bear, endure)

INDICATIVE

ACTIVE

Present	Imperfect	Future		Perfect	Pluperfect	Future Perfect
ferō	ferēbam	feram		tulī	tuleram	tulerō
fers	ferēbās	ferēs		tulistī	tulerās	tuleris
fert	ferēbat	feret		tulit	tulerat	tulerit
ferimus	ferēbāmus	ferēmus		tulimus	tulerāmus	tulerimus
fertis	ferēbātis	ferētis		tulistis	tulerātis	tuleritis
ferunt	ferēbant	ferent		tulērunt	tulerant	tulerint

PASSIVE

Present	Imperfect	Future		Perfect	Pluperfect	Future Perfect
feror	ferēbar	ferar		lātus sum	lātus eram	lātus erō
ferris	ferēbāris	ferēris		lātus es	lātus erās	lātus eris
fertur	ferēbātur	ferētur		lātus est	lātus erat	lātus erit
ferimur	ferēbāmur	ferēmur		lātī sumus	lātī erāmus	lātī erimus
feriminī	ferēbāminī	ferēminī		lātī estis	lātī erātis	lātī eritis
feruntur	ferēbantur	ferentur		lātī sunt	lātī erant	lātī erunt

-us, -a, -um
-ī, -ae, -a →

IMPERATIVE

PRESENT ACTIVE

2nd Person	3rd Person
fer / ferte	-----

FUTURE ACTIVE

2nd Person	3rd Person
fertō / fertōte	fertō / feruntō

PRESENT PASSIVE

2nd Person	3rd Person
ferre / feriminī	-----

FUTURE PASSIVE

2nd Person	3rd Person
fertor / -----	fertor / feruntor

INFINITIVE

ACTIVE

Present	Perfect	Future
ferre	tulisse	lātūrus, -a, -um esse

PASSIVE

Present	Perfect	Future
ferrī	lātus, -a, -um esse	lātum īrī

PARTICIPLE

Present Active	Perfect Passive	Future Active	Gerundive
ferēns, ferentis	lātus, -a, -um	lātūrus, -a, -um	ferendus, -a, -um

GERUND	SUPINE
ferendī, -ō, -um, -ō	lātum / lātū

SUBJUNCTIVE

ACTIVE

Present	Imperfect		Perfect	Pluperfect
feram	ferrem		tulerim	tulissem
ferās	ferrēs		tulerīs	tulissēs
ferat	ferret		tulerit	tulisset
ferāmus	ferrēmus		tulerīmus	tulissēmus
ferātis	ferrētis		tulerītis	tulissētis
ferant	ferrent		tulerint	tulissent

PASSIVE

Present	Imperfect		Perfect	Pluperfect
ferar	ferrer		lātus sim	lātus essem
ferāris	ferrēris		lātus sīs	lātus essēs
ferātur	ferrētur		lātus sit	lātus esset
ferāmur	ferrēmur		lātī sīmus	lātī essēmus
ferāminī	ferrēminī		lātī sītis	lātī essētis
ferantur	ferrentur		lātī sint	lātī essent

-us, -a, -um
-ī, -ae, -a →

Fīō, Fierī, Factus Sum

(to become, be made, happen)

INDICATIVE

Present	_Imperfect_	_Future_		_Perfect_	_Pluperfect_	_Future Perfect_
fīō	fīēbam	fīam		factus sum	factus eram	factus erō
fīs	fīēbās	fīēs		factus es	factus erās	factus eris
fit	fīēbat	fīet	-us, -a, -um	factus est	factus erat	factus erit
fīmus	fīēbāmus	fīēmus	-ī, -ae, -a →	factī sumus	factī erāmus	factī erimus
fītis	fīēbātis	fīētis		factī estis	factī erātis	factī eritis
fīunt	fīēbant	fīent		factī sunt	factī erant	factī erunt

IMPERATIVE (rare)

PRESENT ACTIVE

2nd Person	_3rd Person_
fī / fīte	-----

FUTURE ACTIVE

2nd Person	_3rd Person_
fītō / fītōte	fītō / fīuntō

INFINITIVE

Present	_Perfect_	_Future_
fierī	factus, -a, -um esse	factum īrī

PARTICIPLE

Present Active	_Perfect Passive_	_Future Active_	_Gerundive_
-----	factus, -a, -um	-----	faciendus, -a, -um

GERUND

SUPINE

SUBJUNCTIVE

Present	_Imperfect_	PASSIVE	_Perfect_	_Pluperfect_
fīam	fierem		factus sim	factus essem
fīās	fierēs		factus sīs	factus essēs
fīat	fieret	-us, -a, -um	factus sit	factus esset
fīāmus	fierēmus	-ī, -ae, -a →	factī sīmus	factī essēmus
fīātis	fierētis		factī sītis	factī essētis
fīant	fierent		factī sint	factī essent

BOLCHAZY-CARDUCCI PUBLISHERS, INC.

LATINA MYTHICA
*Intermediate Latin
textbook/reader, mythology*

xiv + 202pp. (2006) paperback, ISBN 0-86516-599-8

COLUMBUS' VOYAGE
*Easy Latin textbook/reader,
American history*

xvi + 40pp. (2005) paperback, ISBN 0-86516-613-7

CONVERSATIONAL LATIN
*Easy Latin textbook/reader, Latin phrase book
and dictionary of modern topics*

416 pp. (2006) hardbound, ISBN 0-86516-645-5,
and paperback, ISBN 0-86516-622-6

WORDS AND IDEAS
Latin vocabulary for English

xxvii + 281pp. (2002) paperback, ISBN 0-86516-485-1

WORDS AND IDEAS KEY
(forthcoming) ISBN 0-86516-637-4

CARMINA POPULARIA
Popular songs in Latin on CD

running time 49:21 (2004) Audio CD, order number 00003

WORDS OF WISDOM
*Latin Proverbs, English translations,
pronunciation, parsing program*

(2000) CD-ROM, ISBN 0-86516-502-5

THE CLASSICAL
MYTHOLOGY WORKBOOK
*Comprehensive mythology presented with
illustrations, exercises and derivatives*

(forthcoming) ISBN 0-86516-573-4

VERGIL FOR BEGINNERS
Easy Latin textbook/reader

(forthcoming) ISBN 0-86516-628-5

BUILD YOUR ENGLISH
WORD POWER
*Latin Vocabulary for English,
grades 4–12*

Student edition: 32pp. (1997) paperback, ISBN 0-86516-354-5

Teacher's manual: 53pp. (1997) paperback, ISBN 0-86516-392-8

CATTUS PETASATUS
*Latin version intended for
oral presentation and reading
(rhyming Latin)*

80pp. (2000) hardbound, ISBN 0-86516-472-X,
and papberback, ISBN 0-86516-471-1

LATIN READINGS
*Easy Latin, mythology, review of grammar,
with graded Latin readings*

Student edition: 109pp. (1985, reprint 1989)
paperback, ISBN 0-86516-044-9

Teacher's Manual: 86pp. (1985, reprint 1989)
paperback, ISBN 0-86516-043-0

ARTES LATINAE
*Self-teaching Latin on CD-ROM,
from grades 4 up*

Level 1: ISBN 0-86516-409-6

Level 2: ISBN 0-86516-410-X

THE LABORS OF AENEAS
*Aeneid told in easy English and
comic presentation*

vi + 108pp. (2003) paperback, ISBN 0-86516-556-4

 WWW.BOLCHAZY.COM